D1159691

THE SHAAR PRESS

THE JUDAICA IMPRINT
FOR THOUGHTFUL PEOPLE

THE
SHAAR
PRESS

Alive!

A 10-step guide to a vibrant life

by
Mordechai Weinberger, LCSW

Foreword by
Rabbi Abraham J. Twerski, M.D.

© Copyright 2015 by Shaar Press

First edition – First impression / February 2015

ALL RIGHTS RESERVED
No part of this book may be reproduced in any form, *photocopy, electronic media, or otherwise without* written *permission from the copyright holder, except by a reviewer who wishes to quote brief passages in connection with a review written for inclusion in magazines or newspapers.*
THE RIGHTS OF THE COPYRIGHT HOLDER WILL BE STRICTLY ENFORCED.

Published by **SHAAR PRESS**
Distributed by MESORAH PUBLICATIONS, LTD.
4401 Second Avenue / Brooklyn, N.Y 11232 / (718) 921-9000

Distributed in Israel by SIFRIATI / A. GITLER
Moshav Magshimim / Israel

Distributed in Europe by LEHMANNS
Unit E, Viking Business Park, Rolling Mill Road / Jarrow, Tyne and Wear, NE32 3DP/ England

Distributed in Australia and New Zealand by GOLDS WORLD OF JUDAICA
3-13 William Street / Balaclava, Melbourne 3183 / Victoria Australia

Distributed in South Africa by KOLLEL BOOKSHOP
Northfield Centre / 17 Northfield Avenue / Glenhazel 2192, Johannesburg, South Africa

ISBN 10: 1-4226-1558-8 / ISBN 13: 978-1-4226-1558-4

Printed in the United States of America by Noble Book Press Corp.
Custom bound by Sefercraft, Inc. / 4401 Second Avenue / Brooklyn N.Y. 11232

מכתב ברכה

בס"ד

שמואל קמנצקי
Rabbi S. Kamenetsky

2018 Upland Way
Philadelphia, PA 19131

Home: 215-473-2798
Study: 215-473-1212

בע"ה יום ג' ל' אב תש"ע

לאוה"ט הרב רבי אברהם ווערטהיימער שליט"א

שמחתי לשמוע שהכרכים על הלכות נדה וטהרת גיזה,
מרוסים ע"ג תשובת הרבה שאלות שנשאלים, ובהם שאלות
חדשות המתחדשות בכל יום שיום לעורר את החמאה
על הראשונים ועל אחרונים הפוסקים

אשרי והן רבים שהבורא ויתרחין יזכה שליט"א, ויכול
הזמן לעיון ולשאת ולתת ולהשקיע בזה, לזכות את הרבים
ולהורם שבלב ולעשות,

כ"ד דבר בדברי תורה כמש מגלמי "יכל ושמחי ומשמחי,
אברכהו כה יצא לאור הבא מהחיל אל חיל, אדות לעולם.

הכו"ח לכבוד התורה
שמואל קמנצקי

מכתב ברכה

דוד קאהן

ביהמ"ד גבול יעבץ
ברוקלין, נ.א. יארק

בס"ד

מ'אות הגאון רבי ישראל סלנטר זצ"ל הי' נודע
שיעול קוראים הלימוד אל מכות הנפש זהו ספר "תורת הבית"
קראתי שים מבסמך שלא שלטלת דקדוק ספר מברך
מרדכי בר. ויוערני שליט"א וראיתי שבא להחזיר עטרת
חכמת הסיכולוגיה לישנה, ספרו הוא ספר שנשא ונותן
בתורת הנפש; ולא זוד, אלא שאברין יוצאים זצא לעזור
העם לה"אציאת, ולאמתו של חורש הבורא, ויצא שהספר הוא
ספר מוכר.

ולכן הנני מברק בהחזר הספל של אשר יכל יבוא שיכל
ה...חפץ לכבוד הסוסקים ד...די ... לה

ד' אד מחט ... ...
פ'ב קוה... ...

Table of Contents

Foreword

by Rabbi Abraham J. Twerski, M.D.

The late ethicist, Rabbi Shlomo Wolbe, in his epic work, *Alei Shur,* points out that the Torah antedated by many centuries the Greek aphorism "Know thyself." He states that without a true self-awareness a person can never have inner peace. Rabbi Wolbe says that the human being is comprised of numerous components, both physical and spiritual, but often these are fragmented. It requires *daas*, wisdom, to bring all these parts into a harmonious, functioning whole.

This is easier said than done. Mordechai Weinberger, in *Alive,* provides us with a detailed method that can enable us to achieve bringing all these parts into a unit.

Most psychologists will agree with what Weinberger points out, that people actually have the solutions to the problems that upset them, but that there are barriers that do not allow them to see the solutions. Weinberger provides a way to identify and eliminate these barriers, thus allowing a person to solve one's problems.

Weinberger points out that there many things about ourselves of which we are unaware, because they are in the subconscious mind. Although we are not aware of them, they can exert a powerful influence on our thoughts, feelings and behavior.

Self-esteem is crucial to happiness, but in our minds there is an accumulation of negative ideas that can crush our self-esteem. Self-esteem is simply a true self-assessment of all one's pluses and minuses.

It is obvious that if a person has a distorted perception of reality, one can hardly make an optimum adjustment to reality. *Every person is the major component of one's reality, and a distorted self-perception inevitably results in problems.*

There are two main reasons a person may not have an accurate self-concept. Actually, they are diametrically opposed. (1) A person may not want to face one's character defects and (2) A person may not want to know one's strengths and abilities.

We may easily understand why a person may want to be oblivious to one's faults, but why would someone not want to know one's strengths and abilities? It is because such knowledge would obligate a person to live up to one's potential, and if a person is lazy, one would rather not know one's potential.

King Solomon, the wisest of all humans, devotes much of the Book of *Proverbs* to *indolence*. He points out that only a fool would not take advantage of one's G-d-given strengths to further oneself in life.

A person who does not live up to one's potential cannot be happy.

Weinberger addresses the various factors that can cause a distorted self-perception. Knowledge of these and their correction can lead to happiness.

Alive is not a book that one can read as one does a novel. Each chapter must be digested and reviewed, and the exercises, should be performed. This requires patience and diligence. Of course, you can get a measure of peace-of-mind by popping several tranquilizing pills, and you can rid yourself of anxiety by numbing your brain for several hours. But the brain is the organ wherewith we run our lives, and it is foolish to render it dysfunctional. Weinberger's proposal can enable one to eliminate the obstacles to optimal emotional health. **This book is an excellent guide for dealing with both the major and minor challenges and stresses of daily life.** Getting the most out of this book will require investing some effort, and King Solomon has told us that anyone who does not wish to exert the requisite effort to improve oneself, fulfill oneself and thereby achieve happiness, is being very foolish.

There may at times be need for help from a psychotherapist, but *Alive* can give you the ability to solve many of your problems by utilizing your innate strengths even those of which you may be unaware.

Acknowledgments

Only Hashem knows the depth of my gratitude to Him, because only He knows where I started. Therefore, only He knows how great is the *siyata d'Shmaya* He has provided to get me to this point and continues to provide as I strive to move forward in my life and my profession. Words would not do justice to the kindness, patience and abundant blessings He has given me. I can only say, "Thank You!"

Among Hashem's greatest gifts to me is my family, starting with my grandparents, R' Dovid and Tzipora Weinberger and R' Zev, *a'h* and Yitu Perlstein *amu'sh*. Each is a hero of faith and courage who came out of the fires of the Holocaust to build radiant lives of Torah and mitzvos. They gave to others when they had barely enough for themselves. They treasured Torah learning and imparted this love to all their children, including my parents, and ensured that this rich, beautiful legacy of living constantly in Hashem's presence would pass onto their descendants. I especially hope that this book and any good that it does will be a *z'chus* for the holy *neshama* of my Zeidy Perlstein, who only a few months ago left this world.

My father, *a'h* and my mother are true heirs to their parents' legacy, and I thank them for all the love and support they have tirelessly given me throughout the years. My father taught me to believe in myself and to set my goals high. My mother, *amu'sh*, has given me constant love and encouragement in everything I have done, and especially in writing this book. But perhaps the biggest gift my parents have given me is a family of siblings — Moishy and Esther Schwartz and Yitzchok and Rivky Weinberger — whose friendship and love I truly treasure.

I would like pay tribute to my wifes grandparents whom I was privileged to know for many years. R' Tzvi and Sara Bornstein *z"l* and Helen *a"h* and Avraham Meer *amu'sh* each lived their lives with uncompromising *mesirus nefesh* for Torah, mitzvos and endless *massim tovim*. I am also deeply grateful to my in-laws, R' Yitzchak and Rashi Bornstein, whose open hearts, loving encouragement and wise advice are always there for me My brothers- and sisters-in-law — Sruly and Chaya Bornstein, Avrumy and Toby Grossman, Pinny and Ruchy Horowitz, Shloimy and Nechumi Bornstein and Moe — reflect the family's beautiful values.

My heartfelt thanks as well to my dear aunt, Miriam Zuker, *a'h* of B'nei Brak and my beloved uncle, Beirach Litwin *z'l* of Golders Green, both of whom were a special source of love and encouragement to me throughout their lives. Their absence is still felt.

Finally, I want to thank from the bottom of my heart my wife Rivky. Hashem gave me all I need to succeed when He gave me my partner in life. She has been the motivation and inspiration for turning my plans into reality, and has given me a beautiful home filled with light and love, and the most wonderful children I could imagine — Shira, Shloimy, Henni, Raizy, Rina and Sara Miriam. Everything I have is to my wife's credit, and she has done it all graciously, freeing me to engage in many community and professional endeavors without a worry. May we be *zoche* to be together until 120 and walk our great-grandchildren to the chuppah.

This book is the result of many people's combined talents and efforts. First, I would like to thank my editor, Chana Nestlebaum, for taking my ideas and giving them form and life in a book that is clear and engaging to read. I wish her continued *hatzlacha,* in her work, which has been making its mark on Jewish publishing for the past two decades.

I feel privileged to have been able to work with the professionals at ArtScroll, which sets the gold standard in Jewish publishing. From Rabbi Avraham Biderman who saw the potential in my first manuscript to Mrs. Judi Dick, whose keen editorial insights brought the final version into its optimum form, to Rivky Kapenstein, whose graphic expertise created a volume that is pleasant and clear to read, to Mendy Herzberg who oversaw the production of this book, I am honored to have had the opportunity to have my book published by the best.

I wish to give special thanks to my dear friend Rabbi Naftali Weinberger, the man who makes things happen. Talent, energy and persistence are his secrets to success.

I am grateful to the Rosh Yeshiva HaRav Shmuel Kaminetsky, shlit'a, and HaRav Dovid Cohen, *shlit'a*, Rav of Gvul Yaavetz in Brooklyn, who took the time to review this book to ensure that its message expresses true Torah *hashkofah*, and who have expressed their support for the important role of mental health awareness in addressing the personal challenges of our times.

My sincere thanks also goes to the Rosh Yeshiva Rav Sholom Kaminetsky, *shlit'a*, and Rebbitzen Miriam Kaminetsky for their invaluable assistance, as well as to Rabbi Yitzchak and Mrs. Goldie Schechter for their gracious contribution of time and effort, and their wise advice.

Every book that addresses mental health issues for the Orthodox community is a tribute to the pioneering work of Rabbi Dr. Abraham Twerski M.D., the visionary who opened this conversation with the Jewish world. I am honored that he consented to write a foreword for this volume and provide his endorsement.

I also wish to thank my clients, listeners and all those who have shared their lives with me. I value the connections I have built with you and the many lessons that *you* have taught me as I observe you facing your challenges and conquering them. As I join you on your journey of growth, I discover more and more about myself. I thank Hashem that I am able to earn a *parnassah* by helping people and at the same time, growing and learning so much from them.

Nothing I have accomplished today would exist if not for the abundant love, guidance and wisdom I received from HaRav Avraham Pam, *zt'l*. I had the privilege to learn with him during the last three years of his life, and to be among the last *talmidim* to whom he granted *semicha*. I wish to acknowledge the Rosh Yeshivah, HaRav Nosson Tzvi Finkel, *zt'l* for teaching me the true meaning of spreading the light of Torah; with the 4,000 *talmidim* learning at the Mir in the years I was there, he was willing to learn with anyone who asked. The times I took advantage of that opportunity were too few, but their impact will last forever.

The Skolya Rebbe, *zt'l*, and his grandson, the present Skolya Rebbe *shlita* with whom my family maintains a close connection, also have a profound influence in my life. I am grateful to have had the opportunity to see first-hand, from all of these *tzaddikim*, the heights a human being can reach.

Finally, I wish to acknowledge you, my readers. If you are reading this book, you are seeking pathways to a richer, more vibrant life. I am honored that you have chosen to invest your time in what I have written, and I am *davening* for you, for me and for all of Klal Yisrael to live lives filled with strength, energy and joy.

Introduction

You've Got It All

A MAN GOES FOR A PHYSICAL. THE DOCTOR DISCOV-*ers that the patient's cholesterol and blood sugar are reaching dangerously high levels. The doctor gives the patient a prescription: a new diet and a half-hour of vigorous exercise each day.*

"Isn't there some pill I can take instead?" the man asks. "I don't have time for exercise and I know I'm not going to change the way I eat."

It is with that perspective that many people come to therapy, as well. "Tell me something, give me something, do something that will take away my emotional pain." Likewise, when I see clients for business coaching, they say, "Make me a success." But after years of working with all types of people, I've realized that anyone looking at me as a solution is looking in the wrong place. When a client asks me, "What should I do?" my answer is often, "Why ask me? What do you think you should do? Why do you want to give me your power to decide what to do?"

In almost every instance, the client discovers that he does know what to do. The solution is inside each and every person. It is often buried deeply, under a heavy mound of negative experiences and negative habits of thought, but if a person sincerely wants an answer to his anxiety, depression, obsessions or dissatisfaction with life, the only place to find it is within himself. As a therapist, I do not give anyone a solution; I can only help people dig down under the heap of negativity until they experience the unbridled, unparalleled thrill of hitting upon their own buried treasure — the talents and abilities, goals and aspirations, knowledge and common sense — that they and indeed each of us possesses.

I sometimes see myself as a plumber: someone who unclogs the works and sets free the bursting fountain of creative energy trapped within us. When I meet with clients, I aim to get them in touch with the answers they already have, and I am always amazed at the clarity of their insights. They know exactly what they need. They know exactly what is holding them back. Their only problem is that all this knowledge is obstructed by a stubborn clog of self-doubt. Once the clog is identified and removed, their strengths and talents burst forth; energy and enthusiasm begin turning lost goals and faded hopes into possibilities — even realities. They come alive!

Over the years, I have found that a great deal of this self-doubt is hiding in the well-protected vault of the subconscious, where it is extremely difficult to reach. This aspect of the mind exerts an amazing degree of influence over our thoughts and actions, and yet, we barely understand how to tap into it and use it to our benefit. At the same time, the more accessible, logical and intellectual part of our minds also exerts great influence; in fact, our subconscious thoughts are often rooted in logic. For instance, an intelligent man who, at the age of 45, still thinks, *I can't learn Gemara*, is probably holding on to an outdated image lodged in his subconscious, but that image got there as a logical conclusion of the learning difficulties he had in his youth.

Seeing firsthand the power of these two aspects of our minds to feed our spirit or, on the contrary, to starve it of energy and enthusiasm, it seemed to me that no therapy could be successful without addressing both the subconscious and the logic. As the situation stands today, most alternative therapies focus on the subconscious, and most classical modes address the logical mind. Rarely are the two joined together so that the therapist is treating both vital aspects of a person's thinking. The void left by this one-sided approach became apparent to me as I began offering therapy. I saw clients who had gone to classical therapists and still did not experience the kind of change they longed for in their lives. On the other hand, there were those who had undergone therapy oriented to the subconscious, and they, too, were still suffering.

One of my primary goals in writing this book is to illustrate how we can truly transform ours lives by addressing both of these aspects of the mind together; some problems reside in one area, some in the other and some in both. And then there is one final piece to the puzzle: our actions. With action, we confirm and reinforce the changes we are making. In each chapter of this book, you will find self-help exercises that will enable you to create movement in your life. Small steps in each area — the subconscious, logic and action — offer immense payback in our overall level of happiness and satisfaction with our lives.

Since the brain is the terrain upon which all the drama of our thoughts and emotions takes place, in the first two chapters of the Appendix I have provided a basic understanding of how the brain works. The information is not technical, but it describes the biological factors that enter into our patterns of thought, feeling and behavior. A third chapter provides a deeper understanding of how inspiration, logic and action are used together in the process of changing counterproductive thinking and habits. I hope the reader will find it a valuable backdrop to the 10 practical chapters that follow.

Having now helped more than 3,000 people to date, I have gained a broad view of the types of "clogs" that obstruct most people's happiness. From this perspective 10 foundations have emerged which, when they are strong, can support a lifetime of growth and achievement, and when weak, wobble and crack under the stress of life. The person who can unblock his inherent power and construct a strong foundation can build a towering life upon it. I have found these foundations to be universal among my clients; they apply to children as young as 5 and adults as old as 85; they apply to religious people, non-religious people, Russians, Israelis, Frenchmen and Australians — to everyone across the board. My purpose in writing this book is to create awareness and to offer initial self-help steps to anyone who wants to live a life of happiness, a life he or she is excited about living.

This book is dedicated to my father, Reb Daniel Yonah Elimelech Yosef ben Reb Dovid, *z'l*. I was privileged to grow up surrounded by his bright visions of my future and his sky-high assessments of my abilities. I was in college studying for my Masters in Social Work, just like 400 other students in my program and 1,600 other students in other programs around New York, but in my father's eyes, I stood out from the crowd. For many years, I brushed his cheerleading aside with a laugh. He was a typical Jewish father who wanted the world for his son, but I saw reality.

Five years ago, my father passed away, and five months later, I was featured on a radio show that attracted 20,000 listeners. I then initiated a service that provides free advice and lectures via telephone (718) 298-2011. To date we have received more than 1.5 million calls. Currently I can be heard on a different radio call-in show that is broadcast in Brooklyn on Yeshivah World, The Lakewood Scoop and Matzav.com. So despite my certainty that I would be one among thousands of therapists taking care of my little corner of the world, the message my father nurtured in me for all those years — that I could make a difference in many people's lives — won out.

This book is here for all those who did not have a father who said, "I believe in you even when you don't yet believe in yourself." It is here to tell you what my father would have told you: "Yes, you have great potential and you can reach it!" I thank Hashem for the 58 years my father was in this world, and hope that through this book, the gift he gave me will benefit thousands more and be a never-ending source of merit for him.

Chapter 1

Step One

Release Your Self-Esteem

The Power of Self-Worth vs. the Trap of Self-Doubt

"HOW DOES HE DO THAT?" LEVI MARVELED AS HE SAT at *a conference table with the rest of the marketing department. His co-worker, Dovid, was presenting his idea for a new advertising program.*

"It's half-baked," Asher Klein, the boss, responded in the middle of Dovid's presentation.

"You have to hear the whole thing, Asher. Give me another two minutes and you'll see, it'll be completely baked!"

Dovid had turned the insult into a joke, Levi noted in amazement. Even Asher laughed. As Dovid pressed on with his presentation, Levi subtly glanced at the boss's expression. Was he getting angry? Was he going to slam Dovid's pitch right back into his face? Levi's stomach was churning with anxiety. He hated these confrontations, even when they didn't involve him personally.

But Dovid didn't seem fazed. In fact, if anything, he sold his idea even harder. "Asher, this completely stands out from anything our competitors are doing. Think about it. You'll see I'm right."

Levi cringed: "Think about it? He tells the boss to think about it?" Asher interrupted Levi's train of anxious thoughts with a question. "Levi, what's your take on Dovid's idea?"

A flush of heat rose to Levi's face. His heart felt as if it were being squeezed. "Um, I'm not really sure," he finally answered. In his mind, however, a voice was screaming loud and clear, "Get me out of here!"

"I still say it's half-baked," Asher told Dovid.

"Well, then I'll stick it back in the oven for a day or two and then see what you think," Dovid replied confidently. Meeting adjourned.

Dovid and Levi both work for Asher Klein, the vice president of marketing. Asher is known as a brilliant, creative businessman and a tough person to please. For Dovid, the job is like an extreme sport, filled with the thrill of high stakes, near-misses and courageous comebacks. He has an easy working relationship with Asher and his co-workers; he puts forth his ideas with confidence, knowing some will fly and some will be shot down.

Levi is competent, respected and well liked by his colleagues. His boss rarely criticizes his work. Yet he sits in his office every day feeling as though the proverbial sword is dangling over his head. When Asher finds fault with another employee, Levi cringes. He feels like someone caught in a hail of rocket fire, overcome with terrified anticipation of being the next one hit.

How do we know if our self-esteem is healthy and strong? Below are some statements that reflect healthy self-esteem:

1. I am comfortable with myself; I don't need others to be like me, and I don't need to be like them.

2. I am a unique individual with a unique role and purpose in this world.

3. Overcoming adversity makes me stronger.

4. I don't allow others to convince me that I can't succeed at something if I truly believe it is worth trying.

5. I can appreciate people who are different or think differently from me.

6. My feelings of self-worth are consistent and durable.

7. I can accept and absorb positive feedback.

8. Setbacks and obstacles don't make me feel like a failure.

9. I am content with the life I am living overall and on a daily basis.

10. I'm grateful to Hashem for giving me life.

11. Even though I have goals I have yet to reach, I am at ease with myself as I am.

12. I anticipate that my efforts will result in success.

13. I wake up looking forward to my day.

14. I act with enthusiasm and energy.

15. I can accept blame and apologize.

16. I feel empathy for others' pain.

The Lock

The result of healthy self-esteem, as Dovid in the opening story illustrates, is that our talents and abilities flow into the world unchecked. Dovid doesn't worry that people will consider him stupid or that others will not welcome his presence and involvement. He feels free to give what he's got, trusting that even if it is rejected, he himself is not being rejected. The simple things are, for him, simple. He can give someone a gift, choose clothing, make suggestions, ask questions, spend time alone and spend time with others, all without nagging self-doubts buzzing in his head.

Because Levi lacks self-esteem, his potential is locked in by fear. Anyone he perceives as above him in some way — the boss, the teacher, the rich man, the *rebbi,* the *rav,* the popular people — fills him with a painful level of anxiety. He wants nothing more than to avoid contact and thereby avoid the scrutiny which, he is absolutely certain, will result in some form of humiliation.

People who lack self-esteem cannot perceive themselves as successful. When they look back at their past, they see a landscape filled with failure: efforts that never came to fruition, hopes that were disappointed and situations that didn't work out. Because they have no trust in their own powers and abilities, they do not believe that they have the means to make positive changes and seek fulfillment of their needs. And if the past and present are hopeless, the future can only appear bleak as well.

Michael was a young married man who, only two years after his wedding, was already feeling unbearable financial stress. His plan had been to finish college and go to graduate school while his wife, an up-and-coming CPA, worked to support them. Then, he would assume the responsibility of breadwinning and his wife would scale down to working part-time and raising a family.

It sounded like a great plan, but when his wife lost her job in the middle of an economic downturn, everything changed. Weeks and then months went by. Their savings dwindled. "I just can't win," Michael's subconscious kept whispering in his ear. "*I knew this would happen. Nothing ever goes right for me. No matter what I try, things just turn against me. Before you know it, Leah's going to be wondering why she married such a dunce, and I don't blame her.*"

"*We're such losers,*" Michael told me. "*Everyone else is having a great time in their nice apartments with their leased cars and we're flat broke. No one's hiring. We'll never get out of this. And now we're expecting another baby. It's only going to get worse.*"

In Michael's view, the past was a failure: an unfulfilled plan of finishing school. The present was an unsustainable nightmare of financial pressure, and the future held no hope. He saw nothing that he could do that would make things better. The entire spectrum of possible solutions — getting help from relatives, getting another job, taking two part-time jobs, finding a business opportunity, moving to a less expensive neighborhood — held no promise of relief for him. He simply could not envision himself as an effective actor on the stage of life. Life happened to him.

With the feeling that we have no impact in the world comes a greatly exaggerated fear of what others might do to us. A person with poor self-esteem feels that he is at everyone else's mercy. He sees himself as a bit of flotsam being shoved to and fro by the tide. He lives in a state of heightened anxiety, afraid to do or say anything that might cause disfavor. He is terrified of making mistakes, which could incur the wrath or ridicule of others and add a new tale of failure to his already epic saga.

Naturally, under such circumstances, he cannot conceive of "taking the bull by the horns" and going after what he wants and needs in life. Whatever gifts he has to give the world, whatever strength and love he has to impart to his friends and family are all trapped behind the barrier of his low self-esteem. Like static on a phone line, the messages of self-doubt create a constant background buzz that scrambles his positive thoughts and plans. There is also an irony in low self-esteem. The people who arouse the most anxiety in us, the ones who make us feel small and vulnerable, often have no more self-esteem than we do. They protect themselves from vulnerability with over-the-top aggression rather than withdrawal. Rather than cringing in the face of authority figures or wallowing in self-doubt, this type of person is the one who makes others cringe. We can recognize him by what he says:

- "YOU'RE *telling* ME *what to do? I know what I'm talking about. I've been doing this for years.*"

- "*What does she know? She's just a secretary.*"

- "*I'm going ahead with this deal no matter what anyone says. I'd rather lose all my money than give him the satisfaction of getting his way.*"

- "*Are you stupid? What kind of question is that?*"

- "*This whole problem would never have happened if you had done what you were supposed to do!*"

- "*I'm giving in on NOTHING. We do this my way or not at all!*"

We might think that such a person has an oversupply, not a lack of self-esteem. It seems as if someone who leaves no room for argument, who admits no need for advice or information from anyone else, who squashes his opponents and dismisses his questioners is someone with supreme belief in his own value and abilities.

In reality, however, someone who cannot accept other people's ideas and scares off criticism with arrogance and insults is a frightened person, a weak person projecting a fearsome facade. He is someone who fears that his self-image cannot survive any assault on his being right. People who suffer from this type of low self-esteem can be intimidating, but they are every bit as locked in as their timid counterparts. They lose out on much of life: They cannot learn from others because they must always be the one who knows, the one who is right. They cannot enjoy balanced, loving relationships or healthy friendships because they step on others to assure themselves of superiority.

Knowing this can help the person on the receiving end of this type of bullying to put the bully's insults and bluster into perspective. It may not be pleasant to experience; it may indeed be necessary to get out of such a situation. However, we can at least refuse to admit this person's words into our subconscious sense of ourselves.

How and Why

How does such a negative self-image invade and occupy a person's subconscious? After all, self-esteem is an inborn trait, a part of our survival instinct. As babies, we all know how to get others to take care of our needs; we scream as loud as we must and awaken or disturb others at any time with no hesitation. As we grow older and develop a stronger sense of other people, we begin to pick up cues that they may not be pleased with our demands. That's a good thing; it prevents us from evolving into implacable monsters. On the other hand, if a child's real needs are met with real rejection, the child loses the foundational belief that he is able to make things happen in his world.

As small children, we are relatively powerless. We depend on our parents for love and affection, food and clothing, order and hygiene and everything we need for survival and wholesome development. If a child does not feel understood, valued and confident that the adults in his life are there for him, he cannot build upon his internal sense of his own value. If his needs go unmet, he develops an inner belief that he is unworthy. If he is often criticized, he develops an image of himself as someone who is faulty and inept. These self-eroding notions are the material of which the child's emotional framework is built. He is like a house framed with substandard lumber; the architecture might be grand, but it will not be able to bear the stress of normal wear and tear.

Conversely, sometimes overly lavish praise and low expectations can erode self-esteem. If the praise does not ring true to the child, because it does not reflect the child's own vision of himself, his subconscious simply will not accept it. Furthermore, when parents gush over non-accomplishments, children perceive the praise as insincere, and therefore meaningless. A general accolade such as "good boy!" can also be counterproductive, because it only holds its value until the child misbehaves and becomes "bad boy!" In addition, if a child gets the feeling that his parents are praising him just to make him feel good, and not because he has actually done something praiseworthy, he may come to believe that they do not consider him capable of anything truly praiseworthy.

Obviously, there will be some criticism in every child's life. There will be unmet needs and misunderstood emotions. Adults may not always be available in the way the child demands. A healthy, robust self-esteem will still develop if the child's overall situation is a nurturing one that feeds his innate sense of himself as a successful person worthy of love and respect. He then has the "seed" of a positive self-image planted in his subconscious, ready to absorb all the nourishment of praise, success and love that enter his life. He feels himself to be a successful, worthy person wherever he goes, whatever he does, even through tears and suffering.

It's when the daily messages entering a child's mind are skewed in the negative direction that the sad subconscious seed of low self-esteem is planted. Once it takes root, it absorbs reinforcement from every setback, criticism and rejection. The child is then programmed to feel himself to be unwanted and unworthy in every situation, from the playground to the *chuppah* and beyond.

The Key

Imagine how life would change for a person who manages to break through the barrier of low self-esteem. All the abilities and talents he holds inside could be set free into the world. He would feel secure in his innate value as a human being and could confidently offer his best as a student, a spouse, parent, employee, entrepreneur and friend. He would feel the excitement of striving toward his goals and living his vision of life. Instead of *I'd love to do it, but it's not going to happen*, his inner voice would say, *I am going to succeed!* He would lose his fear of making mistakes, and would thus be free to try new things and go out on a limb from time to time.

All of this would come to him because he finally realizes that he is a valuable, unique human being and no one can take that away. No criticism, no negative evaluation of him has any impact on his inherent value. **He is like an ounce of gold; the metal is worth the same amount** whether it's crafted into a beautiful bracelet or is just a shapeless lump.

The first key, unlocking our self-esteem, is in many ways a master key, for once we reconnect with our inborn sense of worth, our right to seek our own survival both physically and emotionally, many other doors fly open. Using inspiration, logic and action, we can break through the barrier of low self-esteem and set our best selves free. We can become that person who is comfortable offering himself and all the gifts he possesses to the people in his world. From the child longing to raise his hand in class and give the answer that's screaming in his head to the man who is longing to start a business or make a friend or open a *sefer* for the first time in years, we can break free of our self-imposed limitations and forge ahead toward our dreams.

Unlock Your Self-Esteem

Inspiration

1. **Take stock of your talents and abilities**. Your talents are those inborn strengths and gifts you possess, even if you have not developed them. Your abilities are the areas where you exhibit your talents: the things you can do.

Since many people do not recognize or value their own talents and abilities, they may be stymied when asked to describe them. Below is an inventory of possibilities. As you will notice, they need not be Nobel Prize-winning achievements; they are simply some of the positives upon which your value and success in life are built. Make a list of at least 25 talents and abilities that apply to you and add those not listed here.

My Talents

1. Active
2. Ambitious
3. Amusing
4. Appealing personality
5. Assertive
6. Athletic
7. Authoritative
8. Believe life is good
9. Brave
10. Calm
11. Competitive
12. Confident
13. Consistent
14. Creative
15. Delegate effectively
16. Detail oriented
17. Driven to reach my goals
18. Effective multitasker
19. Emotional
20. Empathetic
21. Enthusiastic
22. Fast worker
23. Focused
24. Focus on the good in others
25. Forward-thinking

26. Gentle
27. Give full attention to task at hand
28. Good with hands
29. Good with logic and puzzles
30. Good singing voice
31. Good social skills
32. Good taste
33. Graceful
34. Helpful
35. Kindhearted
36. Loving
37. Loyal
38. Organized
39. Direct others effectively
40. Mechanically inclined
41. Methodical
42. Motivating
43. Musical
44. Perceive others' needs
45. People person
46. Positive outlook
47. Precise worker
48. Quick thinker
49. Reassuring
50. Reliable
51. Respectful
52. Responsible
53. See the whole picture
54. Self-sufficient
55. Sense of humor
56. Set goals for myself
57. Smart
58. Smile easily
59. Spiritual
60. Strong
61. Thorough
62. Tranquil

My Abilities

1. Balance accounts
2. Comfort others
3. Complete to-do lists
4. Compose music
5. Contribute to the Shabbos table
6. Develop a social network
7. Draw, paint or design
8. Drive a car
9. Earn a living
10. Efficient
11. Express love to family

12. Get children ready for school

13. Give time to others

14. Handy around the house

15. Knit, sew and/or crochet

16. Integrating new information

17. Learn (*Chumash, Mishnayos, Gemara, Rashi, etc.*)

18. Lead prayer services

19. Makes decision's

20. Mediate a dispute

21. Meet my commitments

22. On time

23. Play an instrument

24. Practice a profession

25. Prepare meals for family

26. Prepare a lesson (each subject is its own ability)

27. Provide extras for family

28. Public speaking

29. Read

30. Repair a car

31. Repair machinery

32. Run a business

33. Sing

34. Speak a foreign language

35. Teach others

36. Work

37. Write

2. **Plant new "seeds" of self-image in your subconscious.**

a) Identify yourself as someone who possesses all the talent and ability you have now recognized. That's you! The "you" in the mirror is that gifted, accomplished person you have described. That person can attain any dream he holds inside himself, because those dreams are real. They are the seeds Hashem has planted in us, the seeds of our unique potential as human beings, and when we throw our energy into nurturing those seeds, we are fully alive.

b) Realize that even if you meet failure while striving toward your innate potential, you will feel more energized and successful than someone who mindlessly follows the prepaved road that others have laid out for him. Don't fall into the trap of comparing your path to that taken by others, because only you can define success for yourself.

c) Keep checking your navigation equipment. Make sure you are not veering off course on your way to your goals.

d) Visualize the maximized you. Create a clear mental picture of the person you can become if you simply use more of the abilities and talents you have. See how that person stands, dresses, prays, learns, behaves in social situations, relates to family members, spends time. See him or her at work, at home, at the table. You can even write out your descriptions or draw them to make them real to you. Keep this vision in mind and refer to it often as you face your daily challenges.

3. **Experience the new you.**

Our imaginations can create realities for us. For instance, if we are fearful of the dark, we may imagine intruders and noises that cause us to experience real fear. If we imagine something that makes us happy, for instance, boarding the airplane to embark on a vacation, we feel a palpable surge of excitement in our hearts.

Use that power to taste the kind of life you want to live. Imagine you are someone you admire — a Torah luminary, a wealthy philanthropist, a beloved teacher, a warm, positive wife and mother — whatever suits your nature. Put yourself in his or her shoes and let yourself feel in vivid detail what it's like to live an hour of that person's life.

You may believe that this is just "daydreaming," but in fact, it is setting up a new destination in your subconscious, which reacts just as strongly to your imagination as it does to the facts before your eyes. By firmly installing our optimal goals within our minds, we create a new destination. Our life can be infused with the excitement of heading somewhere we really want to go — and with effort and *siyata d'Shmaya,* we have a chance to get there.

LOGIC

4. **Never compare yourself to anyone else.**

a) We all know that no matter how good we are at something, there will be others out there who are better at it. Therefore, self-esteem cannot depend on comparing favorably with the rest of the world, or even with people who seem to have the identical background, experiences, talents and abilities as we do. You were put on this world to carry out the task that is uniquely yours to accomplish. No one else, no matter how brilliant or talented, can fulfill your role. The precise set of circumstances, the exact mixture of *neshamah,* nature and nurture that makes us who we are is utterly unique, with its own purpose and its own challenges. Your identical twin sister may be a better mother than you are, but not for your children.

b) Even when people excel in an area where you feel you are weak, success depends on the whole picture: the product of the ILA formula. If you remain consistent in working toward your goals, your modest 6 x 6 x 6 (216) will take you further than someone who is a 9 x 2 x 7 (126). (See Appendix for full explanation.)

c) You may well be comparing yourself with someone who looks happy and fulfilled, but is not. The successful CEO living in the mansion next door may live with the unanswered desire to head to *kollel,* rather than the office, each morning, or with a longing to have time for a closer relationship with his children.

d) When you compare yourself to someone else, you are focusing only on one part of that person's total status during one period of that person's life. For example, you feel ugly when you compare yourself to someone who is beautiful. But her appearance is only one part of her life. There are areas in which, without a doubt, your life is more satisfying. You don't know anything about her internal struggles, her family life, or for that matter, what lies ahead for her a day or a decade from now. Would you really want to *be* her, or just *look like* she does?

5. **Analyze and strategize.**

Using your self-inventory, think about your strengths and identify your obstacles.

Make a list of the traits and issues that block your path to the life you want to live, and a list of the tools you have within you to overcome them. Map out a logical route from where you are now to where you want to be. What will it take? What work do you need to do in the areas of inspiration, logic and action?

6. **Start learning.**

Begin gathering the knowledge you need to get where you want to go. If you have a musical talent that you want to develop, find out what instruments suit you, explore teachers or programs that can teach you and start learning. If you want to feel more comfortable speaking in public, find people who do it successfully and ask them for advice. Open your heart to learning; be willing to start from a point of ignorance and seek out new knowledge. Realize that life is always evolving and learning is a constant part of it.

This is part of the greatness of truly great people. For instance, a rabbi renowned for his grasp of Shabbos laws will seek out basic knowledge from an engineer to understand how a certain machine works so that he can determine if it is permitted on Shabbos. The rabbi does not feel embarrassed to ask an elementary question; he is not an engineer. In fact, the greater the rabbi is, the more he will find himself facing questions that demand investigation and learning.

7. **Make Mistakes.**

Mistakes are not the antithesis of success; they are the path to success. Don't bash yourself for mistakes and call yourself inept, stupid or any other negative. Instead, say, "I learned from this." Each day, think of three lessons you learned from efforts that didn't result in the desired outcome. Don't hide from your mistakes. Rather, embrace them as evidence that you are moving, trying and taking action in your life. The only person who does not make mistakes is the one who has stopped growing, and when we stop growing, we start declining emotionally and spiritually.

ACTION

8. **Tell yourself who you are!**

a) Review your list of talents and abilities *every* day.

b) Visualize yourself for two minutes each day as the person you will be when you have fully tapped into your abilities and mastered your talents. Set a specific time to do this.

c) State your talents out loud: loud and clear. This tells your brain that you mean it and believe it. For two weeks, do this 10 times a day. Then do it twice a day for the following four weeks. It works!

9. **Master your talents.**

a) Put real time and effort into developing the talents you have noted. Whether or not you will ever become the best at something, there are many areas in which you can become proficient and experience the thrill of seeing your talents turned into an actuality. Learn to play an instrument. Make a commitment to get up early and put the extra time to good use. Tackle a *sefer* that you want to learn and learn it well. Take a course on baking artistic cakes and make them for friends' *simchahs*. Learn to paint or draw. Get involved in a form of dance, exercise or sport.

When you develop an expertise, whether it's something others know about or not, your sense of your own value increases. It's not about winning admiration for your awesome talent or devotion; it's about winning your own admiration for effort, persistence and achievement.

b) Show what you know. Share your expertise with others. Show someone your painting, share your original Torah thought with your learning partner, teach a new Shabbos song at the table, bake one of your specialty cakes for a school function. By sharing and speaking about your area of expertise, you will be reinforcing your own positive self-image and the image others have of you.

10. **Set goals.**

a) Set the milestone you wish to reach in order to feel that you have gotten beyond the beginner level in your area of mastery. Then set a standard by which you define success. For instance, if your ultimate goal is to learn a particular *sefer,* your first milestone might be that you have learned one-quarter of the *sefer* and are consistently learning it on the schedule you have set. Your final measure of success might be finishing the *sefer* once, or perhaps being able to recall key points from it, or even being able to give a class on it.

b) Keep reinforcing your overall goals by consistently recalling your visualizations and mentally experiencing the life you will have when you achieve them. As long as you keep that vision of yourself fresh and vibrant, it will have the power to steer your thinking and actions in the right direction.

Remember as you put these ideas into action that small improvements make a big difference in your overall feeling of success. Don't be thrown off track by those around you who may challenge or even actively try to discourage your effort to make a positive change. Realize that just by embarking on this effort, you are already giving yourself a self-esteem building message: "I can have the meaningful life Hashem equipped me to have, and I'm willing to pursue it."

While many people think of self-esteem as an invention of child psychologists, it is in fact a concept deeply embedded in Torah thought.

The Lakewood Mashgiach, Rav Nosson Wachtfogel, *zt'l*, is recorded in *Leket Reshimos* (p. 109) as saying that a person who sins should focus on the future rather than his regret of the past. While regret is always an integral part of *teshuvah*, and *teshuvah* is an integral part of a Jew's life, the Mashgiach states that Yom Kippur is the only day that is set aside for reviewing the many ways we have fallen. If not for the power of that day to renew our spirits through *teshuvah*, such a review would plunge a person into depression. Therefore, on all other days it is considered a weakness, not a strength, to dwell upon our past mistakes.

The Take-Away

So many people come into my office overflowing with negative self-talk. All day every day they mull over their mistakes and become paralyzed by hopelessness. We have to realize that this focus will not only fail to repair our past, but it will rob us of our future as well. Mark today as a new beginning and go forward from the here and now.

 The Mishnah in *Pirkei Avos* (2:18) teaches, "Do not judge yourself to be a bad person." The Rambam explains in the *Peirush HaMishnayos* that "if a person thinks of himself as lacking and less valuable than others, he will not strive to grow."

Rav Aharon Kotler, *zt'l*, states (*Mishnas Reb Aharon*, vol. 1, pp.157-159) that a person must view himself as the subject of the verse "You are children of Hashem, your G-d" and "You are a holy nation to Hashem, your G-d" (*Devarim* 14:1-2). Each and every one of us must know that we have G-dliness within us, making us much more than the bodies we inhabit.

Rav Aharon goes further, stating that it is this recognition of our inner holiness that prevents us from sinning. Just as we would not sin in the presence of a great Torah luminary, we would not sin in the presence of the spark of Hashem that is within us at all times. People who act beneath their own standards do so because they do not recognize Hashem within themselves. That is why the most vital step in turning our lives around is to realize how valuable we really are.

The Take-Away

The truth of this idea has proven itself many times in therapy. Sometimes, a family member asks me how I helped a person break away from his destructive habits, and the answer is simple. I helped him connect to his innate power. When we imbue ourselves with a sense of who we really are, our lives take off!

In *Sefer Tzidkas Hatzaddik* (letter 154) Rav Tzadok HaKohen says that a person must believe in Hashem first, and secondly, right behind that belief, he must believe in himself. He adds that we should strive to recognize that the Source of our soul is Hashem, and there is a Divine purpose to everything we do.

The Take-Away

Rav Tzadok HaKohen is saying something extraordinary. Right behind our belief in Hashem is our belief in ourselves and the purposefulness of our lives. How many people feel that greatness within them?

The *Kedushas Levi* (*Parashas Ekev*) teaches that, "A person must say, 'My actions are very important to Hashem. He has pleasure from my actions.' But *chas v'shalom* if a person says, 'What are my actions worth to Hashem?' this is heresy."

The Take-Away

The *Kedushas Levi* tells us how vital our belief in our own importance is, how much our actions mean not only to other people, but to Hashem. There is no room for thinking that we do not matter. If we could keep this thought in mind as we live our lives, it would color our every action and inspire us to live like the VIPs we are.

Does it matter what we think of ourselves? The Gemara (*Makkos*:10b) discusses the concept that "On the path a person chooses to walk, they lead him." The Maharsha explains that the pronoun "they" in this verse refers to *melachim* that are created by our thoughts and actions, whether good or bad. Every choice we make and thought we entertain creates a momentum to continue in that direction, whether it is positive or negative.

The Take-Away

From this concept we see the power of our thought patterns and the power of purposefully thinking about positive actions we wish to take. Saying to ourselves each and every day that we are good, talented, healthy, valuable, lovable and doing even one or two small actions that reflect those traits fuels the positive momentum, both in our habits of thought and in our actions.

Chapter 2
Step Two

Release Self-Acceptance

Freedom to Try vs. Perfectionism

"DADDY, WE'RE PLAYING PICTIONARY!" GAVRIEL exulted. *"Come, play with us!"*

It was a rainy summer evening. The five oldest Goldstein children had come home from day camp and the wind-swept downpour, accompanied by loud claps of thunder, kept them off their bikes and stuck in the house. Binyamin Goldstein was getting some paperwork done while his wife brought their sixth child, a baby boy, to the pediatrician.

Little Gavriel's excited invitation roused Binyamin's dread. He found games boring, and of all games, Pictionary was the worst. He was a terrible artist, and he didn't feel the need to give his children a full view of his ineptitude in that area, as a father, he reasoned, he certainly should not play a game that would cause his kids to lose respect for him.

"Sorry, Gav, I'm kind of busy right now. You guys play," he said mildly.

Now the other four chimed in. "No, Daddy! You play too! It will be much more fun if you play! It's boring with just us."

"Look, I said no," Binyamin stated more firmly. "You can see that I'm busy with my work. Now you can either play yourselves or find something else to do."

Crestfallen, Gavriel led the other children away. They put the game aside and busied themselves tossing sofa pillows back and forth among themselves. The rain pounded its dull beat on the window as Binyamin went on with his paperwork.

Binyamin Goldstein is 35 years old. Gavriel, his oldest, is 11. The next four children at home range in age from 9 to 3 years old. Does Binyamin really believe his artistic abilities are not adequate to satisfy this group? Does he think that Pictionary, a game in which contestants create quick sketches to enable their partner to guess a phrase, requires a very high level of skill? Obviously, the answer to both of those questions is "no." Binyamin does not want to play a game involving drawing because Binyamin doesn't draw very well and as a perfectionist, he is loathe to do anything that does not play to his strengths.

What if Binyamin were not a perfectionist? What if he were not afraid to try something that challenged his abilities, something in which he lacked confidence? What if he did not fear the loss of his children's respect if his rendition of a horse ended up looking more like a raccoon? What if he could even enjoy his children's laughter at his artistic efforts? Then a rainy evening might have looked more like this:

"Daddy, we're playing Pictionary!" Gavriel exulted. "Come, play with us!"

Five eager pairs of eyes searched their father's face for a positive response. Binyamin Goldstein groaned inwardly at the game they had selected. He was an awful artist. Yet the children were so excited and they certainly needed some distraction on this rainy summer evening that kept them all indoors. Binyamin put down his paperwork.

"O.K.," he said with a smile. "But I'm warning you. I'm the worst artist in the world, so if no one guesses my pictures, it's not my fault!"

"No, Daddy, you'll see. You'll be good!" encouraged 7-year-old Aviva.

The family sat down at the table and set up the game. Binyamin's first picture was supposed to be a horse. Five-year-old Yaakov was his partner. "A mouse?" the boy ventured. "A rat? A shark with legs."

The children dissolved into laughter. "A horse," Binyamin announced with fake indignity.

They played for an hour, during which Binyamin's renderings evoked plenty more comical guesses. In the end, Gavriel made an announcement: "No matter who won the game, Daddy won the A for effort." Binyamin agreed, he had won: a warm and bonding evening with his kids.

The "willing to try" Binyamin bought himself a priceless gift with his fearless of display of bad art: a strong, positive experience that his children would cherish. The perfectionist Binyamin passed up this gift to avoid his extreme discomfort with his inevitably flawed performance.

Perfectionism is one of the many human traits that disguise themselves as positive attributes when in fact their effect is almost always negative. People believe that it's good to strive for perfection. In fact, this message enters our consciousness from many sources in our lives. Sometimes we are accurately reading the well-intentioned messages of parents and teachers who set the bar at "perfect," but sometimes we are misinterpreting, believing that, in imposing the obligation to do *our* best, they are actually demanding that we become *the* best.

However, if we buy into the idea that perfection is the standard by which we must judge ourselves, we doom ourselves to a life of chasing an elusive goal while failing to notice and absorb the joy of all we *do* achieve. Worst of all, like Binyamin, we may dread trying anything that is outside our comfort zone, thereby losing out on so much of what life has to offer. We may become isolated by our rejection of anyone who makes us feel less than perfect, and stagnated by our fear of trying something that may highlight some of our weaknesses. For these reasons, there is much truth to the saying that "Perfect is the enemy of good." If you find that in your life, "good" is just "not good enough," you may be caught in the trap of perfectionism. Here are some questions to ask yourself:

1. Do you feel that you must always do better?

2. Do you worry that if you do not excel, you will not have the respect of others?

3. Do you enjoy your current endeavors?

4. Do you truly realize that perfection is humanly unachievable?

5. Do you look far into the future for potential problems or setbacks that might affect your goals and plans?

6. Do you sometimes give up before you start because you recognize that you will not be able to accomplish what you demand of yourself?

7. Are you so tense about achieving the desired result that you cannot enjoy the process of getting there?

8. Do you expect immediate success?

9. Do you feel embarrassed or defeated when you make a normal mistake?

10. Do you accept other people's imperfections and mistakes?

11. Can you settle on a fairly insignificant purchase without having to do a great deal of comparison shopping or constantly second-guessing your decision?

The Lock

Once we accept perfection as a legitimate standard, we tend to apply that standard to everything in our lives. Every decision becomes tied up in questions and doubts. Our progress is hobbled with thoughts such as, *What if it's not right? What if there's something better? What if I didn't understand it correctly? What if I come out looking stupid?* Many ideas die on the altar of perfectionism, while others go forward, but are fueled by anxiety rather than joy.

Naomi and the kids were on high alert as Yossi scanned the living room with the precision of an MRI. The chairs weren't lined up properly. He began nervously rearranging them. In 20 minutes, guests would begin arriving at his home for the parlor meeting he was hosting for his old yeshivah. Why weren't the hors d'oeuvres out on the table yet?

"Yitz!" he yelled into the kitchen to his son. "Get the food out on the table already!"

"Mommy says it needs another 10 minutes in the oven," he called back.

"What? Naomi, why didn't you put it in earlier? And what about the drinks? How are we gonna get everything ready by 7:30?"

"No one comes at 7:30, Yossi. Relax," said Naomi, his wife. "This is supposed to be a nice, laid-back, enjoyable evening."

"How's it going to look if people come and nothing's ready? My Rosh Yeshivah is gonna be here and all my old friends. I can't believe this!"

Relaxed and laid back were the last words on Yossi's mind. His offer to host the parlor meeting, made out of a dose of loyalty to his old yeshivah and pride in his new home, had become a nightmare of incessant worry over the details and tension over the preparations. Not for a moment did he stop to realize that his frantic, harried mood stood to do far more damage to the event than did the delayed display of hors d'oeuvres.

But what if Yossi was able to let go of his perfectionist mindset? His family would have enjoyed the feeling of working together on a big, important project. The early-comers would have joined the effort, offering to ferry the food from the kitchen to the table. No one would have noticed the alignment of the chairs, and most people would have moved their chairs somewhat anyway. Yossi would end the evening with a satisfied sigh rather than a tension headache, and he would be much more likely to undertake addtional parlor meetings in the future. By letting go of perfectionism, he would actually be able to embrace a higher level of accomplishment.

In another guise, perfectionism can look from the outside like utter serenity. For example, Leah appears to her friends to be someone who always "has it together." She has every dish for every Yom Tov meal cooked, sealed and filed in the freezer several weeks in advance. She believes this enables her to be relaxed, but if she looks a little more closely at her inner workings, she will see a relentlessly whirling engine driven to be on top of every situation. It's true that Rosh Hashanah is in the freezer before Rosh Chodesh Elul, but Leah simply displaces the tension most homemakers feel during the days before the holiday to the month before the holiday. When that task is finished, she already feels the pressure of the next task. The perfectionist pushes herself or himself to achieve the goal of completion, yet the goal is always sliding out of reach because life and its demands continue to unfold.

"I wish I could clean the house from top to bottom and it would be done," one client told me. "But there's always a new mess, and the mess makes me nervous. So I'm always cleaning."

Perfectionism can be a cruel taskmaster that keeps us hopping, but it can also cause paralysis. I often see clients who describe themselves as "lazy," when in fact, they are simply overwhelmed by the impossibility of their own expectations of themselves. *I can't do it,* their brain tells them, and they simply shut down. Many people remember experiencing this feeling as students faced with a mountain of homework or a complicated assignment. It's hard to get started because we cannot imagine how we will get to the finish line. People feel this way as well when faced with a big project: a huge pile of papers needing sorting, a "disaster" of a room that needs a cleanup, a household that needs to be packed up for moving.

The advice we give and receive in these situations is "take it one step at a time." But the perfectionist cannot deal with that approach. One completed step of the thousand-step project still leaves 999 uncompleted steps. Even 200 steps still leave 800. The process of gradual, long-term progress creates immense emotional distress for the perfectionist because he or she must live a long time with the discomfort of unfinished, imperfect results. Therefore, for him it becomes impossible to even get started.

The discomfort is even more unbearable when the process involves trial and error. The "error" part of that methodology is something the perfectionist cannot accept. He needs to win the gold, or at least the silver. Anything less, he believes, makes him a loser, and fear of that label stamps out his willingness to start anything new: a business, a career, a skill, a friendship. It even stands in the way of something as simple as playing with his children, as seen in the opening story of Binyamin and the Pictionary game.

Ironically, the mind-set of perfectionism actually detracts from a person's effectiveness because of a psychological phenomenon effect called "ego depletion." This term was coined in the late 1990s by Florida State University psychology professor Roy Baumeister, who conducted experiments to find out how mental stress affects our performance.

We would all assume, even without the benefit of science, that a person may not perform up to his potential if he is under stress while he attempts the task. For instance, someone who worries too much about passing a test may find his mind going blank when he takes the test. However, Dr. Baumeister added a surprising piece of knowledge to that common-sense idea: The stress can even affect our performance in subsequent, completely unrelated tasks. In other words, the person awash in anxiety as he takes his test may drive home with less skill and concentration than normal.

In Dr. Baumeister's experiment, he told his subjects that they were to be involved in a taste test. He sat one group in a room with a bowl of chocolate-chip cookies, and invited them to partake. Another group sat with a bowl of cookies, which they were forbidden to eat, and a bowl of radishes, which they were allowed to eat. All the subjects had been instructed to eat nothing for three hours before the test, ensuring that they would arrive hungry.

When the "taste test" was over, each group was asked to complete a puzzle which was actually impossible to do. Those who had expended their willpower on resisting the cookies gave up the puzzle quickly, while those who had been allowed to eat the cookies persisted for a substantially longer time.

Dr. Baumeister used the term "ego depletion" to describe the idea that we can literally "run out of steam" and have little mental energy left to apply to the next task at hand. He compared the mind to a muscle that could become exhausted from overuse. The perfectionist's constant subconscious agonizing over whether or not something is good enough leaves less mental capacity for concentrating on intellectual activities such as learning or schoolwork, less patience for family members, colleagues and friends and less willpower to stick to goals. Therefore, our perfectionist standards can make perfection all the more elusive.

The How and Why

How does perfectionism infiltrate our thinking in such an overpowering way? As children growing up in the Jewish world, the models of perfection are all around us. From the Torah's spiritual giants to the scholars and saintly figures that populate our history, all the way to the revered leaders of modern times, we hear of men and women who seem to live at a level that is beyond nature and above human foibles. There are those who seem to need little food or sleep, those who give their every moment to the welfare of the community or to Torah scholarship, those who give away their last coin to the poor, those who display incredible brilliance at a tender age and so forth. Reinforcing the examples set by these figures, our *mussar sefarim* urge us onto higher and higher standards, reminding us that there is no standing still. We are either working to rise higher, or by default, we are slipping backward.

While all of these influences are there to illustrate the heights to which a human being can rise, many people create from this paradigm a yardstick by which to measure themselves. They do not take into account the fact that even the great people of our past and present had to climb to the heights they reached. A yeshivah student of 15 cannot measure himself against a Torah luminary of 60.

Perfectionists also dismiss the value of balance, forbidding themselves to say, "This particular issue is just not that important." Here is a speech we will never hear:

"We want to thank our Event Chairlady, Mrs. Goodman, for her reasonable efforts to make this Chinese Auction a nice evening. She didn't get stuck on the details and didn't even make a fuss when we ran out of matching chairs for the food court and had to haul some in from the upstairs classrooms. We also thank her for not pushing everyone to the limits of their endurance."

We will never hear that speech because balance is rarely praised, except by the grateful spouse and children who will some day realize what a gift it is. Naturally, we all wish to be praiseworthy, and so we aim for that which is praised: perfectionism. In

doing so, however, we miss the fundamental truth; we are mea-
sured according to our own capabilities and environment. Hashem
plants each person in the time and place from which that person's
achievements are meant to sprout. For instance, Hashem does not
judge the Torah learning of someone born in America in 1929
against the level of someone who was born in a *shtetl* in Lithu-
ania in 1929. In Hashem's accounting, the American might have
achieved greatness by simply adhering to the laws of *kashrus* and
Shabbos and giving his children a basic Jewish education.

We are each such a unique combination of nature, nurture and
neshamah that it is impossible to apply someone else's yardstick
to our own life; it is only possible to learn from others' virtues.
For this reason, people who want to achieve real, valuable and
lasting growth in their lives are wise to use a "navigator" on their
journey. A person's own *rav,* teacher, mentor or trusted friend
is essential to guide a person on a path that is wholesome and
productive. We all need the occasional "reality check" to ensure
that we are not driving full speed ahead in the wrong direction.

The Key

The negative, anti-joyful hues with which perfectionism colors our lives is proof that it is not meant to be part of the
palette. The same upbringing that shows us how exalted a
human being can become also tells us unequivocally that perfection belongs to Hashem alone. Imperfection is built into
the Creation. The Chofetz Chaim teaches that we can see this
expressed clearly in the blessing we recite after food — "*Borei
nefashos.*" In it, we bless Hashem's multiplicity of creations,
"*v'chesronon*" — and their imperfections: a clear statement
that imperfection is not only inevitable, but a blessing.

How is it a blessing? Someone who accepts imperfection is
not bound and gagged by fear of failure. He realizes that everyone has their strengths and weaknesses; in fact, the Chofetz
Chaim points out that our needs and assets are a large part of

what bind us to each other, enabling us to play the roles of giver and taker. This is what creates the dynamic of chesed, upon which Hashem founded the world. Were we all living in self-sufficient little pods, there would be no society, no give-and-take, and no world as we know it.

By embracing this fundamental fact, we can deal with the ups and downs of our progress and we can deal with our own gaps in ability and knowledge: the writer does not have to feel miserable over his poor bookkeeping skills and the accountant does not have to fret over his non-existent way with words. We can accept that we were each created with a unique nature that includes certain strengths and certain weaknesses. That is how Hashem created the world, and when we accept that, we can sustain our self-image even when we come in last. If we can afford to fail, we can afford to try.

To find that freedom within ourselves, our first order of business is to develop a healthy respect for the value of mistakes. We must say to ourselves over and over and over again, "Mistakes are necessary. Mistakes are productive. Mistakes lead to success."

That might seem too sweeping a statement for the perfectionist to accept. What about careless mistakes that need not have been made? Are they necessary? They are, for they teach us to exercise more care. What about mistakes that cost money or damage or destroy something? What about mistakes that injure another person, such as a car accident? The reasons behind these types of mistakes, which we wish to and try to avoid, involve metaphysical questions of human action versus Divine design, which are far beyond the scope of this book. However, one fact is certain: There is something to be learned from every mistake. Often the most profound, life-changing lessons come from the biggest mistakes.

Mistakes can be compared to strikeouts in a ball game. If someone fears that moment when the ball whizzes past his bat and the umpire calls "strike," and his pride cannot tolerate his teammates' disgruntled faces, he has only one option. He must stay out of the game. If we want to be in the game, we have to learn how to deal with the strikeouts. We have to take pride in the number of times we step up to the plate, regardless of the result.

The Farbers loved guests. They lived in a kiruv community where there were always plenty of people looking for a place at a Shabbos table, and the Farbers were a favorite destination for many. Hindy Farber's mother, Julie, came to visit the young couple one weekend. Julie was an accomplished hostess in her upscale suburban town and she was eager to help Hindy prepare the table for the Friday-night dinner.

"It doesn't look like you have quite enough food," Julie told her daughter. "Want me to run to the take-out store and get some more stuff?"

"It's plenty, Mom," Hindy replied. "I just slice everything a little smaller. No one notices."

"What about this salad?" Julie inquired. "What are you going to serve it in?"

"It's fine in that bowl."

"But this is plastic!" Julie nearly cried. "You can't put this on the table."

"Ma, people come here every week. They get plenty of food and no one refuses the salad because it's in a plastic bowl. If I drive myself crazy with the meal, I won't be able to have guests."

The guests came, the conversation flowed, the *zemiros* were beautiful, there was plenty of food and there were even leftovers. Hindy achieved something worthwhile by allowing herself to fall short of perfect hostess standards. There were a few flaws in her presentation, but because Hindy made the job doable for herself, she was able to obtain the more important benefit of a lively, welcoming Shabbos table. She knew there were people, even in her own community, who served a more sumptuous menu on a more elegant table; it just did not matter to her. She knew that if she had felt the need to make the meals perfect, her invitations would be far fewer and less frequent.

Along with an acceptance of mistakes as a fact of life comes an ability to get past our mistakes. We do so by taking responsibility for what happened, apologizing to anyone who suffered from the error, making necessary repairs and adjustments, and then moving forward. If we allow ourselves to keep rerunning the mistake, we find ourselves suffering the embarrassment and discomfort over and over again. It becomes not just one negative event, but a daily or even hourly recurring negative event which makes the prospect of any future mistake all the more frightening. A person who knows how to move forward can take the lessons learned from a mistake and build something out of them.

Dan went for his first job interview. With his recently minted Masters in business, his expensive interview suit and an "in" with the company, he felt confident that he would have a good chance at the job. However, when the secretary led him into the office of Mr. Robert Rubinov, Dan lost his nerve. Mahogany paneling, antique rugs, museum-quality paintings and Mr. Rubinov himself, with his silver-gray lion's mane atop his fiery features: it was all a bit too much.

"So you're Elliot's nephew," Mr. Rubinov said, sounding a bit disappointed. "What do you know about our company?"

Dan had studied for this question, but now, he could barely remember anything. He mentioned the yearly sales and the company's mission statement, sounding like a schoolkid answering the teacher. The rest of the very brief interview went downhill from there. He knew he didn't get the job.

After the interview, Dan replayed the entire scene. *I sounded so dumb!* he told himself. But then he rebounded. *There's always a first time. I let myself get rattled by him. I have to figure out a way to avoid that.* He asked his mentors how to handle his feelings of intimidation and he practiced many times before his next interview, which went much, much better.

Dan was able to keep moving toward his goal because he knew how to steer clear of perfectionist thinking. He only looked backward long enough to derive the lesson from his mistake. Then he used it to prepare himself for another try. He didn't shy away from trying again; even though he hoped to avoid another mistake, he did not fear the possibility. He had learned one lesson from his first mistake and if there would be a second mistake, he would learn a second lesson.

Mistakes are, in fact, a key ingredient in success. Many great inventions and discoveries are the result of mistakes. The well-known story of penicillin is one example: It was discovered when Alexander Fleming, a scientist, was sorting through petri dishes that he had inadvertently left in his lab over a vacation period. Bacteria were growing all over them. On one dish, however, there was a spot of mold, around which no bacteria grew. From that mold, penicillin was developed. Had Fleming been more of a perfectionist about the cleanliness of his lab, the world would be a different place. **But it was not just the mistake; it was his ability to capitalize on the mistake that bore results**.

As in all the "locks" we are discussing in these chapters, breaking free means liberating ourselves to embrace life's potential. It means reclaiming life's fluidity rather than casting ourselves in stagnant molds that cannot respond to new situations. Shedding the perfectionist mentality lets us adapt to life as it evolves. Things do not always have to be done the same way; they do not always need to be done our way. Neither do the same issues always have to be important to us. A young mother who insists on every dish being washed, dried and put away before she goes to bed may, if she is not locked in by perfectionism, decide as a middle-aged woman that she would rather go to bed earlier and wash the dishes in the morning. She can make that decision without guilt, without feeling that she has dropped her standards; she allows herself to expend her energy on what best suits her needs in the present.

Part of perfectionism is a drive to complete our "to-do" list, and a concurrent feeling of failure when we do not complete it. However, we don't have to go to bed each night bearing the weight of today's leftover chores and tomorrow's new agenda. Completion is great, but until our last day of life, it is only an illusion. Our job is never done, so why categorize the undone items as a failure? Just as we must say, "finished," no matter what we are doing when Shabbos comes in, we must learn to say, "finished," when the day is done. We deserve that sigh of satisfaction that comes with the conclusion of a task, even if the "conclusion" is only partial for now.

To fully embrace our lives, we need to be perfect at only one task: doing the best we can now with what we have now. The person who lives this way lives with joy, takes on tasks with eagerness and goes to bed at night unencumbered by regrets. Here are some ways to get there.

Unlock Your Self-Acceptance

Inspiration

1. **Identify your inner fears of failure.** What are you telling yourself that makes mistakes an unbearable option? Perhaps it is, *No one will respect me* or *Second-best isn't good enough* or *I have to stand out in some way* or *Making a mistake makes me a loser.* Perhaps you worry that you will lose the love of your spouse, parents or children. Discover the root of your fear.

2. **Identify the voices** that insist on perfection. Are they coming from your friends, parents, society, school? Notice how these voices hold you back from reaching your potential. Test the realism of the expectations you perceive: *Is a*

mistake really fatal in this situation, or can it be fixed or overlooked? Am I really stupid, or am I quite competent in some areas? Am I really lazy, or do I actually accomplish a lot with my time?

3. **Experience yourself** without fear. Picture yourself trying something you want to do, completely for your own satisfaction without looking around you for approval. Imagine engaging in the process of trial and error with a sense of ease, freedom and confidence. Be that person who just does it his own way and somehow pulls it off. Imagine making a mistake — burning the main dish, stumbling over your speech, giving a wrong answer — and just acknowledging it with a smile and moving on.

4. **Feel** the focus and energy you have when you work without tension. Feel yourself going with the flow of trial, error and progress toward your goal. Feel the freedom of letting go of your impossible expectations.

Logic

5. **Keep reminding yourself** that perfection is impossible. You are expending tremendous amounts of energy to achieve something that is beyond any human being's ability to achieve.

6. **Acknowledge** that perfectionism is not a positive attribute. This is a vital reframing of a false ideal you may well have been living by since childhood. Perfectionism does not help you reach higher goals. It hinders you, as the theory of ego depletion illustrates.

7. **See yourself in the mirror.** You need to fully understand what perfectionism looks like in action. Since it is impossible for us to subjectively view ourselves, find someone you know who is a perfectionist, and observe him or her. Note the tension and pressure the person exudes and spreads

to others, often not even perceiving their own level of tension. Find an older person who still clings to perfectionist tendencies and realize that without a concerted effort, this mind-set does not go away.

8. **Put one mistake up on a pedestal.** Think of one mistake you have made that taught you something important and led to success. If you find yourself falling into your fear of failure, think of that mistake and its outcome.

Action

9. **Start** by taking a risk. Take on a small project that has thus far intimidated you and take stock of any mistakes you make. Did you find the error painful? Do you see that allowing yourself to make mistakes has allowed you to expand your experiences? Are you engaging in life more actively? Are you happier?

10. **Speak** to people you consider successful. Ask them about their failures, and you will see that every successful person has fallen and risen back up many times. The more successful people are, the more failures they have experienced. The secret is that they are prepared to fall and rise again.

For those who insist on perfection in themselves, who fear making mistakes or demean others who make mistakes, the Torah's viewpoint on perfection is well worth exploring.

The *Shulchan Aruch* (*Yoreh Deah, Hilchos Talmud Torah, siman 246, se'if 10*) states that a *rebbi* should not become irritated with a student who does not understand the lesson. Rather, he should teach it to him several times until he does understand. Nor should the student pretend to understand when he does not. Rather, he should keep asking until he is clear. If the *rebbi* becomes upset, the student should reply, "*Rebbi*, this is Torah and I need to learn it. . ..Please teach it to me."

The Take-Away

The *Shulchan Aruch* is dealing with a normal situation. It acknowledges that some students will find learning difficult, and they have the right and obligation to get their rebbi to teach them until they understand. Getting it perfect the first time around is obviously not required or even expected.

The Gemara (*Gittin* 43:1) records that one day, Rabbah bar Rav Huna rendered a halachic decision. Rav Chisda said that the decision was in error. In response, Rabbah said that "Shlomo Hamelech says, 'This mistake is under your hand.'" The meaning of his statement was that a person can only acquire wisdom in Torah if he makes mistakes. Rashi explains that this is because when someone makes a mistake in interpreting the law, he will delve more deeply until he understands it clearly.

The Take-Away

Even the great Rabbah bar Rav Huna made a mistake, teaching us that we can grow if we are willing to make mistakes and learn from them. If a person of his stature needs to make room for imperfection, we at our level certainly cannot expect to get anywhere without making mistakes, especially as we stretch beyond our limits.

The Gemara (*Pesachim* 22b) relates that Rabbi Shimon Haamsoni would expound on every "*es*" (a seemingly superfluous word that implies an expanded meaning of the next word) in the Torah. When it came to the words of "*es Hashem Elokecha tira*" (Hashem, your G-d, you shall fear) he didn't have an explanation; he could not imagine how the Name of Hashem could expand any further. His students were worried about their *rebbi* leaving out one "*es*," destroying the completeness of his work. Rabbi Shimon, however, told them that the same reward he had earned for expounding on all the other appearances of the "*es*" he would earn for abstaining on this one.

The Take-Away

Rabbi Shimon did not see success as a perfect score. He saw doing his best and abstaining when necessary — even just that once — as success. As long as he acted and accomplished all he could, he knew he had done his job to perfection. If we define success as taking action, then the gaps, flaws and errors inherent in action become part of our success.

In *Pirkei Avos* (2:21) Rabbi Tarfon states, "You are not required to complete the task, yet you are not free to withdraw from it." Rashi explains that if we learn and we aren't able to complete the learning, we will still be rewarded. At the same time, we do not have the option to say, "I'd rather not learn and not receive reward."

The Take-Away

We see countless times that Hashem only wants us to do our best. He wants us to make a start, to stretch ourselves and grow. When we get caught up in the need for perfection or completion, we discourage our own efforts. Rabbi Tarfon tells us, "Just get started."

Straight from the Source

In the Foreword to *Chovos Halevavos,* we learn the proper attitude toward fear of performing imperfectly:

When I thought of proceeding to carry out my decision to write this book, I saw that a man like myself is not fit to compose a work like this....the subject appearing too vast to my eyes, my knowledge too inadequate and my intellectual faculties too weak to grasp the topics. . ..I therefore told my soul to retract the thought and to draw back from what it had resolved on....[However] I knew that many great works were lost due to fear, and many losses were caused by overconcern.....Therefore, I found myself obligated to force my soul to bear the task of composing this book....On Him I place my trust and to Him I ask to teach me the right path which He desires.

The Take-Away

No matter how high we are on the ladder of success, we may always wonder, whether out of humility or self-doubt, why we should be the ones to take on a difficult task that stretches us beyond our limits. It is "part two" of the process — the courage to place our trust in Hashem and dive in anyway — that enables us to reach our potential.

Chapter 3
Step Three

Release Life's New Beginnings

Vitality vs. Stagnation

BORO PARK WAS LEVI'S NATIVE HABITAT. HE HAD grown up there, married and raised his children there. He and his late wife had literally hundreds of acquaintances and dozens of close friends. Now, however, as Levi reached his senior years, life had changed. His children had married and moved to Lakewood. Many of his friends had moved away as well, some to Florida, some to Israel, some to the suburbs or retirement homes.

"I feel really alone," Levi told me. "I want to be around my family. I want to be where I can be part of my kids' and grandchildren's lives. But what would I do in Lakewood? How can I start in a whole new shul and a whole new neighborhood? I can't just park

myself on my kids. I'd have to make a life for myself,
but I'm too old to start making new friends."

"Why are you too old?" I asked him.

"I'd feel so awkward. What am I supposed to say
to people? Who wants some old guy coming over and
shaking his hand and saying, 'Hi, I'm new in town?' I
can't deal with it."

Levi is an expert at living in Boro Park. However, his circumstances have changed to the point where that expertise no longer enables him to have a fulfilling life. He realizes that being close to his family would re-energize him. In his mind's eye, he sees himself taking his granddaughters to the park on a Sunday afternoon, or sitting in the audience as a proud Zeidy at his grandsons' yeshivah events. He imagines how wonderful it would be to spend Shabbos with his children's families without having a long, exhausting drive to get there and get home. With all his heart, he yearns to bask in the glow of the family he and his wife built together. But something is stopping him.

You might find that something is stopping you, as well. Ask yourself these 10 questions to find out how comfortable you are with change and new situations.

1. Are you resistant to meeting new people?

2. Are you stuck in a deadening or damaging situation (relationship, job, school, etc.), simply because you cannot face the prospect of starting something new?

3. Do you resist the advice of caring, trustworthy people who urge you to move onto something new, telling yourself that they don't really understand the whole situation?

4. Do you talk about the same topics over and over, rarely embracing new ideas and interests?

5. Are you afraid to take a risk?

6. Are you fearful when you must perform before a group?

7. Do you dream of doing something new but fear trying it?

8. Do you quit at the first sign of resistance?

9. Do you assume that you won't succeed before you even start?

10. Do you feel that mistakes and failure are beneath the dignity of someone of your status, age or experience?

11. Are you afraid to strive to the next level of achievement?

The Lock

New beginnings are part of the ever-changing landscape of life. Even if we attempt to sit absolutely still, right where we feel safe and comfortable, the earth beneath our safe little spot will inevitably shift and change, and in the process, thrust us into new encounters. For some people, that prospect is so terrifying that they will cling with all their strength to the familiar situation even if it no longer works to their benefit.

A person's discomfort with new encounters stands in the way of a great, ever-flowing river of possibilities in life. For example:

- Getting started in a profession or business is nearly impossible without the ability to network with new people and tackle new skills.

- For people seeking a marriage partner, the dating process becomes an agonizing journey into unknown territory with unknown people.

- Someone stuck in a yeshivah, school or job that isn't suitable might stay there rather than go through the trauma of starting over with a whole new group of people and new ways of doing things.

Almost any forward motion we want to make in our lives requires a willingness to learn new information, try new skills and develop connections with new people. Therefore, the lack of confidence to break out of our comfort zone inevitably leads to stagnation and lost opportunities.

We tend to imagine that confidence is an all-or-nothing trait. There's the extrovert: that robust, confident person with the sparkling smile who always knows just what to say. For him, walking into a crowded room is invigorating. He will walk out with 10 new contacts on his cell phone, a new business proposition and a *shidduch* suggestion for his next-door neighbor. Then there's the introvert; for him, a night at home with a good book is invigorating. He tends to confine his social circle to his family, and can be satisfied with seeing one or two close friends once in a great while.

The truth is, however, the vast majority of people are a little bit of both. Very few extroverts have no fear or self-consciousness in new situations, and most have some capacity to enjoy time alone. On the other hand, very few introverts have no need for new connections and new experiences. The problem is that they have a faulty subconscious program that prevents them from confidently, enthusiastically putting themselves out there in the land of the unknown. They wish they could break out of their insulated world, but they worry that they will somehow humiliate themselves in the process.

What is in this disabling subconscious program? One element is an exquisitely sensitive "radar system" that constantly feeds a person input about where he stands with others. For instance, as he attempts to integrate into a social group, he notices who is speaking with whom, who is looking at him, who has greeted him, how enthusiastically he has been greeted and so forth. Someone with poor social skills may have no radar system at all. A confident person keeps the radar appropriately attuned to the situation, so that only real dangers register. The introvert, however, has his radar system cranked up all the way. His exquisitely sensitive early warning system lets him know if he is in the slightest danger of being rejected.

Moshe sat at his assigned table at the wedding. The band was loud, and so it was difficult to carry on a conversation. Moshe's neighbor Asher was sitting to his right, but Asher was speaking to Yitzy, who sat on the other side of him. Somehow, it seemed that three or four men were involved in that conversation, but Moshe sat frozen, trying to think of something to add that would be worth shouting into his neighbor's ear. Thoughts flitted through his mind, but they all seemed like inane, unnecessary remarks.

"I'm sitting here like a dunce," Moshe thought. "I'm at a table with all my neighbors and no one's talking to me. It's amazing how everyone else has things to say and I'm just out of it." He got up for a few minutes and when he returned, another man was sitting in his seat having a lively conversation with Asher.

"Oh, Moshe, you're back!" the man said pleasantly. "I hope you don't mind that I borrowed your seat for a minute to catch up with my old buddy Asher." He stood up to give the seat to Moshe.

"I'm sure Asher is more interested in talking to him than to me," Moshe thought as he sat down.

There might be a million benign reasons for the way conversations and events unfold at Moshe's table, but his radar picks up every negative nuance. All this input reinforces Moshe's "I'm unpopular" program.

Another difficulty is that sometimes, introverts do not know what steps to take to make friends and develop friendships. They might not realize that this is a skill like any other, requiring purposeful activities such as asking about the well-being of someone else's family, offering to help someone who is making a *simchah* or is dealing with a crisis, keeping in contact with occasional phone calls or texts, participating in conversations, asking people their opinions, inviting people to their home for a Shabbos meal, or any other action that forms a thread of connection between themselves and others.

Similarly, someone who fears the discomfort and inevitable mistakes of a new job might hold himself back from doing the basic groundwork that would ease his way into the situation. He fears asking too many questions because he does not want to appear inept. As a result, he struggles alone with an unfamiliar procedure, a new computer program, terms he thinks he should know but doesn't and so forth. What could be a challenge and learning experience becomes instead an anxiety-ridden ordeal.

If we don't make a purposeful effort toward change and renewal, we find ourselves passively stuck with whatever people and situations fall upon us. This narrow range of choices can breed close, loyal relationships and long-term commitments, but it can also breed trouble. When someone fears having to forge into new territory, he may have a more exaggerated fear of losing the situation he already has. This makes him an ideal target for a manipulative, dominating person. The introvert may be locked into a dysfunctional situation simply out of a powerful fear of breaking free and setting out to create a new situation.

Every day, Aliza came home from eighth grade miserable and depressed. Her best and only friend, Shoshana, picked on her relentlessly, criticized her clothes, ridiculed her ideas and left her out of her wider social circle. When Aliza's mother suggested that she stop spending time with Shoshana, Aliza was horrified. "If I didn't have her, I wouldn't have anyone! No one else wants to be my friend!"

Like this young girl, many people cling to hurtful relationships out of a conviction that it would be impossible for them to make other friends. They managed to slide into this one relationship without having to extend themselves, and therefore, they believe that they will have to wait it out alone until they manage to slide into another one. In the yeshivah world, this can translate into sticking with a *chavrusa* who dampens his partner's learning by dominating the learning, dismissing his ideas or perhaps distracting him from the task at hand. In the business world, it can mean remaining with a partner whose business methods are unacceptable or unproductive. For a family, it might mean staying in a community that is a poor fit. In all situations, fear of a new beginning even prevents us from trying to restructure the old situation into something more satisfying.

The sheer physical discomfort that besets a person who fears new beginnings is enough to stop him from trying. In a classic anxiety reaction, he feels his heart pounding and sweat prickling his skin; his stomach churns, his mouth goes dry and his brain is screaming, *Get me out of here!* The fear of "feeling stupid" keeps people locked into worn-out, unsatisfying jobs and situations in which the main benefit is that their sense of their own competence is not challenged. It prevents them from trying and succeeding at fully using their abilities.

Esther and her husband Aaron got married and a few months later, the young couple moved to Italy to take advantage of a business opportunity. They had agreed that they were willing to settle and raise their family there, and were both excited about starting their life together in a foreign country. In preparation for the move, they took a crash course in Italian, and by the time they took off to their new home, they both had a basic grasp of the language.

From the second they arrived in Italy, Aaron spoke to everyone he met in his fractured, Americanized Italian. His mistakes brought smiles of understanding from some natives, sharp corrections from others and actual guffaws from still others. Aaron kept trying, and by the time he had lived in Italy for a year, he was able to carry on his day-to-day affairs in fluent Italian.

Esther, on the other hand, had always been a great student. She hated the feeling of not knowing what she was doing. If she couldn't do something right, she wouldn't do it at all. She would rather hunt down a person who could understand

English or struggle to make herself understood with hand gestures than venture to speak an incorrect sentence. After five years in Italy, Aaron felt like a native and Esther was still a tongue-tied stranger.

Why did Esther and Aaron, each starting with about the same level of knowledge in the language, have such different outcomes in their mastery of it? Aaron's secret was that he accepted himself as a beginner. He knew he would make a lot of mistakes before he got it right, but he also knew that making those mistakes was *the* necessary step to getting it right. He got flustered and nervous just as Esther did, but he forged ahead anyway. When someone corrected him, whether with a smile or a smirk, he appreciated the input. He tried the sentence again right then and there.

Like Aaron, anyone starting something new, whether it is as major as a complete career change or as minor as joining a new carpool, can find the freedom to achieve when he accepts his rank as beginner — and begins. With that mind-set, we can step forward into the situations life presents to us, thus turning our dreams and potentials into realities. We can connect with the fabulous variety of people who enter our sphere, thus enriching our own lives.

The How and Why

Human beings are social creatures. How, then, does the prospect of making new social connections become so antithetical to some of us? Aren't we supposed to long for those connections? Aren't they the ticket to a happy, healthy, fulfilling life? What happens to turn this natural source of joy into a heart-thumping anxiety attack? Furthermore, from our earliest days we have an innate desire to learn and experience our world. Why does that robust curiosity that drives a toddler to rummage through cabinets and pull at locked doors shrivel up and die?

Some people have an overly sensitive nature. Whether this is because of a lack of self-esteem or just an extreme personality trait, this sensitivity makes all the awkwardness and insecurity of beginning a new activity or forging a new relationship too painful to endure. Just as someone who easily burns in the sun will stay away from the beach, a person who is easily burned emotionally will shy away from situations in which uncomfortable feelings are almost sure to emerge.

The fear of failure and rejection is another strong motivation for steering clear of new beginnings. While nobody likes failure, a more extroverted person can accept it. Rather than worrying that there is something wrong with him or feeling embarrassed by the situation, the extrovert thinks, *Oh, well, I guess this wasn't for me.* Since he is able to process the failure or rejection and move on, he is able to take the risk inherent in new situations. Someone who perceives rejection as a humiliating disaster, however, does whatever he can to avoid the risk. This is especially so if he has experienced a painful rejection in the past.

It's not always the potential for pain that keeps a person from entering a new situation. Sometimes the demand for perfection is the roadblock. Because we must begin at the beginning, we will always start a new endeavor with most everyone else already well ahead of us. There is no other choice. There will always be a first day, a first time, a first try, and it will never be as comfortable as the 25th day, the 25th time or the 25th try. As we noted earlier, people who cannot accept themselves as beginners cannot embark on new beginnings.

At some stages of life, of course, a beginner is all we can be. A child starting his first day of nursery school has no choice but to deal with all the drama and trauma of unfamiliar surroundings. Most of us make our way through these situations, cultivate friendships and settle into a comfortable norm. That comfort, in and of itself, can become another obstacle to stepping into a new situation. The long-lost skills that got us through the first day of yeshivah, the first day of high school, the first time at the in-laws' Shabbos table and so forth are tucked away somewhere in our minds, but we are reluctant to dust them off and use them again. We are not even sure they still work. Rather than face potential failure, we stay in our comfort zone.

One last reason for a lack of confidence is a lack of necessity. People who are naturally complacent with the status quo have little motivation to move out of it. They sometimes fail to recognize the need to expand their horizons and find out too late that ultimately, stagnation ends up being a poor policy. There comes a time when we realize that we are losing by failing to integrate ourselves into some group: our child's school, a workplace, a community or shul. Or, we realize that our life has become an empty routine that cries out for revitalization. At that point, we find ourselves faced with a situation we do not quite know how to handle.

That's where experience comes in. If we allow ourselves to step into new situations, we learn how to do it. In the "action" segment below, we provide many simple, pragmatic steps we can take to relieve that knot of tension inside us and fortify ourselves with the courage to move forward into a world of new possibilities. These ideas are useful for everyone from a child going to a new summer camp to a girl heading to seminary to a man starting a job to an elderly person moving into an assisted living facility.

While all of these methods can ease the way into a new situation, there is still important internal work that must be done to enable us to get rid of the fear at its source. If we can rewrite the program that prevents us from opening up to the world around us, we literally rewrite the story of our lives.

The Key

What happens when we reach inside our subconscious and unlock our deep, inborn desire to experience the world and people around us? The impact is so much more than what it seems. It's not just a matter of being more comfortable at weddings or less anxious about meeting a potential client. It's a matter of liberation; we become free to explore the myriad opportunities that come our way and to vastly expand our imprint on the world.

When we master the art of new beginnings, we create a life of new beginnings. Life's changes might still unsettle us, but we no longer waste our energy trying to repel them. Rather, we embrace them and trust in our ability to learn, adapt and ultimately grow from our challenges. All of these benefits and more can be ours by using the Second Key.

Unlock New Beginnings

Inspiration

1. **Hear the inner voice** that reacts with excitement at a new prospect. That voice is your nature calling out to you, lighting up the path that is specifically yours to take. With that spark of excitement, you'll be fully charged with the energy to move full speed toward your goal.

   You'll know what speaks to you when you pay attention to your emotional reactions to various possibilities. When you imagine yourself involved in a certain career (not the schooling or training it takes to get there, but just being there), does that image excite you? When you imagine living in a certain community, do you see yourself as thriving? Listen to that happiness; it's your subconscious mapping your optimal route in life.

2. **Hear your inner doubts**. Do not try to ignore them or downplay them. Your subconscious needs to be heard, and once that happens, the concerns can be tabled until such time as they become relevant. Doubts are like nagging "to-do" items that keep interfering with your thoughts until

you write them down. So write down your doubts without feeling the need to solve them at the moment, and you will find that you are able to move forward.

3. **Visualize the new you.** Imagine the excitement you will feel when you embark on your new experience. Picture the light in a child's eyes as he experiences something for the first time, and let yourself open up to that sensation. Realize that what you may believe to be a lack of desire for renewal and growth is really just the fears and disappointments of the past, hiding the pilot light that still burns in your heart. See yourself reignited, fresh and youthful, doing the positive, productive, exciting new things your nature longs to do. Spend three minutes a day vividly visualizing and living the new you.

Logic

4. **Know** that all beginnings are challenging, no matter how accomplished you are in other areas. Someone who has learned a foreign language to the point of fluency will still struggle and make mistakes when he tries to learn a different language. The person who can crochet intricate designs will probably suffer through a few botched projects when she decides to branch out into knitting or sewing.

The purpose of expecting mistakes is to cultivate patience for the process. If you know that, with persistence, it takes two years to master a certain skill, you can find the confidence to keep pushing even when, after a few weeks, you still feel like a beginner. If you don't set up false expectations, you won't be undermined by normal trial and error.

Example: The Steins sent their daughter to seminary in Israel. Mrs. Stein told her daughter, "I know you want to love it from the first minute, but there's a lot to get used to. So don't even ask yourself, *Am I happy?* until Chanukah time." Indeed, the daughter was homesick and overwhelmed with the work and the unfamiliarity with her surroundings. But with her mother's words in her head, she put her unhappiness in a mental "file" to be examined in full at Chanukah time. By then, she was settled in and loving her experience, just as she had hoped.

5. **Recognize your signs of life.** The flutter in your stomach and the pounding of your heart when you try something for the first time is a *good* sign. It means you're alive and growing. If you are 70 and feeling that sensation, it's something to celebrate: you haven't stagnated! If you're 14 and feeling it, it's also something to celebrate: you're not afraid to take the risk, even when it's frightening. Let your logic override what feels like fear, and translate it into the excitement and thrill of plunging into new territory.

6. **"Ride the wave"** of your inevitably up-and-down emotions as you embark and carry through on your new experience. Expect to feel energized and confident one minute, and then full of doubt the next. The secret is to avoid panicking when the negative feelings surface, and also to avoid deflating the positive feelings with thoughts like, *I better not get too excited. What if it doesn't pan out?* Remember that everyone who accomplishes anything goes through these stages over and over.

One helpful strategy is to create a support system. Find two or three people (so that no one person is overburdened) whose judgment you trust and speak to one of them when you find yourself overwhelmed with doubts. An objective eye can help you break out of your own emotionally colored perspective and enable you to see the whole picture. You will find that with a change in outlook, every situation is manageable.

Action

7. **Learn the rules**. Starting something new — especially new relationships — is a process we can learn to master.

   a. **Engage yourself**. If you are developing new social relationships, make sure to spend actual "face time" with the person so that you can build a bond based on shared conversation and experience. If you are starting a new job or skill, set aside time to take action and engage in activities toward your goal. Talk to knowledgeable people; learn by observing and doing rather than just thinking and reading up on the topic.

   b. **Allow for disagreement.** Do not feel rejected or undermined if others have opinions different from your own. Friends can "agree to disagree." In the spiritual world, people can take many paths toward growth. In the world of business and professions, there are many models for success. Be open to what others have to offer without going on the defensive.

   c. **Create continuity.** Every step you take should be concluded by planning your follow-up step. That way, you do not have the constant feeling of starting from scratch and you will be primed to continue on your path. When you "keep the motor running" you don't have to keep restarting the ignition.

   d. **Be patient.** It's not hard to understand that a skill takes time to master or a business takes time to show a profit. What we may not see as clearly is that friendship, too, takes time. Even if we find that we are compatible with someone, it is often months or even years after we meet that we really feel that he or she has become an important part of our lives, and vice versa.

8. **Set a goal and timetable**. Depending on what you are trying to accomplish, you should be aiming for anywhere from six months to two years down the road. Less than that sets you up for failure, and more than that changes a realistic goal into a fantasy.

   After you set your goal, set certain benchmarks for assessing your progress. Be like a business that pays its taxes on a quarterly basis; it doesn't judge its revenue on a day-by-day basis, nor does it wait until a year has gone by. Rather, it evaluates what it has achieved over the course of a few months. At that point, the management can determine if a course adjustment is necessary. Once you pick your goal and your benchmarks, write them down and put them someplace obvious to help you stay on track.

9. **Take your first step!** A vocational school advertises its program with the motto "Turn 'one day' into Day One." So take that first step out of your comfort zone. Here are some ideas suited to various goals.

   - New friendships: Call someone you'd like to befriend; get out of the house (take your kids to the playground, go shopping, etc.) and introduce yourself to one new person a day; attend a lecture or social event and speak to the person sitting next to you; offer to do someone a favor.

   - Starting or expanding a business: Speak to people in the same field; research products and suppliers; research advertising and website development; get a mentor; map out a step-by-step plan with one step to take each day.

   - Changing careers: speak to people in fields that interest you: find programs that will provide you with credentials; take prerequisite courses; plan how you will fund your training; make a to-do list and take at least one step a day.

- Putting old fears and issues to rest: Offer to be the *baal tefillah* or speak at a family gathering; drive on a road that you're fearful to drive on; discuss topics buried under the rug; seek out advice from someone you respect; investigate methods and embark on a campaign to overcome or, at the very least, restrain one negative trait or habit.

- Re-energizing and renewing yourself: Take a course or attend a *shiur*; travel somewhere you've never gone before; take art or music lessons; join a gym; take a quick getaway vacation; plan a visit to friends or family whose company you particularly enjoy; get involved in a community project.

10. **Be consistent.** It is critical to be consistent in keeping to your short-term commitments so that you reach your long-term goals. It's also vital to keep trying new experiences. Don't just pick one idea and let the rest of your life stagnate. The more you open yourself up to new beginnings, the more you will have faith in your ability to succeed, which in turn leads to even more growth. It is understood that you can't take on too much. The idea is to see new challenges as opportunities rather than threats. The reward for shaking yourself up and moving forward is nothing less than a fully lived life.

We all want to achieve our purpose in this world, but many people wonder how they are supposed to know what that purpose is. They wish Hashem would send a personal letter detailing the mission. But in fact, Hashem does reveal our mission to us; it is embedded in the opportunities, situations and people that cross our paths. Each is there for a reason, intersecting with our lives because there is something for us to accomplish through them. When we shed our fear of new beginnings, we open the door to the people and experiences that enable us to become who we are meant to be.

Do you ever wonder how a pilot summons the courage to make his first solo flight? How the acrobat finds courage to hurl himself into his first triple back-flip? How a surgeon finds the courage to cut into a human body for the first time? They know they lack the benefit of experience, and yet, they take the leap.

The Gemara (*Berachos* 10a) relates a time when Chizkiyahu, the king, was deathly ill and Hashem sent Yeshayah, the prophet, to deliver a message to him. The message was that the king had forfeited his place in both this world and the next because he had never married and had children. Chizkiyahu answered that he refrained from marriage because Hashem had let him know that his children would depart from the ways of the Torah. Yeshayah told the king that he did not have the right to try to interfere with Hashem's plan; he must simply fulfill his duty to marry.

Chizkiyahu then suggested that he marry Yeshayah's daughter so that the combined merit of the two families might overturn the decree of having wayward children. "I have a tradition from my grandfather (King David) that 'Even if a sharp sword is posed at your neck, never give up hope for Hashem's mercy.'" The Gemara ends there, but we later learn that Chizkiyahu does indeed marry the daughter of Yeshayah, and he is saved from the decree of losing both worlds.

The Take-Away

Of the many lessons this Gemara illustrates, the one that I find most helpful and liberating to people is the idea that even a king has to step out of his comfort zone, despite knowing he may not be successful. Moving forward and growing in this story is literally a do-or-die mission. For us too, emotionally and spiritually, growth is a do-or-die mission. Stagnation is not a viable option. Hashem wants us to master the art of stepping forward, armed with faith and courage, into uncharted territory. Even the prophet learns from this story that it is never too late to change our destiny.

Midrash Rabbah (*Vayeishev*: 85) discusses the selling of Yosef, relating that Yosef, Reuven and Yaakov were all overcome with sadness. Meanwhile, "Yehudah was occupied getting married (to Tamar). Hashem was busy creating the light of Mashiach (who will be a descendant of this union)."

The Take-Away

The selling of Yosef brought dark times upon the family of Yaakov, but even in the darkness, Yehudah found the energy to begin again and re-establish his family line. He was already old, had already lost two sons, but he started again. In doing so, he planted the seed from which Mashiach will sprout. This, too, was the amazing response of so many Holocaust survivors. They had lived through incomprehensible darkness and suffered crippling losses. Yet, with whatever they had left, they started anew. Old or young, new beginnings give us vitality.

The *Chumash* records countless Divinely mandated journeys, starting with the command of "*lech lecha*" issued to Avraham, to which he responded instantly by leaving his home and family and following Hashem to an unknown destination. All of the *Avos* continued in this spirit, picking up and moving wherever Hashem directed them. Wherever they went, they met with challenges, overcame and prospered. Later, their descendants, the *B'nei Yisrael*, followed their Forefathers' ways by following Moshe *Rabbeinu* into the Wilderness and moving from encampment to encampment as Hashem directed. They left Egypt not knowing how they would survive, yet confident that they were traveling toward their destiny.

The Take-Away

Many people fear stepping into the unknown. They want everything planned and guaranteed before they make their first move. They try to predict every potential problem and often become so bogged down that they become paralyzed. The entire *Chumash*, however, is a travelogue of lessons learned "on the road." At all ages and stages of life, our Forefathers followed the road Hashem laid out for them. They found the strength to meet the tests and challenges they encountered and in doing so, fulfilled their potential. This is a lesson that can give us tremendous encouragement when we face a new situation and fear taking that first step.

Chapter 4
Step Four

Release Free Choice

Choosing Your Life vs. Default Mode

The story of our lives is the story of our choices: how we use each moment of life we're given, how we spend our resources, what words we choose to speak, where we put down our roots, what we eat for dinner and which route we take to work. Big choices and small, life altering or seemingly mundane, we are in a constant state of deciding, and each of these decisions helps to pave our path in life.

As Jews, however, some paths are already paved for us. When we come to a question that has already been settled by *halachah* or *minhag,* we need not wonder what to do. There is, in that case, only one right decision. This chapter is not about those types of questions. When we discuss the value of "choosing your life," we are discussing only those choices that are ours to make. When we speak of "social norms" or "community standards," we are not talking about religious obligations, but rather the choices we make *within* the parameters of Torah and mitzvos.

It is within this wide world of choices that many people get lost, mindlessly falling in line with the crowd without even realizing that they are robbing themselves of some important aspect of their own personal identity. At the same time, we are not advising that people dwell on what they perceive as missing from their lives. *Pirkei Avos* (4:1) tells us clearly that the happy person is the one who is "happy with his portion." This is a chapter about balance. We must first understand who we are and what inspires us, but then we must understand what is actually possible and realistic in our lives. At that point, we can find the balance: What can we do to tap into our sources of inspiration right here, in the life we have?

When Chaya arrived home from seminary in Israel, she was almost 19 years old. Her parents were eager for her to begin some kind of training toward a career. "I'm going into speech therapy and Shoshi's becoming a dental hygienist," her friend Batya told her. "Everyone's going into some kind of medical job. There's lots of good programs for that."

Chaya, however, had a different idea. She was an artistic girl with a flair for clothes, and she longed to become a dress designer. "What?" Batya said.. "Are you serious? Who becomes a dress designer? Name me one girl you know from our school who is a dress designer! You need a normal job that will help pay the bills."

Chaya held out for awhile, but eventually followed her friends' more practical path. She enrolled in an accelerated course to become a speech therapist, and four years later, was married and gainfully employed in her field. As the years went on, however, she began to think that perhaps there was something wrong with her.

"I just can't get up in the morning and I feel tired all day long," she told her husband. "Maybe I'm depressed or I need

a vitamin. It just seems like the same old thing every day. If it weren't for Shabbos, I don't know what I'd do."

Why was Chaya feeling so lifeless? Why did she face her day-to-day routine with a sense of dull dread rather than energy and engagement? Among the many superficial reasons was one underlying problem: she was not living *her* life, the life that sprang from her unique talents and interests. Hashem had given her a powerful creativity that she had set aside unused. Instead, she was doing what everyone else in her social circles had done, simply because it was the "normal" thing to do.

Her career was not a bad one. Indeed it had many positive perks; she had autonomy, made good money and helped other people. It may well have been more practical and lucrative than the career she had wanted. However, it didn't tap into her unique wellspring of energy and passion. It was something she *could* do, but not something she wanted to do. Thus, she had to rally herself every morning to face the day. She told herself to be mature, to adjust to reality and be grateful for what she had, and while her mind accepted this advice, her heart did not feel it. After years of this effort, she was left feeling spent. She didn't know why, and therefore, she did not know what she could do to help herself.

When Chaya abandoned her personal goal in favor of going with the flow, she squelched her desire to become who she wanted to be and lost contact with a significant inner source of joy and satisfaction. Ask yourself the following to discover if you, too, are trapped in the grip of social pressure and unexamined "norms," or are living a life rooted in your own true nature.

1. I ask myself why I do what I do.

2. I recognize when something in my life is no longer working for me, and I make changes.

3. I am willing to retry something that previously did not work.

4. In areas that are not determined by *halachah*, *hashkafah* or *mesorah*, I don't fear being seen as an individual. I do not have to do what everyone else is doing simply for the sake of blending in.

5. I can follow my path without needing to be "in the face" of those who disagree with me, or ascribing negative intentions to their perspective.

6. I operate on the basis of both knowledge and energy; I seek information and guidance before I act, and once I feel I know what I'm doing, I act on it.

7. I see change as the natural part of living.

8. I feel comfortable asking for guidance from a Rav, a friend or an expert and accepting their advice.

9. I'm aware of my talents and abilities, which are my tools for making changes.

10. I can visualize myself living free of the habits that limit me.

The Lock

Social norms are a powerful force. On the positive side, they keep us securely on track, doing what needs to be done without having to analyze our options anew at every juncture. For example, we do not have to weigh the risks and benefits of getting dressed every morning; we just do it, because that is what everyone does. Manners, hygiene and many other details of daily life are also the product of social norms.

On the other hand, social norms and pressure can keep us locked into non-productive or even destructive attitudes and behaviors. Sometimes, as in the story of Chaya, we follow the crowd because we become convinced that if so many people are doing something, it must be right for us, too. We resign ourselves to the sadness of giving up our own vision, and perhaps even elevate it to an act of noble self-sacrifice that is "just my lot in life."

In some cases, what appears to be the less-than-perfect situation is indeed a person's "lot in life." We need balance and perspective to examine our lives and determine if change is proper, worthwhile and necessary. The "I did it my way" and "I've got to be me" mentality can have severe drawbacks; it can hurt others; it can provide us with weak excuses for abandoning our obligations and backing away from the challenges that Hashem has provided to spur our growth.

In fact, while many people suffer from the inability to recognize and pursue what they want in life, many others suffer from the opposite: a refusal to accept anything challenging or difficult. While knowing ourselves is a vital pillar of mental health, a lack of willingness and resiliency to deal with imperfect situations undermines the entire structure of a person's life. Rather than dealing with the difficult people and circumstances in life, a person may decide, *It's making me unhappy and it's not for me*, feeding into a self-centered, "disposable" proclivity to drop jobs, relationships and commitments that require work. The key is to find the balance; to understand what we can and should change, and what we can and should accept.

We need courage and Heavenly assistance to break out of a rut, but we also need these essential assets in order to embrace the present imperfect situation and mine the joy and satisfaction buried in that particular spot. People have found inner peace in a Siberian prison; they have also found misery in a life of wealth and adventure. The starting point, however, is knowing who we are and where our passions lie.

Because social norms are a product of our environment, troubles can arise when we choose an environment that is at odds with our own priorities. For example, someone with simple tastes may find life difficult in a community that is very materialistic. He will find himself forced to keep up, or cast into the role of a misfit. On the other hand, if he settles into a community that shares his priorities, he can live according to his vision of himself without having to fight for it. Many aspects of our lives, from style to speech to social activities to perspectives on life itself are colored by the environment we live in.

It is when the norms of our world negate meaningful parts of our natures that we find ourselves discontented, depressed and "just going through the motions," often without even knowing why. Much as we might want things to be different, we may believe that they never will be. "The more things change, the more they stay the same" is an underlying belief many people carry around in their minds. However, it is a belief that Jewish thinking rejects and real-world experience proves false. The annals of history are replete with individuals who changed themselves, which changed their circumstances, which in some cases, changed the world.

By the time Meir and Leah had gotten halfway through the engagement of their daughter Miri, they had tapped out every source of funding they could access. Their house had a refinanced mortgage, their credit cards were maxed out and they owed money to several gemachs as well. They had purchased fine linens of a quality they would never in their lives get to sleep on. They had outfitted Miri with three new sheitels for a price that could have replaced Meir's dilapidated car. They had set aside money for their share of a "bare bones" wedding for 400. "She needs to have what all her friends have," Leah kept telling Meir.

Then came time to furnish the couple's apartment. The couch had to be leather. The dinette set had to have a marble top and wrought-iron chairs. The mattresses had to be luxury quality. "We can't keep going like this," said Meir. "We have to do what everyone else's parents do," said Leah.

The engagement that had filled them with gratitude and joy now seemed like a Trojan horse, a crippling assault hidden inside a great gift. They felt growing resentment over the unspoken demands of the couple and the in-laws and the community's stratospheric standards, and they felt guilt over their resentment. Where was the joy in the simchah?

The parents had two choices: depart from the spending seen as normal in their community or drown in debt. Filled with guilt and remorse, they finally spoke to Miri. "Here's the money we can give you to furnish the apartment," they said. "You decide what to buy with it."

"O.K.," Miri said. "Thank you, Daddy! Thank you, Mommy! Don't worry. We'll get what we need."

The parents' hearts refilled with happiness, because not only was the unbearable bloodletting of money over, but also, their daughter's beautiful personality had shone through. She was indeed ready to become a wife and mother.

Change in this situation seemed impossible as Meir and Leah were driven deeper and deeper into debt by the demands of a "normal" wedding. Change only became possible when they came to believe that it was necessary. When they were able to shake off the demands of social norms and do what was appropriate for them personally, the financial drain that seemed unstoppable was suddenly plugged. They were free to choose a sensible, responsible method of meeting their daughter's needs without burdening themselves with an unsustainable debt. Their daughter's wedding was restored to what it should have been all along: an occasion that everyone could celebrate.

We can never free ourselves to choose a better way, however, if we do not even allow ourselves to acknowledge the flaw in the current situation. Without such an awareness, Meir and Leah would have committed themselves to a lifetime burden of heavy debt without realizing there was an alternative. People living in a listless, default mode would think, *This is life. That's the way it is and I better just get used to it.* If they don't look inside themselves to find out where their wellsprings of inspiration reside, they cannot tap into the resources they possess for reclaiming their vitality.

Sometimes, our own rationalizations are the first and most unbreachable obstacle to breaking out of a rut.

Shmuel grew up in an old-fashioned European family. His father was a strong, tough man who had survived World War II by living in the forests. While he loved his children fiercely, he rarely showed affection. He worked long hours to support his family and considered involvement with the children to be the mother's exclusive realm.

Shmuel believed that his father's way was the right way to raise children. However, his 12-year-old son Yisrael was becoming withdrawn and restless. "He needs more attention from you," Shmuel's wife told him. "Maybe you should take him out bowling or something."

"I'm not his buddy," Shmuel insisted. "I'm his father. I'm here to let him know what's right and wrong, not to take him bowling. My father didn't play with me, and he was a good father and we were good kids!"

"Yisrael's not you," his wife continued. "He needs a lot of encouragement."

"Look, I work hard for this family," Shmuel countered. "That's plenty of encouragement. Food on the table and clothes to wear are very encouraging. I'm not letting the parenting experts tell me how to be a father."

"Shmuel, you were there at PTA with me when his rebbi even suggested that you spend more time with him," Leah argued. "His rebbi is not a parenting expert, is he? Your father was a good father for you. But Yisrael needs you to be a good father for him."

If we cannot even see that there is a problem, we will be bound securely to the default mode we were trained to follow, no matter how destructive it might be. Shmuel is not making a choice in his parenting style; he does not even see that there are choices other than to be locked into conflict with his son. He is the living illustration of the Yiddish saying, "To a worm in a jar of horseradish, the whole world is horseradish." His world-view is confined to what he's seen, what he knows and what he believes, whether it works in his favor or not.

For some people, the problem is not a lack of awareness, but a faulty definition of strength. In Shmuel's case, he may have an inkling that his relationship with his son needs repair, but he views any change in his manner as capitulation to the "parenting experts." He defines strength as rigidity rather than the self-confident flexibility to try Plan B when Plan A isn't working. Free choice is nothing but an illusion for those who cannot see their own mistakes, admit to mistakes when they do see them and switch tracks when they find themselves headed in the wrong direction.

The How and Why

When we use our power to make conscious choices, we are tapping into the part of us that makes us uniquely human. Going blindly with the flow, letting our surroundings and past experiences lead us unthinkingly into brick walls is an expression of the more instinctive part of our nature. A fascinating study of monkeys paints the perfect picture of how this type of mindless, counterproductive decision-making plays out.

The study was conducted in 1965 by a researcher named Dr. Gordon Stephenson. Dr. Stephenson took five monkeys and placed them all in a cage that contained a ladder. At the top of the ladder, the researcher placed a banana. An assistant stood near the cage armed with a hose that sprayed ice-cold water. Whenever a monkey ascended the ladder to retrieve the banana, the assistant sprayed the other four monkeys with the ice water.

Not surprisingly, the monkeys began to attack any of their group that started up the ladder. They had learned that one monkey climbing the ladder brought the others discomfort, and so they enforced discipline on the entire group, forcing them all to forgo the banana so as to save them from the ice-water shower. Eventually, the experimenter no longer needed to spray the water. The monkeys were trained to stay off the ladder.

The next step in the experiment was to take out one of the original five monkeys and replace him with a newcomer. Having never experienced the ice-water shower, the new monkey naturally headed up the ladder. However, it quickly learned that its attempts would provoke an attack by the others in the group. Once that new monkey was trained, another of the original group was removed.

One by one, a new monkey was introduced and trained to replace one of the original five monkeys, so that by the end of the experiment, there were none in the cage that had ever been sprayed. Nevertheless, they had all learned to attack any monkey that tried to climb the ladder to retrieve the banana. None of them knew *why* it was necessary to prevent one another from climbing to the top, nor could they discern whether this rule served any positive purpose. They attacked those who failed to conform to the rule simply because that's what was done in their cage. Even if they were hungry, they did not recognize the option of climbing up the ladder and getting a banana to eat. Their decision to eschew that ladder and the banana at the top was not a decision at all, but the result of behavior modification that overrode all needs, abilities and desires.

Obviously, we are not monkeys in a cage. However, to the extent that we bypass our thinking process and just follow the crowd, we relinquish an important piece of our humanity. As we noted before, in many areas of life the decisions have been well thought out by greater minds than ours and we are wise to follow the paved path. Certainly, in areas of *halachah*, *hashkafah* or *mesorah*, we are not permitted to forge new paths on our own and must discuss any variations with a Rav. However, many areas we think are set in stone are really not; they are merely cultural norms that have developed within our social groups. In those matters, when following the crowd or adhering to old habits works against our ability to live vital, productive lives, we have to identify the lock and break free.

Often, this means untangling a thick knot of preconceptions we've managed to create over the years. After all, we all learn by following. A baby imitates the world around him. From talking to playing games to writing, reading and tying shoes, a child's repertoire of skills comes from copying what he sees around him. As we become socialized, the copying becomes more subtle. We fall into the patterns of others around us, doing what we perceive as "normal." Sometimes our unhappiness arises not out of any real lack or void, but simply out of comparison to the norm.

"I remember the bungalow colonies we used to go to in the summer when I was kid," recalls Devorah. "They were really nothing more than shacks. But in those days, most of the kids didn't go to overnight camp and there was no place for them to play in the city. So we'd leave our nice air-conditioned apartments and go live in the mountains for two

months. We'd be outside all day long. We had a pool and a ball field and it was heaven.

"Then, one year, one of the families renovated their bungalow. It was all brand new. It had a big front porch and a modern kitchen and four whole bedrooms. After that, we all hated our bungalows. All of a sudden, they really looked like shacks to us. It's funny, as long as everyone was living in a run-down two-bedroom house with kids sleeping on a highriser in the kitchen, we were fine with it. It was normal and no one gave it a second thought."

Devorah's observation holds true for a vast swath of our attitudes and practices. When something is perceived as "normal," we do not tend to analyze its risks and benefits. On the positive side, we can be happy with little if everyone else also has little. On the other hand, we may accept norms that are bad for us. Therefore, we may eat the way others eat, even if the five-course Shabbos meals are literally killing us. We may stay up too late and feel tired all day because the norm in some communities is to make phone calls and do business at all hours. We do these things even when they don't work for us, even when they harm us, because we are trained to copy those around us.

One of the most prominent ways the crowd mentality shows itself is in fashion. Even in the Jewish community, which maintains its own standards of appropriate clothing, the dictates of fashion prevail. But who chooses the next trend? Somewhere out there, a few individuals take the lead, and almost by telepathy, everyone else follows. A saleswoman in a ladies' clothing store in Brooklyn reveals that, "All I have to say is, 'lots of people are buying that,' and the customer wants it."

On the other side of the coin is *bechirah:* free choice. No matter how we have acquired our negative habits, we still bear responsibility for our actions. In this regard, the first choice we make in any major area of life is the most potent one, for with that, we can keep ourselves out of situations that foster destructive habits. In other words, don't get into or stay in the destructive relationship; don't move into the spiritually uninspired community; don't take the first steps down the wrong path; don't smoke the first cigarette.

Nevertheless, it is impossible to avoid *every* poor choice. Whether our choices affect our physical health (food choices, exercise); our productivity (procrastination, poor work habits); or our emotional health (fear, negativity, anger), we are bound to find ourselves habituated to some behaviors that block our full embrace of life and its possibilities.

We can be slaves to habit and social pressure, or we can be free. Our Torah and *mussar sefarim* remind us that we are not the five monkeys in the cage; we are Jews who possess a G-d-given power to choose, with each step we take, the direction of our path in life. With Hashem's help, we can take the key that is in our hand and unlock that power to discover within ourselves new dimensions of energy and potential.

The Key

What does it mean to tap into our innate power to make real, significant choices? It means having the chance to live the life that is uniquely ours to live: the life that springs from our true strengths, talents and ideals and draws energy from these bountiful inner resources Hashem has given us. It means having a full range of remedies and approaches available to address the challenges in life. Thoughts, such as *I never did that before, Nobody does it that way, What will people say? My friends will think it's foolish,* lose their power to trap us in counterproductive habits and thinking. Instead, we look around with open eyes at the possibilities; we weigh with an open mind the options *halachically* available to us; we accept with an open heart the sound advice of those we respect and admire, including ourselves. Our inner voice asks, *What makes me feel alive?* and *How can I accomplish that?*

Often, we find ourselves working within a social system that does not seem to be custom tailored to our needs. A particular office, school, neighborhood — even a family — may not fit all its members in every way. We set up a false dichotomy when we believe that a social system is "all or nothing." A social group can be wonderful, warm and supportive in most ways, and yet there still can be certain norms that work against us. For instance:

When Rabbi Leibowitz decided to leave full-time learning and become a rebbi, he imagined teaching second grade. He could picture the bright, open faces of a class full of 7-year-old boys. His somewhat corny sense of humor was always a hit with little kids, and he was a great storyteller as well. He knew he could keep a class spellbound, and get them hooked on learning in the process.

However, Rabbi Leibowitz was not only an entertaining young man with a playful nature; he was also a highly regarded talmid chacham. "Second grade is not for you," his friends and rebbeim told him. "You should be teaching the older boys. You should be doing serious learning, not beginning Chumash." Finally, Rabbi Leibowitz came to believe that second grade was indeed beneath his capacities, and he was quickly grabbed by a high school to teach the 10th-grade class.

Day after day, instead of looking forward to his class, he felt a mild disappointment. The boys were fine, but there was no fun or playfulness in the job. His storytelling talents lay dormant, as did his silly jokes and all the games and contests he had planned as he had dreamed of teaching his second graders.

Finally, one day, he spoke with an older friend. "I can't shake this depressed feeling," he said. "It's just not like me.

I thought I'd be that great rebbi that came in like a ball of energy every day, but instead, I feel like I'm only half there. I really wanted to teach second grade."

"So why didn't you?"

"Because everyone said it was foolish. They said a guy like me belonged in mesivta. I felt like it would be embarrassing somehow to take second grade."

Shortly after this discussion, Rabbi Leibowitz had a thought. Who says I have to be embarrassed? I'm going to teach second grade! *From that moment on, even as he tended to his 10th graders, the fog lifted from his mood. With energy he hadn't felt in years, he began applying for positions and eventually found one for the upcoming school year. His career became a source of happiness that spilled over into the rest of his life.*

Rather than leaving teaching altogether because he could not find happiness doing what everyone told him he was supposed to do, Rabbi Liebowitz found the happiness available to him in the profession he had chosen. He looked inside himself and recognized what he really wanted, looked outside himself to find the path to his goal, and then took action.

For the first 20 years of Shua's life, he spent every summer at his family's beach house. He cherished every memory: the salt air, the sound of the waves in the quiet morning hours, the sun glinting off the water, the tingle of cold water on a hot day. When he was 21, however, he found something worth far more than sun and sand; he found Torah, and immersed himself in a baal teshuvah yeshivah. A few years later, he married.

For many years, the excitement of his new life outweighed any regrets over the life he left behind. But now, as a father of young children, he was finding the summers sad and confining. He wanted to give them the thrilling freedom of running along the shore, playing in the sand and splashing in the waves. That longing piqued a sense of nostalgia and injected an unwelcome tinge of discontent into his life.

"Life was a lot simpler before,"he confided in me. "Now everything is so complicated and I feel so guilty. I know if I were a good Jew, I wouldn't need the beach. No one else needs the beach. They're happy with a pool."

As I spoke to Shua, he realized that despite his discontented feeling, he loved his life. He also came to the realization that the Torah does not forbid a Jew from going to the beach; it was only the environment of most beach areas that presented the problem. Shua wanted and needed to reclaim a significant part of himself that had been locked away.

"Do you think you could find a private beach for a day or a week once a year?" I asked him. He lit up. "I have an old friend who has a place out in the dunes on Cape Cod. Maybe..."

Shua arranged a midweek vacation for his family at his friend's beach house. They needed a dune buggy to get out to the isolated, perfectly private spot. "We did it the right way. Completely kosher," he later told me proudly. "And it was just what I needed." Rather than allowing frustration to fester, Shua looked inside himself and discovered what was separating him from his inner sources of joy, looked outside himself for a solution and took action.

Balance is the key to successfully exercising free choice. Rabbi Liebowitz and Shua both worked to zero in on the reason their zest for life was drying up, and balance that against what was possible for them within the parameters of *halachah* and other non-negotiables, such as their responsibilities to their families. Rabbi Liebowitz did not quit his job; he found a satisfying position. Shua did not sneak off to the beach with his children or become depressed about his choice of lifestyle; he found a kosher way to satisfy his heart's yearning. This kind of adaptation must, of course, be done with guidance, because a person's strong subjective feelings in these areas can easily lead him to define anything that bothers him as "optional."

As is obvious to anyone who has lived a couple of decades or more, our "heart's yearning" is not always within reach. However, there is almost always some way to stir the embers and let their heat warm up our lives. For instance, even if Shua didn't have a friend with a beach house, he could have found some other way to get a little sun and surf into his life. Perhaps he could have taken his children fishing or on a boat ride. Rabbi Liebowitz might not have landed a second-grade teaching position, but perhaps he could have led a Pirchei group to engage his sense of fun and humor. Chaya might not be able to change professions at her stage of the game, but her talents would no doubt be welcome as a costume designer for the local high school's play. Sometimes a taste of a rich, delicious dessert is all we need to satisfy our appetite.

While we all have our default mode, the person with real freedom to choose can recognize when he is stuck. His life can then move forward rather around in endless circles. He is not afraid to strike out in a new direction, even if he finds very few who are traveling the same road. He uses all his faculties, plus all the resources available to him, to discover creative solutions and productive approaches. He may not be able to choose the circumstances of his life; no one can. However, he can and does choose what he does with the life G-d gives him.

Here are 10 steps to unlock the power of free choice:

Unlock Free Choice

inspiration

1. **Feel** what is going on inside you. Listen to the voice within. Is there a misalignment between the life you believe you could have and the life you're living? Identify what stirs your enthusiasm, happiness and hopefulness.

2. **Imagine** living the life you would be excited to live, even if it is not possible right now. Don't think about the steps

you would need to take to have that life, or the obstacles you would have to overcome. Leap from the present to the ideal and experience yourself in that place. This is the means by which your mind re-sets its GPS. When the goal becomes vivid enough, you will find yourself heading in that direction, finding joy in the journey even if you do not actually arrive at your chosen end point.

3. **Bring** Hashem into the picture. Ask Him to guide you toward choices that will bring you to your full potential.

Logic

4. **Question** why you do what you do. Is it what Hashem wants you to do? Is it the right thing to do? Is it what you want to do? Does it work for you? Are you doing it because that is what everyone else in your class/town/ neighborhood/ shul does? Understand that while "the system" (whether in the workplace, the family, school or community) may work overall, you need not adhere to every last detail of it if it doesn't conform to your personal path (except regarding issues of *halachah* and *hashkafah*).

You do not need to knock the system, change the system or berate those who are part of it, even if you believe that it is flawed. Let people find their own way when they are ready. Right now, your job is to find *your* way List those things you feel compelled to do and those things you feel stymied from doing. Think ahead to where change in these areas would lead you. What would the gains and the drawbacks be for you and others in your life?

5. **Re-examine** the obligations and limitations you have accepted upon yourself. Ask yourself, *Do I really want this, or am I behaving like the monkey in the experiment?* Do you really want to purchase a certain type of car or live in a certain-size house? Is it really essential that

your children go to a certain school or camp, or that you marry someone with a certain pedigree, or that you present guests with a certain quantity of gourmet food? If you think about this, you will probably recall times in your life when you were forced by circumstance to give up something you thought was essential, only to discover that you really did not need it after all.

For example, an eighth-grade boy was applying to yeshivah high schools for the coming year. His parents believed he belonged at Yeshivah A, where his older brothers had gone. All the "good boys" from their community went to Yeshivah A, and the parents were convinced that anything less would devastate their son. However, this boy was not quite up to the level of learning that Yeshivah A demanded, and the Rosh Yeshivah politely explained to the parents that their son would do better elsewhere.

The parents were wealthy and well connected. They used every connection they had to try to convince the Rosh Yeshivah to give their son a chance. They offered to hire tutors to help him keep up. They hinted broadly at the large donations they would be making to show their deep appreciation. Nevertheless, their son was not admitted. Instead, he went to Yeshivah B, where he thrived. When the next son's turn came to apply to high schools, the parents had a different outlook. "Let's look around and see what's best for him," the father said.

6. **Appreciate** your uniqueness and status as a thinking person with your own passions and goals. Realize that your individuality is not an obstacle or a flaw, but a blessing. Thinking and analyzing your choices is a great gift and a mark of wisdom.

7. **Accept** that life is ever-evolving and that people are always changing. What works in one situation may not work in

the next. Be ready to acknowledge mistakes and flaws in what you are doing without feeling that this makes you a bad person. Think of your life in terms of 10-year blocks rather than "from this day forward" so that you will leave room for new priorities and new situations. Revising and adapting are a reflection of growth, and acknowledging mistakes is the prelude to that growth.

For example, an anxious mother does not allow her son to drive on the highway when he first receives his driver's license. Two years later, she still does not allow it. The son argues constantly with his mother about this topic, since this limitation causes him a lot of inconvenience and embarrassment. The mother argues that her son's life is more important than his pride, and she will not budge on her position. One day, as the mother speaks to a friend whose son is the same age as hers, she realizes that her position is no longer appropriate. "I guess I just didn't realize that you really are not a kid anymore," she tells her son. "Just be careful."

Actions

8. **Make time** to think, take stock of your life and analyze where you are. Write down five things you wish to explore. Often, our default mode takes over simply because we do not take the time to analyze and plan our lives. We do things the way we've always done them because it is quicker and easier than trying a new way. To make time for thoughtful analysis, make a set appointment with yourself, for instance, every Rosh Chodesh.

9. **Ask** someone who is honest and gentle for an objective opinion of where you might be stuck in an unproductive habit or attitude. Use that person or another person as your safety net to help you realign yourself if you head offtrack.

10. **Push yourself** to take one habit, thought or limitation that you know is holding you back and do your utmost to break it! Write down the steps you intend to follow. If necessary, take it on in incremental steps. For instance, if you decide that you want to get to sleep earlier so that you are more alert and energetic during the day, you will probably not be able to suddenly shut the lights and fall asleep two hours earlier than usual. Instead, push yourself to get to bed 15 minutes earlier than normal for a week or two, and then add another 15 minutes and so forth, until you are getting enough sleep. It is better to take small, grounded steps than grand ones that will be difficult to sustain.

Once you've embarked on the road to discovering and actualizing your unique gifts and passions, don't give up. Keep moving forward step-by-step, and you'll be delighted to find fresh new streams of inspiration along the way.

Straight from the Source

Every social group and every family has its "culture" that determines which traits and achievements are most valued. But what does Hashem value? Two Gemaras offer an insight. In *Taanis* 21b, we learn about Abba, the bloodletter, who received a daily greeting from the Heavenly Academy. In contrast, the great Abaye received a greeting only on Erev Shabbos, and Rava only on Erev Yom Kippur. Abba's merit was the modest and discreet way in which he performed his medical procedures and his free services to Torah scholars.

Likewise, *Taanis* 24b highlights the merit of a simple *melamed* who taught Torah to children. He would not charge those who could not afford to pay and moreover he would entice them to learn by rewarding them with fish from ponds that he owned.

His prayer was successful where the great Rav failed in soliciting Hashem's immediate response to a prayer for rain.

The Take-Away

In these stories, we see that Hashem showed extraordinary favor to seemingly ordinary men whose only claim to fame was that they used the talents they had been given to spread Hashem's Torah. I often see people who let the crowd set their standard of success. But they end up striving to become what they are not, rather than tapping into their own talents and giving Hashem the best they've got.

 The Mishnah (*Shabbos* 10:1) designates types of clothing and jewelry that are not permitted to be worn on Shabbos. One item is a necklace called a *ketula*. Rashi describes a *ketula* as a wide, tight-fitting choker that women would wear to make their faces appear fuller, since in those days, plumpness was viewed as a sign of prosperity.

The Take-Away

We learn from this Mishnah that people have been apparently always been willing to suffer to meet the social standard for beauty. Heaviness used to be the standard because it signified that the woman could afford abundant food in times when malnourishment was common. Today, the standard is the opposite, but people still suffer, sometimes to the point of starvation and often to the point of obsession, to attain the look that they believe will make them fit the criterion for beauty. Yet starving ourselves is no more logical than choking ourselves. Balance in life only comes when we accept ourselves.

The Gemara (*Avodah Zarah*:19a) relates that Levi and Reb Shimon, the son of Rebbi, sat before Rebbi and completed a *sefer*. Rebbi offered them a choice of what to learn next. Levi chose *Mishlei* and Reb Shimon chose *Tehillim*. Reb Shimon prevailed and they began learning *Tehillim*. When they reached the verse that says, "My desire is in Hashem's Torah," Rebbi explained it to mean that a person should learn the facets of Torah that his heart desires. With that, Levi rose and said, "You have given me permission to leave."

The Take-Away

For someone to have success in Torah learning and develop a true, lifelong love of it, his heart must be in it. Following the crowd will not spawn success. Rather than feeling excitement and interest, we will begin to feel bored and burdened, and from there it is easy to decide, "Learning isn't for me." The idea that we have an obligation to seek learning that speaks to us comes from no less an authority than Rebbi, the author of the *Mishnayos*, the teacher of the oral Torah for all generations.

The *Shulchan Aruch* (*Yoreh Deah* 240:25) rules that if a son wishes to travel to learn with a certain *rebbi* with whom he feels he will be successful, and his father prohibits him from going because of dangers in that place, the son is not required to obey his father. The Rema continues in this vein, stating that the son can also override his father if the father is keeping him from his choice of marriage partner (provided the choice is within the realm of a proper Jewish marriage). Regarding these *halachos*, Rav Avrohom Pam *zt'l* often cautioned his students that, while they have the right to make their own decision, they should realize that their parents have their child's best interests in mind. Their input should be taken seriously. In the end, however, where to learn and whom to marry are a person's individual decision.

The Take-Away

Through these *halachos*, we see that the Torah embraces the idea of individuality. It recognizes that a child is not just an offshoot of his parents, and that he may respond to learning and people differently than they do. If we take this concept to the next level, we can see that if we are told to think for ourselves even when our parents are the ones trying to steer us, the urge to seek our own path would be all the more justified when it's the anonymous "everybody" trying to set our course.

Chapter 5

Release the Power of "No"

Setting Boundaries vs. Fear and Guilt

"I ALWAYS WORRIED THAT I WASN'T CUT OUT FOR motherhood, and now I know I was right," said Rachel, a mother of four small children. "I manage all day long to deal with the whining and fighting and messes. I try my best to give them affection and keep my cool. But when it gets to be past their bedtime, I'm out of patience.

"They stall and stall. It's one thing after another. They need a drink, then they need the bathroom, then they're hungry for a snack and then they have to brush their teeth, then the big ones remember some homework sheet that needs to be signed, then it's another round of drinks. Play some music, read a story. I keep doing what they ask thinking, 'How can I send them to bed hungry *and thirsty? How can I send her to school with her home-work unsigned?' But it just never stops until I scream and threaten. Then they're quiet and I feel miserable."*

Rachel told her story with the demeanor of someone confessing to a crime. She had come to therapy for help in repairing what she assumed was an anger issue regarding her children. In her view of motherhood, setting a firm boundary of a healthy, normal bedtime for her children meant denying them basic needs like food and water, which she could not do. Neither, however, could she provide the hours of room service and entertainment her children had grown accustomed to receiving. Rather than saying "no" in a firm and reasonable way, she ended up exploding and feeling guilty.

Alex was a very wealthy, accomplished individual who sought therapy to restore a crumbling family situation. "I don't know what they want from me," he said of his wife and children. "They just don't appreciate what I do. Do they know how much money I've raised for the yeshivos in this town? Do they have any idea how many people I see every day who need help for this problem and that problem? I've probably married off more brides around here than the busiest shadchan!

"It's ironic. For everyone else in town, I'm a hero. But my own wife and kids don't appreciate it at all. My wife says, 'You're always running away.' My kids constantly interrupt me when I'm on important phone calls and complain that I like my cell phone better than I like them. I'm only trying to do the chesed a guy like me should be doing. Other guys have wives who help them and kids who are proud of them. Why do I get grief instead of support from my family?"

For Alex, the demands of the community are non-negotiable, while the time he invests in his family is subject to constant compromise. He does not believe that a person to whom Hashem has given so much has the right to say "no" to those who are lacking. Nevertheless, he is by default saying "no" to many of his family's needs. His wife's and children's complaints express their feeling of being cast aside.

Because they lack boundaries in their lives and the knowledge of how to set them effectively, both Alex and Rachel are losing out on satisfaction in their well-meaning, highly productive lives. Are you?

1. Do you fear that saying "no" to someone will cause them to dislike or become angry with you?

2. Do you find yourself apologizing to people for making your own needs a priority?

3. Are you always helping others and often getting complaints rather than appreciation?

4. Do you often put other people's needs ahead of your own or your family's?

5. Do you often feel regret at the end of the day for the things you did *not* accomplish?

6. Are you often late, overscheduled, not getting to do those things you had planned?

7. Do you consider "no" a bad word?

8. Do you find yourself feeling resentful over how much (or how little) others do for you compared to what you do for them?

9. Are you able to be pushed into doing more than you feel capable of doing?

10. Do you find yourself feeling angry, tense or resentful after you agree to do something?

Giving, and the compassion that drives it, are hallmarks of the Jewish people: our inheritance from our forefather Avraham, who is described as the paradigm of *chesed*. We are taught that Hashem created the world in order to have a recipient for His kindness, and thus giving is the very purpose of creation. When the world became devoid of *chesed* in the times of Noah, Hashem deemed to destroy it. It is no wonder, then, that as a culture, religion and people, we have trouble denying others that which they ask of us. We equate "yes" with goodness and "no" with selfish cruelty.

However, everyone knows that there can be "too much of a good thing." The world and the human being operate best when kindness flows within contraints. To illustrate, think of a river that flows between two strong banks. Because the water is confined, it rushes forward with tremendous force. If we restrict its flow further by building a dam, the water can generate enough force to power an electrical plant that lights up an entire region. In comparison, a river that overflows its banks destroys everything around it. Ultimately, as the water spreads farther and farther out across the land, it loses all its power. It becomes a large, stagnant puddle.

Limitations are not the antithesis of *chesed*. Rather, they enable *chesed* to become a force for the good.

As we take on responsibilities in life, we find that whether we want it or not, we acquire our own little kingdoms. Parents create their children's world and therefore the parents loom large in their child's life. Grandparents, through their special bond, also exert an influence on the very structure of a child's view of life. Employers create the atmosphere in which their workers either thrive or wither. Teachers govern the world of their students. To be effective as the rulers of their kingdoms, they all must know how to lead: That means saying "no" to that which is counterproductive, dangerous or immoral, which is in essence saying "yes" to that which is productive, safe and morally correct. This requires constant weighing and re-evaluating of our situations.

For example, when a mother has two children who are 2 and 4 years old, she might say "yes" to hanging up their clothes. She sees it as a way of caring for her household. However, by the time these children are 6 and 8 years old, she will most likely find that the expenditure of effort is unreasonable. She will say "no" to the clothes strewn around their rooms and teach the children to do the task themselves. That "no" is, in reality, a form of giving, for it gives her children the chance to develop the essential life-skill of personal responsibility. It also allows the mother to channel her energy toward more productive immediate goals, rather than allowing it to leach out into an unnecessary effort.

Even if we are not in a position of official authority, each of us still has our own personal "kingdom" to run, and therefore, each of us must establish some "laws of the land" for ourselves. For example, a student may have to stand up to peer pressure or to a bully. A yeshivah boy might have to say "no" to a learning partner who does not foster his needs. A young man or woman might have to say "no" to an unsuitable potential marriage match. An employee might have to refuse overtime or taking on more work than he can handle.

For each of these instances of "no," there is a "yes" embedded within. The student who deflects peer pressure says "yes" to a clear conscience. The employee who says "no" to overtime says "yes" to the activities he pursues outside of work, whether it is family, learning, a hobby or just some downtime for recharging. Since we live in a world of physical boundaries and time constraints, we are always standing on one side or the other. Saying "yes" to everything is not feasible.

When we make "no" a forbidden word in our vocabulary, we essentially set the wheels of our lives upon a muddy rut in the road. We become stuck in the irritation, exhaustion, anxiety and ineffectiveness that come with being all things to all people, believing that there's no "nice" way out. Worst of all, we do not even get to enjoy the satisfaction of knowing we are kind and giving people, because to someone to whom setting limits is an anathema, there is always more guilt over what wasn't done than gratification over what was done: "I gave him $100 but he needed $200. Maybe I should have given him the $200. But I really didn't have it to spare. Maybe I should have borrowed it or given him a postdated check. If I had enough *bitachon* I would have given him the whole amount."

To live a balanced, productive life, we have to pull our wheels out of the mud and set them on the solid ground of reality. There is no doubt that sometimes, we are indeed called upon to go above and beyond our limits, but for many people, "sometimes" is "always." Once we come to terms with our need and obligation to set appropriate boundaries between ourselves and others — even our parents, spouses and children — we are free to forge ahead with all we've got. Rather than spilling uselessly or destructively over weak riverbanks, our kindness and compassion can surge forward and light up the world.

The Lock

As children, we start off on the receiving end: a tiny bundle of needs and wants, without any sense of limitations. Soon, however, we begin to become educated in the art of giving: sharing toys, giving in to the other child, waiting our turn, doing favors and chores for our parents and teachers and, as we grow older, taking on more serious *chesed* endeavors such as raising money for our schools or for those in need, visiting the sick and comforting those who are in mourning. All of these experiences enrich us as human beings and elevate us as Jews. Rather than locking in our personal strengths, doing *chesed* sets them free in the world and strengthens them as well.

But just as a glass of wine enhances joy but a bottle of it brings incapacitation, *chesed,* too, has its healthy and unhealthy measure. This part of the picture tends to escape our notice. We become like the proverbial camel that takes on a load of straw.

Can he bear one more piece of straw? Of course he can; it's only straw. But piece by piece, his load grows heavier until it reaches a point at which one additional piece of straw breaks his back. When we translate "yes" into love and kindness, and "no" into selfishness, we are easily manipulated by those who wish to add a little more straw to our load. We take on another, another and still another demand until at last, our backs are sagging precariously under the strain.

"Hi. Daddy, how are you?"

"Baruch Hashem," says Chaim, gearing up for the question he knows is coming next. His son Aaron cherishes the illusion that Chaim is an ATM, and that all life's problems can be solved with a friendly "Hi, Daddy" phone call. On the other hand, Aaron's new wife has pretty expensive tastes, and Chaim certainly wants to do his part to keep the newlyweds peaceful and happy.

"I hate to bother you," Aaron says, "but we bought that new armchair for the living room this month and now I'm kind of short for the bills. I really didn't think we needed it, but Leah said she couldn't invite her family over if we didn't have enough places for people to sit. And you know Leah, she likes things to be nice."

Money was tight for Chaim, and his thoughts were less than charitable: Maybe Leah's family could have bought the chair if they were so particular about their seating? Or maybe Chaim could have taken the spare armchair in the family room? It wasn't leather, but it wasn't bad. It only took a nanosecond, however, for those thoughts to dissolve against the new motto of his generation: "Close your mouth and open your wallet." What was more important, $400 or his son's marital harmony?

Chaim doled out money he could not afford to give. He felt resentful over it; he hadn't purchased even one piece of new furniture for his own home in years. He said "yes" when reason, practicality and emotion all weighed on the side of "no." By hinting to his father that the money was necessary to keep his marriage happy, Aaron manipulated his father into a situation where Chaim felt that to withhold the money would have been a shortsighted act of selfishness.

Not only did Chaim's line of thinking lock him into a financially draining situation; it also locked his son into an unhealthy dynamic with his wife. Rather than facing their financial realties together as a couple and making practical decisions, Aaron scurried around covering the gaps so that his wife could live in a blissful fantasy in which all things were possible. In reality, both Aaron and Chaim allowed themselves to be manipulated by the fear of displeasure their "no" might incur, and their desire to please another person.

Their "yes" to financial mismanagement, however, was a "no" to many other benefits: Aaron lost out on the chance to develop true adult independence and a true partnership with his wife; Chaim lost the ability to prioritize his spending as he saw fit, and he even lost out on the quality of his relationship with his son, which was now marred by constant stress and resentment.

A person who cannot set limits is locked into dilemmas that seem to have no solution. When the consequences of "no" are too much to bear, a person's bargaining power evaporates. He is basically at the mercy of those who are pulling the strings. Often this mind-set turns a person's work-life into a 24/6 stress test.

When 50-year-old Tzvi walked into my office, I assumed that he was well over 60. His hair was thinning and gray. He was a bit paunchy and walked with a slow, tired gait. His face was sagging and sad. His complaint, chronic insomnia, seemed to explain his careworn look.

Tzvi had been employed at his current job as a computer network consultant for five years after two years of unemployment. Since the company's clients often needed overnight technical assistance, the consultants all knew that they would be called upon from time to time to work at odd hours.

However, the company had down-sized, and Tzvi was now being assigned more of these jobs than he could handle. His life was falling into a shambles as a result. His body clock was thrown completely off kilter, so that even when he tried to get a normal night's sleep, he couldn't settle down. He had no energy or patience for anything or anyone, much to his family's dismay.

"What would happen if you told your boss that you can only take, say, one overnight a week?" I asked him.

"No way! This is my job and I can't whine about it. What kind of loser would they think I am?"

What kept Tzvi locked into this torturous routine? He believed he had no right to say "no." Fearing an image as a "loser," he allowed his employers to squeeze him twice as hard rather than hiring enough employees to satisfy the company's needs. To break free of this trap, he had to set the boundary, at least in his own mind, recognizing that he should not continue to accept inhumane demands that could ruin his health or perhaps even kill him. Until he took that step, he was like someone whose house was on fire but didn't even realize that he could and should look for an exit.

Once Tzvi mentally said "no" to the situation, even if he kept doing as his boss demanded, his eyes would be open to the necessity of finding alternatives. He might look for another job, perhaps in a different field; he might take the risk of telling his employer that he has certain limits; he might work out a compromise such as more vacation time or fewer hours. Until he enunciated that "no" in his mind, however, he would feel stuck with both feet in a mire of misery.

We see from both Chaim's and Tzvi's stories that fear is a powerful barrier that blocks the word "no" as it marches from our minds to our mouths. Often, however, it is the positive emotions of kindness and idealism that won't let us demur. As we discuss in the Appendix, the limbic system of the brain is the primary seat of emotion, and it operates without a sense of time or practical limitations. In that chapter, we note that many charitable endeavors are launched by people whose the limbic dominates their thinking; even if the mission seems impossible, their emotional drive to get it done will inspire them to take it on against the odds. "I don't know how we'll do it, but we will!" is the battle cry behind many great accomplishments.

Despite the good that such "sky's the limit" optimism can achieve, not every idea is worthy of this kind of effort. If we do not take some time to analyze the reality of a situation, we may find ourselves committed to a time and energy-draining activity that truly does not fit our situation.

Zahava lives up to her name, which means "gold." She is the oldest of a large family and her mother counts on her help. When her teacher asks her to volunteer to do homework with a local girl whose mother is ill, Zahava responds with an instant, "sure!" She imagines heading over to the girl's house after school, sitting with her for an hour and then getting back to her own house in time to eat dinner, do homework and get her two youngest siblings ready for bed.

By the end of the first week of this routine, everyone is upset with Zahava. The girl she is helping needs more time. Zahava gives her some, but not enough. She leaves the girl dissatisfied and comes home to her own homework, which she does quickly under the deadline of her siblings' upcoming bedtime. She is delayed in getting her siblings to bed, forcing her mother to abandon other chores to take over that one. The problem is that Zahava has scheduled six hours of activity into five hours of time and it just doesn't work.

Not only are we not always able to do what others ask us, but we are also not always the right one for the job. In Zahava's case, a girl with fewer family commitments would have been more effective as a homework tutor. If Zahava had said, "Sorry, I'd love to do it but I just wouldn't be able to give her enough time," the teacher could have found a more appropriate candidate. Zahava's "no" would be transformed into a "yes" for the girl, who would have gotten the attention she needed, a "yes" for Zahava's schoolwork and a "yes" for the siblings waiting eagerly for her bedtime story.

For both Tzvi and Zahava, setting limits is also difficult because it requires saying "no" to someone in a position of authority. We are raised to respect parents and teachers, and must for practical reasons do the bidding of those who keep us employed or keep our businesses up and running. Within these relationships, we sometimes do not even recognize "no" as an option on the menu.

Of all these situations, the one that is most subject to confusing perceptions is the one most saturated with love and duty. The parent-child relationship can easily be poisoned with guilt and manipulation when boundaries are not set:

"Where are you going?" Atara asked Yaakov.

"I've got to run over to my mother's house. Her washing machine broke and she wants me to take a look at it."

"Oh. But what about Zevi? You told him you'd take him to buy a bike today. It's already 4 o'clock and the store closes at 5:30. Besides, why didn't she ask you to fix it when you were there for breakfast?"

"I don't know. Listen, I'll take Zevi next Sunday," Yaakov responds. "You know my mother. If I don't go now, she'll be calling me every hour on the hour until I come."

Atara sighs in frustration. "Look, Yaakov, I love your mother dearly, but things can't continue this way. It was one thing when we were newly wed, but now you've got your own family to think about. You can't always drop everything and run over there!"

"She's lonely," says Yaakov. "I know it's hard for you, but as she never tires of reminding me, 'I'm still your mother.' I'll try to make it quick."

Is Yaakov right to drop everything and answer his mother's call? The couple's argument signals that they need to decide together on a boundary. Perhaps his mother's loneliness truly warrants extra attention, or perhaps his mother is trying to maintain an inappropriate amount of control in her son's life. Perhaps Zevi will benefit by seeing Yaakov honor his own mother, or perhaps Zevi really needs his father to keep the date they made. Where the boundary is drawn depends on the specifics, but a failure to draw one can lead to a chaotic, conflict-ridden family life in which too many people have their hands on the controls.

People who adopt the "never say no" mind-set are often convinced that the alternative is a self-centered life in which we hoard our time, money and energy for our own pleasure and satisfaction. They believe that setting limits means we never go the extra mile, never put ourselves out for a person or a cause, never feel the exhilaration of over-the-top effort and achievement. In reality, however, our boundaries stake out a fruitful, fertile life in which we direct our efforts in directions that are important, meaningful and feasible for us. And we can, because our energy is available, there for us to pour into the needs that are rightfully ours to fulfill.

The How and Why

Much like perfectionism, the reluctance to create and adhere to boundaries rises from the false pretense that we are capable of anything and responsible for everything. We are raised to admire those who go above and beyond the norm. Even in the secular world, the hero is the one who sacrifices his life for others: the fireman who runs into a burning building, the soldier who jumps on a grenade to save his comrades, the mother who goes without so her children can have. In the Jewish world, where *chesed* has its roots, our long and difficult history has given us a millennia-long chronicle of incredible sacrifice. The 20th century alone provides story after story of people great and small who gave more than any human being could be expected to give.

Could any of us give our only pair of shoes to a barefoot man in the dead of winter? Could we give away our Shabbos candlesticks to someone who needs money to marry off a child? Give the last of our food money to a widow whose children are starving? Risk our life to don a pair of tefillin? Go door-to-door begging money for a poor man who is too ashamed to beg?

Even if we leave aside the indelible images of suffering, can we rise to the paradigms of *chesed* in today's world? How many people could join Hatzolah and drop everything to answer emergency medical calls day and night? How many could do the work of a *rav* or a community activist, dealing all day every day with questions and problems ranging from the vital to the absurd? How many can start an organization that eradicates a dreaded disease or raises millions of dollars for sick children or delivers tons of food each week to needy families? How many could even find the time to do the deliveries?

Against this backdrop, a person who has his or her hands full raising a family, making a living and trying to be a responsible member of the community is bound to feel like a chronic underachiever. Because we, as Jews and simply as human beings, really do value and enjoy the feeling of helping others, we readily accept the idea that we should do more. We live on the precipice of "yes," just waiting for the little push that makes us jump in and take on another obligation. When we find ourselves in over our heads, we don't question the wisdom of having taken the plunge; rather, we wonder why we are not as capable as others seem to be.

Another false premise that prevents us from setting limits is the idea that if we don't do it, it won't get done and disaster will ensue. We subtly airbrush Hashem out of the picture, imagining that we are running our corner of the world and there is no one else who can step into the situation. We anxiously, frantically struggle to move our world in the direction we see fit at the pace we desire, forgetting that it's all under control. While it is true that we each have our individual mission in life, and that the challenges we face can lead us forward in that mission, it is not true that we must do it all alone.

Chava was on the phone to her son Shmully's fourth-grade rebbi for the third time this week. She was a mother who "stayed on top of things," and was convinced that all her kids needed her constant monitoring. Although Shmully was an average student, she sat for hours every night with him, reviewing his studies and supervising his homework, certain that this was the only way to ensure his success.

"It would be great if you could compliment him on something he says in class," she tells the rebbi. "He might seem like an outgoing boy, but believe me, he doesn't have any confidence in himself."

"I try to call on all the boys and encourage them as much as I can, Mrs. Stein," said the rebbi. "Certainly I'll do the same for Shmully."

"Right, but he really needs it more than most other boys," she reiterated. "Maybe if you could call on him, say, once a day at least, that would help. We could bring in some prizes and you could give him one every couple of days when he asks a good question. Could you do that?"

"I heard very good things about him from his last year's rebbi, Mrs. Stein," the rebbi said. "I don't think we'll benefit him by singling him out so much. Why don't we give things a few weeks to settle and then we'll see where we're holding."

"Look, I'm sorry if I'm a little anxious, but I'm his mother and I have to make sure things go right so he'll have a good year and be ready to start Gemara next year and end up in a good high school. I don't have to tell you what that means to a boy."

Whatever Hashem's plans might be for Shmully, Mrs. Stein is determined to run interference and make sure nothing gets past her. She believes that if she does not manage every detail of his fourth-grade school experience, his prospects for high school will be ruined. The boundary between Shmully's responsibility and her own is fuzzy at best, and therefore, she feels obligated to wear herself out living his school experience. It never occurs to her that other people also influence Shmully's school life and that he might succeed even without her micromanagement. Or, he may fail despite it or perhaps even because of it.

In all of the situations above, the common denominator is a melding of the individual's identity with that of others in his life. As one mother once lamented, "You can only be as happy as your least happy child." That is because to a mother, her children's happiness seems inseparable with her own. However, if we accept that premise, that means that in order for a woman with eight children to be happy, eight other people with their own lives, problems, challenges and flaws, must also be happy, all at the same time. The odds are clearly stacked against the mother.

Setting boundaries vastly increases the odds. While we all want to be loving, empathetic people, and saying "yes" to others builds those traits, "yes" is only a loving response when it emerges from within healthy boundaries, unadulterated by guilt, resentment or fear. Tapping into the power of "no" gives us a balanced life, a life in which we recognize that we can only do our part, and Hashem does His part. Then, the help we give others will truly build them and our relationships with them. Sometimes, a kind, caring but firm "no" is the greatest "yes" of all.

The Key

The master key for unlocking the power of "no" is to realize, accept and fully believe that healthy boundaries are truly an expression of love, and that the opposite, relinquishing our personal sovereignty to everyone else's needs and demands, can do great harm. We are not even necessarily pitting our own needs against those of others in this paradigm; in almost every case, when we erode our own positive energy, we hurt others in the process. The typical example of this is the oxygen mask that descends from the ceiling when an airplane encounters distress. Parents are told to put on their own masks before they help their children. If the parent isn't functioning, the children have no one to help them.

In the effort to convince ourselves that limits are not bad and wrong, a vital step is to realize that Hashem built limitations into the Creation. He made day and night; the workweek and Shabbos; life and death. None of these forces can exist in the same time and place as its opposite. If Hashem tells us that a moment in time cannot be both Shabbos and a weekday, surely we cannot expect to make a moment both sleeptime and worktime. Furthermore, this concept of opposing forces pervades the universe. At every single moment, somewhere in the world, light is dawning while somewhere else, night is falling. While babies are being born, people are passing from the world.

Everything in creation exists in its moment in time and its spot in space. We are allotted a certain number of moments in our lives, and each of them can be used only once. Therefore, if we say "yes" to one thing, we are of necessity saying "no" to another, at least for that moment — and vice versa. We cannot possibly say "yes" to two disparate things at one time. Even the most expert multitasker can only put his hands to one task, his eyes to one sight, his mind to one analysis at a time.

We unlock the power of "no" when we internalize the fact that this is really, truly a positive power. We have to recondition our thinking to understand that it is right and good for us to budget the limited hours of our lives wisely and productively. It is right and good for us to protect our time, resources, energy and joyfulness. And here are some ways to do it:

Unlock the Power of "No"

Inspiration

1. Identify how you feel when you have to say "no." Are you fearful? Do you dread it? Do you feel guilty or wrong?

2. Feel the loving emotions behind a balanced "no" to a child or someone else to whom you are close. Feel your desire to do what is really best for that person, out of your sincere care for him or her. Feel when your "no" expresses care for yourself, so that you can have energy and joy to give. Feel when you are setting boundaries to encourage the other person to use his or her own strengths.

3. Identify where you learned that saying "no" is bad, and test the reality of those messages. Do they apply to you in your life right now?

Logic

4. Mentally tally the things you accomplish in a day. These are all the things to which you have said "yes." Understand that they have only been accomplished by saying "no" to other things you could have been doing during that time. For instance, if you visited your grandmother in the nursing home at lunchtime, you did not use your lunch break to meet your friend or to pay your bills.

5. Tell yourself that even though there are 40 things that need to get done today, there is only enough time for 10. Choose the 10 tasks you will undertake today and say "no" to the others.

6. Recognize that as you get older and your life becomes more complex, you will have to delegate more tasks to others, saying "no" to the things other people can take on

so that you can say "yes" to the things that require your particular strengths.

Actions

7. Say out loud words you would use to say "no" to something you have agreed to do in the past, but feel is not feasible for you to do now. Imagine the situation and role-play your part.

8. Practice setting limits and sticking with them. For instance, decide to spend 20 minutes on a task and then stop when 20 minutes are over. Try to set yourself a schedule for yourself and stick to it. Say "no" to your own and others' attempts to distract you from your schedule.

9. Practice saying "no" in a way that explains the "yes" that is on the other side of it. For instance, "I can't do that job right now because I have to finish something else," or "I can't take business calls after dinner because that is when I learn with my son (take a walk with my wife, go to my class, etc.)."

10. If you have people who tend to manipulate you and can't take no for an answer, realize that saying "no" once does not penetrate their consciousness. You have to say "no" at least three times to be heard, so practice saying your "no" sentence three times, practically word for word:

   You: "I would like to do that, but right now I'm taken."

   The Other Person: "Can't you do that later? Right now I really need you to do this."

   You: "Really I'd like to. But as I said, right now I'm taken."

   TOP: "I know you're busy, but this is important. If you don't do it now, it might end up being too late."

You: "Gee, I'm really sorry you didn't ask me earlier when I might have been able to help you. I would like to, but you know, right now, I'm taken."

TOP: So you're saying you really can't do it?

At this point, your "no" has at last been heard.

While we all admire the supermen and superwomen who seem able to achieve the impossible, we sometimes misconceive the mind-set that gets them there. They are not people who have no limits; rather, they are people who know how to set limits and say "no" when necessary, so that all their power and energy are channeled to productive purposes. We see this concept illustrated by many Torah sources that urge us to do our maximum in our own lives and for others. However, they also caution us to be aware of what that maximum really is.

Sefer Hanhagos HaChofetz Chaim (p. 278) records the Chofetz Chaim's advice on "doing it all," as the topic was discussed in the letters of Reb Pesachyah Minkin. In a conversation with the Chofetz Chaim, Reb Pesachyah received the following advice: Do not learn more than your stamina can endure. Get fresh air, take an evening walk or just sit and rest to prevent your body from becoming weak. "Pushing oneself extra is the advice of the *yetzer hara*," the Chofetz Chaim is reported to have said. "This will weaken the body, and then the person will have to lose a great deal more time from his learning." He recalled that in his youth, he had pushed himself too hard and had become ill. His doctor ordered him to refrain from learning for two years.

In *Sefer Kitzur Toldos* (p. 4) there is another account of the episode. The Chofetz Chaim relates that when he was 20, he experienced exhaustion that destroyed his ability to concentrate on learning or praying or anything else that required focus. He understood that the exhaustion arose from the pressure he put upon himself to learn without rest. Doctors had nothing to offer him, and only time — a full year — could move him past the crippling symptoms. "After toiling in a complicated *halachah* for three or four hours, I have to stop," he wrote in later years. "I am not allowed to overwork my mind."

The Take-Away

The Chofetz Chaim was not lazy. He was not looking for an "out." On the contrary, he is one of the most accomplished and influential Torah luminaries of recent times. Yet he teaches us that recognizing our limits, saying "no," is not only acceptable, but it is necessary. The person who runs himself ragged, whether it is for learning, for *chesed*, for work or family, will ultimately burn out. Thus, as the Chofetz Chaim teaches us, the *yetzer hara* is the real winner when we say "yes" to everything.

One more interesting sidelight of the Chofetz Chaim's account is his admission of overwhelming exhaustion. People often ask me why it seems that so many psychological disorders have only surfaced in the past few decades, and it may well be true that they are far more prevalent now than they once were. However, we see here that mental exhaustion was acknowledged and addressed by one of the generation's greatest figures.

We see this point depicted again in **Rebbitzen Kanievsky: A Legendary Mother of All** (ArtScroll) in an episode in which the Rebbitzen, who provided help and advice for a never-ending stream of Jews, became overwrought by one particularly jarring situation. The author (p. 261) relates that she took an anti-anxiety medication to calm down, and the footnote explains that this had been prescribed for her for the rare occasions on which she was physically overwhelmed by others' pain.

The Gemara (*Pesachim* 113b) lists various types of people whose lives are not worth living. Among them is the person who has pity for everyone. Rashbam explains that this type of person has no peace, because of his concern.

The Take-Away

Even kindness and mercy need a limit, as this Gemara teaches us. While mercy is a commendable trait that can bring much good into our lives, if our empathy is so strong and pervasive that it eats up our joy in life, our life loses its value.

The Chazon Ish (*Igros Chazon Ish,* Letter 29) made himself available for a wide range of *Klal Yisrael's* needs, spanning every topic under the sun. Once in a while, someone would ask a question to which he did not want to respond. The person would pester and persist; such persistence, the Chazon Ish wrote, constitutes an *aveirah* in itself.

He stated, "Mental stress on a person is harder than physical stress. Therefore, I have the right not to take upon myself your request to do tasks that are hard on me....However, I don't want to send you away empty.....The Ri says that to put a person in such a predicament is a violation of the Torah's prohibition against working an animal beyond its endurance."

The Take-Away

The *Gedolim* have boundaries defining what they will and will not undertake. Furthermore, the Chazon Ish tells us that we do not even have the right to ask someone to do something that we know will be difficult for him, because he may say "yes" out of sympathy for us or fear of insulting us. In other words, the common idea that "it doesn't hurt to ask" is not always true. Furthermore, if it is not permitted for someone to ask us to do something that is too difficult for us, it is certainly permitted for us to say, "Sorry, I can't." Even if the stress is "only" mental, the Chazon Ish tells us that the stress is real.

The *Mesilas Yesharim* (*Perek* 2, *Middas Hazehirus*) reveals that one of the *yetzer hara's* prime tools is to convince us that we must rush from one thing to the next, or multitask everything all at once. When we're in a hurry, we don't stop to think. In fact, this strategy of forcing people to rush from one task to another was used by Pharaoh to keep the Jews in a state of mindless confusion. Because we lack any kind of focus in such a frantic situation, we are also crippled in our effort to find some way out of it.

The Take-Away

Downtime is not wasted time. It is necessary for our functioning and growth. We need time to assess, to plan, to think our thoughts and feel our feelings. People believe that if they turn down a request because they want the time to themselves, they are doing something terrible. But in truth, running non-stop from one thing to the next leaves us far more vulnerable to mistakes, confusion, depression and burnout. Sometimes, by not doing someone a favor, we're doing him the biggest favor of all.

Chapter 6

Release Your Nature

Playing to Your Strengths vs. Fighting Yourself

"I FEEL LIKE I'M ALWAYS FIGHTING WITH MY TEENAGE
son, Yitzy," says Daniel. "Just at an age when we should
be getting closer, it seems that there's always an edge."

"What types of things do you fight about?" I ask him.

"Mostly it's his attitude. He takes his sweet time
about everything. I mean, he's not a bad kid, not at
all. He walks to the hospital every Shabbos and visits the patients. He's the type of kid his friends can
count on for a favor. And he's a learner, too, when
he's motivated. But that's the trouble with him; he's
got no self-discipline when it comes to getting to shul
or yeshivah on time. He waltzes into Shacharis 15
minutes late every Shabbos. I say to him, 'Look, Yitzy,
if you can make it every week at 8:45 on the dot, you

*can make it at 8:30. Do me a favor, don't embarrass
me. Come on time.'"*

"So how does he respond to that?" I follow up.

"Oh, he's 100 percent agreeable. But then nothing
changes. Why can't he do the one thing I ask him to
do? Even if he doesn't feel like it, I feel like he should
listen to his father. He'll walk two miles to visit strangers, but he won't make me happy by getting up 15
minutes early to get to shul on time!"

Prodding a little more deeply into Daniel's background, we
come to realize that he, too, used to find timeliness challenging. As a boy, he had trouble being on time for school and
shul. It wasn't that he couldn't get up in the morning; it was
just that he often got caught up in something else as he made
his way through his routine. The distraction was sometimes his
desire to hear one more song on the beloved music tape he
played as he prepared for school. Sometimes it was his devotion
to the vegetable garden he was growing in his yard; he couldn't
walk away without pulling a few weeds and giving the plants a
shpritz of water. By the time he got back on track, he was late.

Most notably, Daniel testifies that he worked long and hard to
drum the "dreaminess" out of his personality. He pushed himself
to excel in yeshivah and gave himself no "wiggle room" at all. As
a young man, he was known for his zeal, never arriving at yeshivah a minute late, leaving a minute early or taking off time for
anything but absolute necessities. "I realized that if I didn't want to
be a loser, I had better stop being 'nature boy' and stop getting all
involved in music, and just get with the program. By the time I was
Yitzy's age, I had gotten serious, And it's time he gets serious too."

One of Daniel's problems with Yitzy is that when the father
looks at his son, he sees a negative aspect of his own nature
staring back at him in a mirror. It's as if Daniel had gotten a
nose job and now he sees his old nose on Yitzy's face. Daniel's

discomfort is all the greater because he has long ago labeled a significant part of his nature as the material of which "losers" are made. On one hand, he had accomplished a great feat of self-improvement, turning himself from a lax and dreamy pre-teen into a self-disciplined, hard-working young man. On the other hand, however, he believed that this progress could only be made by surgically removing his love of nature and music. It was as if he had decided that since his right hand worked better than his left hand, he would cut off his left hand.

Part of our work in rebuilding Daniel's relationship with Yitzy is to awaken Daniel to the fact that everything works better with both hands. If Daniel can reclaim the more creative, emotional nature he has abandoned, he will find not only his own life vastly enriched, but he will discover common ground upon which to meet and help his son.

Sandra grew up in the peace-and-love hippie era of the 1970s. She was a perfect hippie, eager to help the poor and save the world. She earned a Masters degree in social work and devoted two decades of her life to working for various antipoverty programs and non-profit agencies. In the view of the world that pervaded Sandra's professional, social and family circles, competition was a bad thing. Therefore Sandra, a brilliant and articulate woman, subdued her innate desire to excel. She convinced herself that her "elitist" perspective was wrong and bad.

Somewhere along the road, Sandra became religiously observant and got married. As expenses began to mushroom in tandem with her growing family, she began feeling constrained by her social-work job. An opportunity arose to start an online business, and although she was tempted to jump in, she was beset by guilt. "I feel like I'm selling out," she told me. "All these years, it was never about money. And now, now that I'm a religious Jew and I'm supposed to be more spiritual, this is when I start obsessing about markups and profit margins? This is when I'm going to dedicate my time to peddling more junk in the marketplace? But on the other hand, I feel like I'm at such a dead end with social work. I need stimulation and concrete goals. I need something to make me feel sharp and accomplished."

What Sandra is discovering is that no one is one dimensional. We all possess several natures, some more dominant than the others, and some that are even in opposition to the others. She has devoted many years to the care and feeding of her emotional nature, empathizing with others' problems and putting her desire to compete and excel on the back burner. In seeking to start a business, she is not "selling out" as she fears, but rather, is rescuing her squelched "challenger" nature that was crying out for air and water. She worries that she is losing her identity by leaving a "helping profession" for the business world, when in fact, she is enabling another essential dimension of her identity to emerge.

But what would have happened if Sandra had not crushed her competitive nature, but rather had integrated it into the life she was living for the first decades of her career? What if she had subscribed to the idea that someone can be both caring and competitive; that someone can value others while also fully embracing her own power? She may have found her life as a social worker far more satisfying. Perhaps she would have started an organization to alleviate some pressing social problem. Her mental acuity and competitive spirit could have made her a successful philanthropy entrepreneur who raised millions of dollars for her cause. However, like Daniel, Sandra chose to cut off the nature she considered unacceptable, rather than putting it to work in her life.

People often wonder why others can't see things they way they do. How can the neighbor not see that she is spoiling her children? How can the husband not see that his wife wants him to put down his cell phone and talk to her? How can the mother not see that her daughter really needs that new dress? How can people be so selfish, so blind, so out of touch? Not only do we ask these questions about others, but often, after the fact, we are forced to ask these questions about ourselves.

Part of the answer to this mystery is that each person has his or her own natures, and it is through these natures that we perceive and navigate our world. Our natures are what define us: our sources of joy, growth and satisfaction, as well as our obstacles and challenges. The sensitive situation that seems obvious to the emotional person might entirely escape the notice of the logical one. The inspirational lecture that delights the spiritual person might bore the kinesthetic one into a stupor. The community project that thrills the activist will probably cause the playful type of person to run in the other direction.

Understanding our own natures lets us work effectively with the tools Hashem gave us for our journey through life. We tend to recognize this principle more easily when dealing with other people. For instance, if we understand that our 3-year-old child is fiercely independent, we realize that we'll have to give him enough time to get himself dressed with minimal help from us. To interfere too aggressively would invite the child's resistance and turn the procedure into a frustrating battle of wills. Instead, the wise parent leaves enough time for the child to dress himself, thus fostering the positive trait of independence and helping the child develop the skills to do the job more efficiently. Just as common sense dictates that we "work with" the child's nature to bring out the best in him, we must "work with" our own natures as well. Just as this approach brings out the best in the child, it also brings out the best in ourselves.

The infinite combinations of human natures comprise the palette from which our world is painted. If we study a realistic oil painting, we discover that nothing is monochromatic. For instance, an image of a blue silk dress is made up not only of strokes of blue, but perhaps includes streaks of brown, white, yellow, purple and other colors. The darker colors give the creases in the silk its depth, while the lighter colors give the fabric its shimmer. As individuals, we too are multicolored. Each of our differentiated and sometimes conflicting natures offsets, highlights or balances the others, giving us full depth and dimension. As a society, too, our varied natures create a balanced whole. The activist might enlist the kinesthetic person to perform the hands-on part of his project. The spiritual person might later hear about the incredible *hashgachah pratis* with which the project was blessed, and inspire many more people with the story.

To live vibrantly, we must discover and work with our natures. To create wholesome, productive relationships with others, we must discover and work with their natures. While we do have the obligation to work on improving the negative aspects of our natures, the first step is to identify the natures themselves. Whether one wishes to cut his meat along the grain or against it, he must first find the grain.

The Lock

When we do not inquire into our own natures, we may suffer from confusion and dejection, wondering why we cannot seem to find a comfortable niche in life. The famous children's story, *The Ugly Duckling,* plays out this theme vividly:

A mother duck sits on her eggs until one day, they hatch. Just one egg, which is larger than the rest, remains unhatched. The next day, that one also hatches, revealing a large, awkward gray "duckling." The duckling lives in misery and rejection among the other ducks, until one day, he encounters a flock of swans and realizes that he is not a misfit duck at all, but rather, he is a perfect swan.

Many people live with misery and rejection because they believe that they are defective, when in fact they are exactly what they were designed to be. The person whose nature is more intellectual might think of himself as "lazy" because he does not have the physical energy of someone whose nature is more kinesthetic. If, on the other hand, he recognizes his nature, and that every nature has its strengths and weaknesses, he can stop deriding himself. Maybe he needs to build up his physical energy level — force himself to pitch in when physical jobs need to be done, or make sure he gets enough exercise to stay healthy — but he does not have to assign a harsh label to his proclivity. He may be far from lazy when it comes to intellectual pursuits.

We can also become consumed by inexplicable feelings of envy as a result of misreading our own natures. We see someone who excels in a certain area that has eluded us, and it drives us crazy.

"It's as if I can't allow my brother-in-law any success in life," said Leib, a 32-year-old man who worked as a warehouse manager. *"I make great money, I have adorable kids, a wonderful wife, and my brother-in-law is 28 and not even married yet. He should be jealous of me. But instead, you know what drives me crazy? His law degree. I try not to speak negatively about him, but whenever I see him, which is often, my mind is busy thinking, 'Mr. Professional. Mr. College Degree. Thinks he's so smart.' What's* wrong *with me?"*

The answer to that, we soon discovered, was that Leib saw in his brother-in-law the successful manifestation of a nature that Leib, too, possessed. Law might have been just the career to unleash the power of his logical nature and competitive spirit, yet Leib had never considered it. The training seemed too long and expensive, and he knew he would make more money in his present job, at least to begin with, than he would make as an entry-level lawyer. The fact that Leib reacted with envy to his brother-in-law's achievement was a powerful clue to Leib's own latent nature. Had his brother-in-law become a doctor, Leib would have felt nothing; he hated the sight of blood and found science deadly dull.

Friction also develops when we fail to realize that every nature is a package deal. Each comes with its strengths and its weaknesses. This is often a disturbing revelation for married couples. A woman might adore her strong, protective hero of a husband until she realizes that there's a certain demanding, bossy side to his personality. Another woman might admire her husband's sweet, easygoing nature, but discover that it is interwoven with a lack of assertiveness. A husband might be proud of the way his wife delights in playing with her little children but cringe at the crayons, blocks and books that cover the floor and tables. Another husband may admire his wife's great organizational skills and professional achievements, but find fault in her lack of spontaneity.

All of these confusing blockages can be dissolved to some extent by understanding the natures that create them. We are never allowed, as Jews, to look at a flaw in ourselves and say, "Oh, well, that's just the way I am." We are in this world to work on our flaws and through that work, to achieve our potential. Our natures can sometimes spawn our imperfections, but they are also the source of the strength we have for improving ourselves. To live our lives to the fullest, we must lay claim to all of our natures and create with them a three-dimensional picture of who we are and what we can be.

The How and Why

Who knows us better than we know ourselves? How could it be that we harbor inborn natures that we do not even recognize? Those questions seem less puzzling when we think about them from an objective perspective. How many people do we know who do not seem to really understand themselves? How many people can we read like a book, yet they seem largely unaware of their own patterns of thought?

Susan is a lonely, older woman. Lori is her friend and neighbor who works at home on her computer. Susan often calls Lori in the middle of Lori's workday, always with some important issue for which she needs Lori's immediate input.

"There's no one else I trust to tell this to," Susan usually says *as an introduction to what she realizes is an ill-timed phone call. Susan believes that she respects Lori's time and only interrupts her workday when there's something important to discuss. It's obvious to Lori that Susan is lonely, and uses her "issues" to convince herself that it is not social neediness, but something more important, that motivates her phone calls.*

Susan sees herself as an activist, a person who recognizes what's wrong in the world and burns to fix it. She feels the need to "bounce her ideas" off Lori, her trusted friend. In reality, however, Susan is an emotional person with a deep need to connect to others, and Lori is a willing and available connection. Lori sees this clearly, but Susan does not see it at all.

Our ability to recognize our natures rests partly on what types of natures we believe are worthy and respectable. In an intellectual family, the physical, hands-on nature might not receive much nurturing. In a family in which organization is prized, an intuitive nature might be squelched. School and society also play a powerful role in defining natures that are considered positive and worthwhile. We are often told that we will not succeed if we do not develop some set of traits that may or may not exist within our natural make-up.

As a result of all this input, we can indeed live a long time without knowing ourselves very well. We can struggle against what seem to be insurmountable odds as we try to become what we are not and try to bury the traits that stubbornly keep bubbling up from within us. Nevertheless, a world of insight and positive power emerge from our knowledge of ourselves.

The Key

Thus far, we have been discussing the concept of "natures," and we have identified a few more commonly recognized categories. Here we will offer a more complete picture. There are 18 distinct natures that describe a full realm of traits, strengths and weaknesses we find within the vast majority of people. As we noted earlier, no one bears just one of these natures. All of us have many, with two or three that dominate. The first step to understanding your natures is to recognize them. Which categories apply to you?

1. **Logical:** You base your world on thought; you primarily value that which makes sense. Your emotions do not enter into your decision-making.

    Strengths: You deal well with emergencies because you do not get swallowed up in the emotions of the situation. You are a good problem-solver and prioritizer. You absorb information. You are honest and straightforward with your praise and your criticism.

    Weaknesses: You tend to be emotionally unavailable when others need to feel your care. You have trouble listening to others' problems when they are seeking empathy and instead feel the need to offer solutions. You have difficulty feeling moved or inspired.

2. **Emotional:** You base your world on emotions, seeking situations in which you can express and receive love. You need affection and feel hurt if it is denied. You are open with your emotional expressions, laughing and crying easily.

    Strengths: You are highly empathetic and feel for others. You may cry for joy at someone else's *chuppah* or in sorrow at a funeral. Your feelings drive you to give generously to *tzedakah* even when it is beyond your means, and to undertake projects that may seem logically impossible. You exude warmth and people enjoy being around you. You are open to inspiration.

    Weaknesses: You become angry when your goals are frustrated. You resent being forced to prove your point and give up easily when obstacles arise. On the other hand, you may insist on continuing on a course that does not make sense. You may tend to feel depressed and anxious.

3. **Healer:** You thrive on helping others and are willing to take on difficult tasks against great odds in order to do so. You feel others' pain and perceive their needs without them having to express it outright.

   Strengths: You are altruistic, willing to put others' needs ahead of your own and will come through when others cannot. You refuse to see anything as impossible. You will even use the last of your strength to give one more try to achieve something worthwhile.

   Weaknesses: In putting others first, you may deny necessary support to yourself and your family. You avoid saying "no" to any request, and sometimes even jump into a situation when you are not wanted or needed. You may sometimes "kill with kindness" someone who needs the experience of working a situation out on his own. You resent people questioning your motives for giving so much of yourself.

4. **Kinesthetic:** You are a hands-on person who experiences life on a sensory level. You like to be around people and relate face-to-face rather than by email or phone. You show warmth with a handshake, hug or slap on the shoulder. You like to give and receive impressive gifts.

   Strengths: You approach a job with energy and enthusiasm. You're a take-charge person who is not afraid to issue directions to anyone. You live in the present, enjoying what you have and avoiding worrying about the future. You are vigorous and enjoy physical work. You are able to challenge and argue without making it personal.

   Weaknesses: You have trouble accepting opposition and raise your voice when you are arguing. You are not sensitive to other people's emotional make-up and may end up hurting others unintentionally. Because you do not think about the future, you may not do what is necessary to build a career or business. You may seek short-term satisfaction at the expense of long-term goals.

5. **Maven:** You are the person with the inside information on everything. You know where to get the best deals. You know everyone and to whom they are related, to whom their family members are married, where they went to school and so forth.

    Strengths: You have great intuition about business and investments, and you are willing to share your information with anyone who is interested. You love being on the scene when deals are sealed or events are taking place. You love being "in the know," and being a source of information for others.

    Weaknesses: You more often play the bystander rather than an active participant in the deals and events you witness. At times your intuition is wrong, but since your "in the know" reputation is your most valued commodity, you cannot admit a mistake. Therefore, you sometimes blame others for mistakes. Your desire to be the source of information makes confidentiality a great challenge for you.

6. **Challenger:** You thrive on competition. You love to prove your point and will go to great lengths to get others to agree with you. You never tire of debating the issues that are important to you. You are, however, open to new information and can form a new opinion based on facts. You love to attempt something others claim is impossible.

    Strengths: You can stand up to a challenge and do not fear opposition. You will fight even if the odds are against you. You are willing to take up "lost causes." You are a leader.

Weaknesses: Your argumentative nature can create enemies. You might appear insensitive, bullying or manipulative in your passion to win.

7. **Leader:** You exude a natural sense of confidence that makes those around you feel safe. You seem able to handle any situation that comes your way. With you around, people feel that everything is under control.

   Strengths: You are a born leader who has no trouble directing people older than you or in higher positions than you. People trust you and follow your lead. You take a lot of responsibility on yourself and you get things done.

   Weaknesses: Your confident demeanor sometimes hides a lack of knowledge or ability to handle a particular situation. When things don't work out or you are blamed for problems, you may become despondent. You may take too much upon yourself and be unable to handle it. People feel free to criticize you, believing it doesn't affect you.

8. **Spiritual:** While this is a nature that every Jew possesses, and to which we all must find ways to connect, for you, spirituality is reality. Your view of the world is based on Hashem and spiritual values. You connect emotionally to prayer and mitzvos. You see Hashem's presence in nature and in your life. You love to hear stories of *hashgachah pratis* (Divine providence) and to see it in your own life. You seek ways to become closer to Hashem.

   Strengths: You inspire others and give them encouragement in their lives, both by your example and your words. You are a free-spirited person who cares little for material things. You will take a difficult path or give until it hurts if you feel that this is what Hashem wants from you. You feel Hashem acutely in your life. Your soul responds deeply to music. You love peace.

Weaknesses: You do not handle money, time or structure efficiently. Your household or office may be disorganized. You avoid conflict at all costs.

9. **Intuitive:** You have a high level of native intelligence; you just seem to know a lot about a wide spectrum of different things. You seem to know what lies ahead. You read other people accurately through their words, facial expression and body language, and know how to talk to others in a way that reaches them. Your perceptiveness lends itself to good judgment in matters like business or *shidduch* proposals. You appreciate having time alone to think.

   Strengths: People love and admire you. You see the best in everyone and relate to everyone at their own level. You know what to say and what not to say to a broad range of people. As a result, you generate peaceful relationships that lend themselves to a peaceful life.

   Weaknesses: Sometimes your sensitive radar picks up vibes that are simply inaccurate, and you proceed based on those false perceptions. When people betray your trust or treat you with hostility, you are deeply hurt and can become cynical and depressed. While you understand others, they do not always understand you, which can make you feel isolated and betrayed. Your keen awareness causes you to focus on whatever is wrong in any situation.

10. **Critic:** Your eyes turn first to the flaws and mistakes. You aim to fix what's wrong, even within yourself. You foresee problems realistically and avoid wishful thinking. Your greatest goal is excellence in all matters in which you are involved, and you focus on fixing whatever is wrong right away at all costs.

    Strengths: You can be a great manager who sets the bar high and brings out the best in others. Your eye for detail picks up on mistakes in a wide variety of areas, and your problem-solving perspective helps you find solutions. You push the envelope and end up achieving more than anyone expects.

Weaknesses: Your perfectionist nature can be hard on you and others. You often overlook other people's emotions in your quest to drive them to excellence. You are seldom satisfied because everything can always be better.

11. **Playful:** You find the fun in life, no matter how old you are. You smile and laugh easily, always looking for the positive in situations. You are slow to anger.

    Strengths: You have a positive outlook on life. You can connect with people of all types and all ages, and know how to make others smile.

    Weaknesses: You shrink away from a crisis, finding someone else to take charge. You sometimes fail to take others' worries seriously, believing that they can coast past difficulties in the same way that you do. You do not understand how others can feel hopeless or depressed.

12. **Idealist:** You are always looking for the highest goal and best route to that goal, and you have a natural sense of how high that can be. You are self-motivated to keep striving and are a role model for living up to one's potential. You have exceptional appreciation for all of Hashem's creations.

    Strengths: You focus on bringing out the best in yourself and others and work to help others achieve excellence. You are self-aware and committed to self-improvement. You thrive on peace and are willing to work for it.

    Weaknesses: You are self-critical and critical of others, and rarely feel satisfied because your ideals are never totally met. You have trouble understanding why people do not see right and wrong as clearly as you do. When people reject your advice, you feel depressed and angry.

13. **Imformational:** You are very thoughtful and love information. You can spend hours researching almost any topic because knowledge fascinates you. You appreciate people for what you can learn from them. You prefer books to social interaction, but you are kindhearted.

   Strengths: You see the world with a sense of wonder and amazement. You are constantly learning and know about a great range of topics. Your mind operates on a higher plane that keeps you above personal disputes and enables you to live a peaceful life.

   Weaknesses: You are uncomfortable with emotions and have trouble relating to people as people. You are unable to negotiate conflict and therefore avoid it at all costs. You tend to be an introvert and live largely in your head, bypassing much of life's real experiences.

14. **Activist:** You come alive in a crisis and thrive on dramatic, highly emotional situations. You are a natural networker who loves to meet people and make connections.

   Strengths: You are able to form and maintain a wide network of contacts. You are aware of your strengths and accomplishments. You see other people's strengths and value what they have to offer. You have unlimited energy and can spring into action at a moment's notice and work around the clock when necessary. You are willing to go to great lengths to help someone in need.

   Weaknesses: Focused on getting the job done, you might step on toes, lose your temper or insist on doing things your way. Sometimes you overestimate your own capacity and end up having to drop an undertaking before it is completed.

15. **Planner:** You can look at a situation and see where it is leading. You are good at weighing the possibilities. You have charisma. You get things done.

    Strengths: You are effective in undertaking projects and anticipating what will be needed to succeed. You have the patience to follow through until you achieve your goal. You are able to connect to others emotionally, empathizing with their problems and finding solutions.

    Weaknesses: You might use your foresight to manipulate people, and may turn hostile and hold grudges against those who do not see things your way.

16. **Manager:** You know how to motivate people to do things they may not want to do. You know how to delegate responsibility. Although you tend to be blunt, people understand that you are trying to achieve a goal and usually do not take your statements personally.

    Strengths: You are capable of managing a large staff and inspiring them to act. You can handle criticism. You are not hesitant about telling others what needs to be done, even if they are in a higher position than you.

    Weaknesses: Your bluntness and forceful personality can sometimes hurt others. At times you appear to be taking over other people's jobs and threatening their positions.

17. **Reserved:** You can think your thoughts and come up with jokes and interesting comments without having to speak them. You don't have to prove yourself to others. You know who you are and are comfortable in your skin.

    Strengths: You are rarely involved in conflicts, because it's enough for you to know you are right without having to prove it to others. You are an excellent listener, since you are not preoccupied with what you are going to say next. Because you rarely speak impulsively, you avoid saying insensitive or hurtful things. You tend to develop a mature, well-rounded perspective on matters.

Weaknesses: People may mistake your reserve for shyness or unfriendliness. You have difficulty expressing enthusiasm and emotion even when you feel it. If you do not push yourself to express excitement, your spouse and children may feel a lack of warmth and appreciation. Your employer may feel you lack "fire." You may pass through life without ever communicating all the valuable ideas and feelings to those who would benefit from them.

18. **Social:** You are focused on the world around you. You love to be among people and are bored with solitary pursuits. You come alive in social situations and in public roles. You're the type of person that "everyone knows."

Strengths: You are able to strive for your goals without hesitation. You are well equipped to participate in your community, profession or any other group in which you become involved. Your aptitude for making connections makes you a great "matchmaker" whether for marriage, jobs, business opportunities or any other area in which networking is important. There's always action around you, which draws others toward you and wins you admiration.

Weaknesses: You can come across aggressive and may sometimes steal the spotlight. Your wide focus may stand in the way of developing close relationships. Family members may sometimes find you uncaring. Your outgoingness sometimes leads you to speak without thinking, sometimes hurting others or imparting misinformation.

If we think about various situations that arise in life, we can see how each of these natures would respond differently. For instance, if a child has a medical issue, the Activist will get busy finding referrals to the top specialist in the relevant field. The

Emotional person will concentrate on soothing the child's worries and pain. The Factual person will research the condition and learn everything he can about it. Chances are, most people will take some combination of these approaches, starting with the reaction that arises from their most dominant natures. When we understand how our natures influence our reactions, we also realize that we will have to push ourselves to cover the bases we are not as inclined to cover. For instance, the Emotional-natured person must still gather information and seek referrals.

Very often, Hashem gives us a highly effective tool for "pushing ourselves" to refine our natures. It is called "family." If our parents, spouses and children think and do things differently than we do, we have two choices: We can endlessly wrangle for dominance, or we can adjust and modify our own traits to maintain peace and balance. If we perceive their way of doing things as wrong or bad, we are bound to keep fighting. If we see it as an outgrowth of their nature, we will realize that we can't win. Fighting with someone doesn't change who they are. Therefore, we adjust ourselves, and in adjusting, we grow exactly along the path Hashem laid out for us when He placed us in this marriage and family. Likewise, their adjustments to us fuel their growth.

Once we have identified the range of human natures, our goal must be to recognize and accept the natures that are our own. To become the best we can be, we must first embrace who we are, and here are some ways to do it:

Unlock Your Nature

Inspiration

1. Which three or four natures do you feel connected to? Even if your logic tells you differently, recognize your inner feeling. For instance, you may feel that you are an Activist at heart, even though in reality you hesitate to get involved in projects.

2. Let your imagination experience the natures with which you feel connected. Allow the nature to express itself and feel the power of living in that mode. For instance, if you are someone who tends to let others do the talking but you know that you have some of the "maven" in you, imagine yourself speaking up at a meeting or in class.

3. Identify what is missing or interfering with your ability to embrace that nature. Realize that the obstacle was from Hashem. For example, if you have an untapped "healer" nature, but have been unable to express it, consider taking an EMT course.

4. Integrate all your natures into your image of yourself. Let go of your efforts to fight them and instead, imagine where they can take you.

Logic

5. Analyze the things you think and do in an average day and identify the natures that are active and inactive in your life right now.

6. Recognize opposing natures within yourself and accept this lovingly, rather than deriding yourself for being the "ugly duckling."

7. Look at your spouse, parents or siblings and realize that Hashem connects us with people whose natures can help us grow. How can the people in your life help you grow?

8. See all the varied natures within you and around you not as flaws but as blessings which enable the world to survive.

Action

9. Write down your natures in the order of their prominence in your personality and identify those that you have not yet fully accessed. Identify the negative effects of ignoring or

denying those natures and the positive effects of embracing them.

10. Work on mastering those natures. When you are alone, take some time to practice expressing them. For instance, if you have been squelching a kinesthetic nature, get up and dance or do some push-ups. If you are keeping a spiritual nature under wraps, take a few minutes to have a conversation with Hashem or to sing a *zemer* or listen to a *shiur.*

 The Torah recognizes that Hashem creates each of us with a different set of personality traits. We learn from many sources that this is a concept that is embedded in the very fabric of Creation.

The Gemara (*Shabbos* 156a) records a list of personality traits based on the act of Creation that occurred on their day or time of birth.

Rabbi Chanina (ibid.) discusses the influence of the constellation under which a person is born. Traits imparted by this force include the propensity to be: distinguished; unable to keep one's secrets hidden; affluent; passionate; wise; subject to suffering; subject to having his plans frustrated; righteous; driven by blood lust and a whole range of others.

Take-Away

While the Torah demands the same standards of behavior from every Jew, it also recognizes that from the moment of birth each person has a unique set of strengths, weaknesses and motivations.

Rambam (*Hilchos Dei'os* 1:1) says, "Each and every man possesses many character traits. Each trait is very different and distinct from the others." Traits he names include calmness or anger, pride or humility, pleasure-seeking or ascetic, materialistic or simple. Each trait, he says, can be carried to an unhealthy extreme. In Halachah 4, the Rambam advises as to how we are to deal with our traits: "The straight path: This is the midpoint temperament of each and every trait that man possesses. This refers to the trait that is equidistant from either of the extremes, without being close to either of them."

The Take-Away

Rambam not only acknowledges the differing traits within people, but offers advice as to how we can live productively with the natures we have. We are not supposed to say, "That's just the way I am," and let our natures run rampant. Rather, we are supposed to assess and understand ourselves and then work to channel and balance the traits that are ours to use in achieving our unique missions in life.

Chapter 7

Step Seven

Release Your Support

Seeking Encouragement vs. Going It Alone

SOL HAD A GREAT BUSINESS IDEA. IT COULDN'T FAIL. *Sol loved pancakes, and he knew that the non-kosher diners worldwide flocked to a certain franchise restaurant noted for its pancakes. It was a place that specialized in pancakes of all sorts — blueberry, chocolate chip, apple, mini-pancakes — it made Sol's mouth water just to think about it.*

"The kosher market will LOVE this," he told himself. When a local restaurant location went up for lease, he quickly forged a plan for his Kosher Pancakes House and swung into action.

"A guy in my office used to manage a pancake franchise," his friend told him. "He could give you the inside scoop."

"Go over this carefully with your accountant," Sol's brother-in-law warned him. "There are always hidden costs you're not going to think of."

"Why don't you get a consultation with my Uncle Eli?" suggested a friend. "He's an expert on business start-ups."

"I'm not having everyone weigh in on this and drive me crazy," Sol told his unsolicited group of advisers. "Believe me, I know what I'm doing. I managed Pizza Palace for eight years. You think I don't know the restaurant business?"

Everyone clammed up and watched silently as Sol zoomed ahead like an express train. They all knew he was stubborn and impulsive; they just hoped that this time, he'd be lucky, as well.

Sol thinks he is a strong, independent man. Is he? That depends on how we define strength. If we define it as popular culture does, then Sol is indeed the classic rugged individualist. He is tough and unwavering, unfettered by any doubts about the rightness of his decisions. No one tells Sol what to do.

But what happens to Sol's business idea as a result of his "strength?" It quickly ends in disaster. First of all, he does not lay the basic foundation of finding out whether there is a market demand for the product he wants to sell. Do enough kosher consumers love pancakes the way Sol does? It turns out that most of them still want a bagel for a breakfast. Then there is the business model itself; having managed a pizza shop tells Sol nothing about how much profit he needs to make, how to price his menu items, how many employees he needs to hire and dozens of other details that make or break a business.

The "rugged individualist" is in fact not someone so strong that he doesn't need others. He is someone so weak that he cannot stand to have his ideas challenged by others. Real strength shows itself in the ability to learn from everyone. A strong person solicits and accepts advice from others. He can admit when he's wrong and apologize if necessary. He is not too fragile to let others into his life; he admits that there are people and issues that concern him. Most of all, he knows that he needs people to cheer him on when the going gets tough, and to pat him on the back when he does well.

Laura and Joe met in Israel while each of them was enrolled in a program for college students interested in exploring Judaism. When they married, they were both fully observant, but neither of them had exactly fallen in with the mainstream of religious Jewish life. They brought their children up in a way that they defined as "unique" but which the children, ultimately, found confusing. When the oldest child, Yaakov, began showing signs of rebellion, his yeshivah principal recommended that the parents seek advice from a rabbi in the community who was experienced with such challenges.

They respectfully listened to the principal, but later, discussing the situation together, they decided that no one in the community could really advise them. What they told each other was, "No one's going to get where we're coming from." What they meant, however, was "There's so much we don't know and we don't want anyone discovering it."

By the middle of the next school year, Yaakov was in a deep emotional ditch from which it would take years for him to emerge. His parents no longer cared what anyone might think about how they ran their home. They desperately searched for help.

For Sol and for Laura and Joe, the idea of seeking advice was more disturbing than the disasters the advice might have averted. Imagine how Laura and Joe might have established and raised their family if they had found one or two mentors who understood their unique challenges. Instead of worrying about being exposed as ignorant, they would have had the encouragement of people who knew them well and valued their strength and courage adopting an observant life. They would have had a guide to help them along an unfamiliar road, rather than trying to find their way without a map. They would have heard those cherished and infinitely powerful words: "You're going to get through this."

Imagine how Sol might have proceeded if he had possessed the strength to hear others' ideas about his business plan. He might have taken an informal survey to find out how many people would choose a pancake house as their breakfast destination. He might have found out that his menu would have to be more varied to bring in the flow of customers he needed. He might have discovered that he could not make enough profit with his idea, and saved himself the loss of a significant investment. Instead, he would have had the chance to tweak the idea into something with a better chance of success.

Every successful businessperson has a team. If an entrepreneur doesn't hire and delegate, his business cannot expand. It will remain a one-man show.

But a team is not only integral to the functioning of a business; it is vital to our own personal functioning as well. We all need a "team," even if it is comprised of just two or three people, to encourage us, believe in us and, when necessary, help us get back on track. We need the "go-to" people who see our potential, and are insightful, honest and kind enough to prod us toward it with the right balance of encouragement and constructive advice.

The "go-it-alone" person thinks that needing someone to root for him is a sign of weakness. In reality, however, it is a sign of being human. Our sense of what we can accomplish in life is very much linked to the messages we receive from those around us. Anyone who has ever won an award starts his acceptance speech with a list of people he wishes to thank for believing in him and keeping him going. Praise and encouragement are not just the dessert; they are the meat and potatoes, without which our spirits starve. We need to hear and feel this positive input not only as children, but throughout our lives. If we are lacking it, we must find it, just as we would be compelled to find food if we were starving. High achievers know they need others; they admit others into their lives and recognize the value of their input.

Are you a "go-it-aloner" or someone who taps into the vast pool of people who are willing and able to share their experience and wisdom with others?

1. Do you believe that a strong person is one who is always right?

2. Do you believe that asking advice is a sign of weakness?

3. Do you have anyone from whom you ask advice?

4. Is there anyone who knows what you are seeking in life and encourages you in your efforts?

5. Do you value other people's input or feel that it slows you down or confuses you?

6. Do you feel that you don't need anyone to tell you, "You can do it"?

7. Did you ever abandon a project that seemed to have too many obstacles, only to see someone else accomplish it?

8. Is your first response to advice that of rejection? Why?

9. Do you view criticism as a personal attack?

10. Do you feel that sharing a failure with someone exposes your weakness?

What distinguishes the type of person who seeks others' input is his healthy core of self-esteem. As we explained in Chapter 1, how we integrate other people's opinions of us depends on how we, in our deepest subconscious, define ourselves. That definition is the "seed" planted in childhood and nurtured throughout our lives by the input of the world around us.

If the seed is that of a scruffy weed, no matter how much praise we pour on it, only a scruffy weed can grow. Therefore, if we tell a person who thinks poorly of herself, "You did a wonderful job," she will not suddenly start feeling wonderful. Instead, she will feel that she just fooled someone into thinking she's wonderful, and that the fallacy is sure to be revealed. On the other hand, if someone's self-esteem is an acorn, an oak will grow, even if occasional criticism is poured upon it. Such a person can hear the words "I think you made a mistake," and still feel the strength and dignity of the oak.

We see from this that our greatest support must come from within. If we have that, we can bear the weight of other people's ideas, suggestions, comments and critiques. If we are weak within, we can't risk it. We fear it will break us, and so we build a high fence around ourselves and keep others out of our decision-making and growth process. And we lose. We lock out exactly those people who could push us past our limitations: the people who believe in us more than we may believe in ourselves.

It would seem, therefore, that the only people who are capable of benefiting from others' input are people who least need it; those with rock-solid self-esteem. All of the rest of us would be stuck in our fearful little cocoons. Yet that is not the case, because if we become aware that our deeply rooted self-image is a negative one, we can use the positive input of others to help us replant. That awareness is not so difficult to attain; we need only listen to our inner response when someone points out our strengths or successes. Do we negate it, thinking, *If only he knew the truth,* or confirm it, thinking, *I really do have something to offer!*

If we test the ground of our inner world and find it weak and wobbly, we may need to reach out to someone who can help us reinforce it. A rav, a coach or a therapist — some third party who we can assume is not just "being nice" — often can be the one to fill this role. That objective person can help us break out of our negative view of ourselves, helping us to focus on our capabilities and achievements, and step-by-step, integrate them into the structure of our inner world. As we feel more capable, we will take more action, accomplish more and acquire more reinforcement.

Anyone — whether blessed with a positive, can-do attitude and a track record of successes, or challenged with self-doubt and self-imposed limitations — can take life to the next level by bringing a few, well-chosen others on board.

The Lock

Why does it seem so dangerous to some people to seek the counsel of others? A useful way to understand this phenomenon is through the classic work of Abraham Maslow, a groundbreaking psychologist who, in 1943, authored a paper called "A Theory of Human Motivation." Maslow established a structure that remains in use today, called the "hierarchy of needs." It's a pyramid, at the bottom of which are the most basic human needs. At the pinnacle are our more advanced and elevated pursuits. Maslow's theory states that we proceed up the pyramid only when the needs at the previous level are met.

What are the levels of the pyramid?

- The bottom, most basic level is survival; air, water, food and all the physical functions that guarantee our survival as individuals and as a species.

We can see the effects of deprivation in this area in people who have had to fight for their lives. For instance, many Holocaust survivors who endured starvation spent their lives worrying incessantly about having enough food. Some would insist that their children finish every last morsel on a plate, or would stock the pantry and refrigerator to the bursting point or save even the smallest leftover portion. Even if they became quite wealthy, they never felt secure that there would be food for them tomorrow.

When people are worried about staying alive, that concern rises above all others.

- The next level is safety. That includes physical security, employment, adequate resources, moral safeguards, family, health and property. Obviously, our physical safety demands our complete focus. We see the effect of physical insecurity in children of abusive parents. Friendship, school achievement, religion or any other life-enhancing pursuit fall by the wayside as the child simply tries to avoid pain and humiliation. It's a full-time job.

- Above that are the emotional needs of love and belonging. At this level we need family, not just to keep us safe, but to nurture us. We need friends, connections and affection.

When our emotional needs are unmet by the people with whom we share our lives, we fail to develop a positive sense of ourselves and our value . As we have already seen throughout this book, this is the muddy rut in which many people's lives become mired. Such a person will not strive for anything bigger than some affirmation that he's O.K.

On the other hand, when our emotional needs are met, we can absorb the praise and positive input others offer. We have a place in our hearts that believes them and grows from their encouragement.

- The next level is esteem. Here is where we begin to strive for achievement, where we seek a feeling of competence, confidence and respectability. When we are able to operate at this level, we start identifying our nature, our gifts and assets. We begin developing our potential.

- The top of the pyramid, the highest striving of a human being, is self-actualization. This is where he or she develops a belief system, creativity, spirituality and an inner sense of morality. Someone at this level is seeking a higher purpose and meaning in life. He wants to help the world and achieve something with lasting value.

From this model, we see that a sense of safety and validation is the key to setting us free to climb to higher goals. On the other hand, when the basics are missing, we become stuck at that level and unable to strive for higher attainments.

"Now are you proud of me?" might be a reasonable question for a first grader to ask his father, but it is a tragic statement when it comes from a 40-year-old, even if the words are never said outright. It is tragic because that person is still building the foundation of life at a time when he or she should be putting the finishing touches on the upper stories.

Without that foundational sense of security, we simply cannot afford to let others in.

How and Why

The life experiences that lock us into a "my way or the highway" mentality, or keep us shrinking away from people who might help us, are really part and parcel of many people's upbringing. There's the 2-year-old getting scolded for pouring water on the kitchen floor when in his mind, he is cleaning it for Shabbos. There's the first grader being told to stay in his seat when he desperately needs the bathroom. There's the fifth grader being told he "should have listened" when he asks the teacher to repeat something he didn't understand. There's the teenager being told that he must remain in Yeshivah A when he would be so much more comfortable and successful in Yeshivah B.

So often, the amount of attention and inquiry an adult would have to invest to really understand what a child wants and thinks is just not forthcoming. Sometimes there seems to be too little time for it, and sometimes the adults are just so sure that it doesn't matter. Lacking validation of their thoughts and needs, many children grow up unable to validate others' ideas. Often, once they arrive at the point where they are doing the talking, they don't stop to listen. They never learned the skill of constructive communication, and they never learned to trust others to give a fair hearing to their ideas. The best strategy seems to be to cut others out of the picture.

A child growing up in these circumstances may also flee from others' input because he so seldom gains from it. Imagine if every time the doorbell rang, it was a neighbor coming to complain. We would probably stop answering the door. On the other hand, if the doorbell usually brought the UPS man bearing gifts from our many admirers, we would spring up happily to answer. In the same way, a child who receives mostly motivational input — recognition of his talents, praise for his efforts, encouragement to go further — is bound to welcome it, whereas the child who mostly hears complaints eventually stops responding to the doorbell.

People who have an unusual way of looking at life may also find it difficult to run their ideas by others. They are so accustomed to being ridiculed and knocked down that their default mode becomes, *No one understands me anyway.*

Finally, as mentioned earlier, asking for and following advice seems, to many people, to be a mark of weakness. They may feel that they lose "ownership" of an achievement if they included others in the process. They fail to realize that their seeking and heeding advice is yet another achievement to their credit; they were wise enough to take that course and humble enough to accept guidance.

The Key

Moishy began playing a complicated classical piece on his violin. Only a few notes into it, his teacher stopped him.

"You're running the notes together," he said. "Each one has to finish. Don't be in such a hurry."

Moishy resumed. A moment later, his teacher interrupted again, "No, no, that's a D-flat. You have to look at the music."

Moishy resumed. The 45-minute lesson continued this way, with dozens of corrections, stops and starts. At the end, the teacher smiled warmly at his student. "You're doing great," he said. "You're really getting there."

After the teacher left, Moishy's sister commented, "Boy, you really don't do anything right, huh? He has to stop you every two minutes."

"That's what's so great about him," Moishy answered. "He hears every little detail. And he doesn't bug every kid he teaches about these things either. He told me that he only works so hard with me because I have the talent to really get somewhere. Even I can see how much better I'm playing now."

No violinist ever achieved mastery without a teacher to demand precision. No athlete ever excelled without a coach to push him to his outermost limit. No *talmid chacham* ever reached greatness without a *rebbi* to listen to his *chiddushim*. We all need people who care enough about us to hear our ideas, to encourage us when we're losing confidence and correct our course with respect and love. We need those who know the difference between knocking others down and helping them to strive to higher levels, like the violin teacher who managed to impart, through his constant instruction, his faith in his student's ability.

If our parents fill this role in our lives, we can consider ourselves mightily blessed. But even then, we often need to seek out new supporters as we take on new roles in our lives. If your father is a dentist, he might have difficulty mentoring you in your real estate career. If your parents had two children, they might have no clue in guiding you in handling the challenges of eight offspring. Therefore, we have to look around us and find the people who are equipped to help us steer the course laid out by our own personal situations. If we access those who can help us rather than doing it all ourselves, we can become more than ourselves.

The key is *not,* however, to hand over control of our lives to others. The vitally important first step in seeking mentors is to recognize that it is up to *us* to *choose* who we wish to invite into our lives. No one has the right to stake a claim on our personal sovereignty. We need to find the people who will help us to reach *our* goals and strive toward *our* dreams. How do we choose such a person? Here are some criteria:

- Someone who will give you time.

- Someone who is willing to share his or her experiences with you.

- Someone who has faced challenges similar to yours and knows what it means to fail and rise up from failure.

- Someone who has humility, who will feel that he is gaining from the relationship with you just as you are gaining from him.

- Someone with judgment and wisdom that you respect, whose corrections you would accept.

- Someone who knows how to encourage you in a way that penetrates and feels real.

- Someone with whom you are comfortable admitting failures, mistakes and doubts.

- Someone who doesn't feel he "owns" your success or owns *you* because of the input he has had in your progress.

A good mentor is a person who sees your value; he doesn't look at you as a broken vessel in need of mending, but rather, he sees you as complete. He helps you to formulate your vision for yourself and he believes in your ability to actualize that vision, using the very tools and gifts you already have.

"Sarala, you're such a great girl," Sara's teacher told her during a heart-to-heart conference. "If you would only put in a little more effort, I know you'd rise to the top of the class."

Sara had heard this "encouragement" from more teachers than she could count in her 11 years of schooling. No one believed she was really trying because she was clearly much smarter than her grades showed. All she could think about was, "How many more days until I graduate." She was down to about 520. Seminary, which would add another 300 or so days to the "sentence," was out of the question.

Then she spoke to Mrs. Kramer, her Navi teacher. Mrs. Kramer had no advice about getting to the top of the class. In fact, she confided in Sara that she, too, had been a fairly lackluster student. Mrs. Kramer wanted to talk about Sara's plans for herself: Summer job, career training, marriage.

She helped Sara see that, even in the midst of her "boring" classes, she could cull lessons needed for the future she planned. "Even if all you learn how to do is push yourself to focus when you're bored, you'll be learning something you'll be able to use probably every day of your life," Mrs. Kramer told her. They created a game in which Sara kept track of how long she stayed tuned in to her Jewish history class: the one she found most deadly dull. With this and many other Sara-friendly strategies, Mrs. Kramer kept Sara going for those last 520 days, and was instrumental in finding her just the right seminary, where she finally felt engaged and inspired.

In that one year, Sara gained what had been missing for the previous 12 years. Finally, Torah and mitzvos found a place in her heart, rather than rattling around noisily in her brain. "Baruch Hashem for Mrs. Kramer," she said many times throughout her life.

As unproductive as it may be to accept advice from people who do not recognize and value our goals for ourselves, it can be equally dangerous to limit ourselves to people who tell us what we want to hear. A crew of "yes-men" accomplishes nothing.

We reach our best selves by building connections with people who have achieved what we wish to achieve. Whether we are looking for spiritual, emotional, financial, professional or any other kind of growth, we must find people who have reached the level we hope some day to reach. They must not be so far above us that they can't relate to our point of view, nor so close to us that we do not trust their perspective above our own. Finally, we must always remember that in the last analysis, the buck stops with us. We make the final choice as to what advice to follow, and we must claim responsibility for the results of our choices.

Each of us can have a "board of advisers" filling in our gaps of knowledge, offering the perspective forged by experience and telling us the words we all need to hear every single day, whether we're 4 or 44 or 84: "You can do it!" Build your dream team and jump-start your life.

Unlock Your Support

Inspiration

1. Find your dreams and passions. Think of your goals as real and attainable, not "pie in the sky." Imagine living the life you will have when your goal is achieved.

2. Trust yourself to choose someone to guide you toward this goal. Use the guide above to make sure the person can

serve as a real asset, and make sure to clarify the extent to which you want this person's involvement.

Logic

3. Know that ultimately, you are the one making decisions. Your coach is offering an opinion that you may incorporate into your life as you see fit.

4. Understand that by seeking advice, you are showing strength.

5. Choose two or three people to guide you so that you will have a wider range of perspectives.

6. Ask them for balanced feedback. You want to know what you can improve, but you also want and need to know what you are doing well.

7. Do not feel obligated to take advice from everyone who chooses to give it to you. The more public your position is, the more people will feel impelled to offer you suggestions. You could write down unsolicited advice for later consideration if you wish, but you will not be able to function if you take every person's criticism or suggestion to heart.

Judy and Sharon opened a flower shop. They were new to the business, but they took a small storefront on a major shopping avenue and the customers began to stream in.

"No tulips?" said one customer. "You really have to have them this time of year. Otherwise everyone will just get their flowers at the supermarket where they have tulips."

"Two dollars per rose?" another customer observed. "Let me give you a little advice. If you sell them for a dollar and a quarter, people will be running in here for the roses. Then you'll get their business and they'll come for the other flowers too."

And so it went, day after day. The local experts offered their advice, and Judy and Sharon tried mightily to satisfy them. After all, they were new at this.

The roses sold like wildfire at cost price, but the customers didn't buy anything else. The tulips, which were pricey, could only be purchased in large quantities. A few sold and the rest wilted. Judy and Sharon set up a "suggestion box" and took a business course.

Action

8. Tell yourself that you have the help you need to reach your goal. You're equipped to succeed. Most people feel more confident doing something difficult when someone else comes along for support. Now you have support. Say it out loud: "I can make it!"

9. Speak to the person or people on your team once a week and get plenty of feedback. Concentrate on getting positive feedback to keep yourself motivated.

10. Be a mentor/supporter for someone else. Be the one to tell them: "I believe in you," "Your goals are attainable," "I had that problem and here's how I fixed it," "Be patient and success will come," "I learn so much from you!"

Straight from the Source

The Torah is filled with mentor-student relationships that have enabled greatness and wisdom to pass down through the generations until today.

Yehoshua never left the side of his mentor, Moshe Rabbeinu, and as a result of his willingness to absorb all that Moshe could teach him, he became Moshe's successor in leading *Klal Yisrael* through the crucial juncture of entering and conquering Eretz Yisrael. How could any man have had the confidence to step into the place of an incomparable leader, someone who had the closest possible connection to Hashem and the passionate love and loyalty of the nation? He needed encouragement, and Hashem provided it.

First, when Hashem directed Moshe to appoint Yehoshua as his successor (*Bamidbar* 27:18-23), Moshe was told to ordain him in front of the Kohen and the nation, and give him a measure of authority even while Moshe was alive. In this way, the nation would have no doubt that Yehoshua was indeed the legitimate successor. Then, in *Devarim* (31:24), Hashem encourages Yehoshua further, telling him to be "strong and courageous" and promising him that he would have Hashem by his side as he led the nation into the Land of Israel. Hashem repeats his words of encouragement again in the beginning (*Perek* 1) of *Sefer Yehoshua*, after Moshe has passed away and the new leader was in charge. Over and over, Hashem tells Yehoshua, *"Chazak ve'ematz,"* be strong and courageous.

The Take-Away

The reason Yehoshua was chosen as the rightful heir to Moshe was because he attached himself to Moshe as a master and teacher. He attached himself to the greatest man of his time, the greatest prophet of all times, and sought to learn from him. Obviously, Yehoshua had no illusions that he could or should reach his potential all on his own. We find that anyone who reaches great heights in any area of life can name the people who got him there.

We also see from this sequence of events that Hashem encourages Yehoshua not just once, but many times. Parents often say regarding their children, "I already told him I was proud of him. He knows." But these *pesukim* show us that even when the encouragement comes from none other than Hashem, it bears repeating.

The Gemara (*Bava Metzia* 85a) tells of the meeting between Rebbi and R' Yose, the son of R' Elazar, who was the son of R' Shimon bar Yochai. R' Elazar had died young and left his son, R' Yose, to fend for himself.

When Rebbi encountered R' Yose, he was living a disreputable life on the streets. However, Rebbi recognized his potential. He took in the lost young man, ordained him as a rabbi, and sent him to learn with R' Shimon ben Issi ben Lakonia, his uncle. R' Yose often complained to his uncle that he preferred his old life, but his uncle would reply that a person of R' Yose's stature could not sincerely prefer his old life.

Eventually, R' Yose become a great scholar and went to learn in Rebbi's academy. Rebbi recognized R' Yose's voice, and proclaimed, "'The fruit of the righteous is a tree of life, and he that wins souls is wise.' 'The fruit of the righteous' refers to R' Yose, the son of R' Elazar, the son of R' Shimon ben Yochai and 'he that wins souls' refers to R' Shimon ben Issi ben Lakonia."

The Take-Away

From R' Yose's viewpoint, we see from this story that illustrious lineage is not enough to guarantee greatness. Everyone, even the grandson of R' Shimon bar Yochai, needs people who believe in him and work to build him up. From the viewpoint of the mentor, we learn that we must sincerely impart our vision of the other person's potential and begin treating him like the important person we expect him to become. Rebbi saw R' Yose as he could be, not as he was. He overlooked the outward appearance and zeroed in on the greatness at his core, having him ordained as a rabbi, even before he had earned it.

R' Shimon ben Issi ben Lakonia ran up against a common obstacle in dealing with alienated youth. "My life was much more fun before you got hold of me." Because the uncle persisted in keeping his lofty vision of R' Yose alive, and because he believed sincerely in his vision, he was eventually able to transmit that vision to R' Yose. Had he given up on R' Yose at the moment R' Yose gave up on himself, thinking, *Once a street kid, always a street kid,* the ending would have been much different.

In *Parashas Vayeishev* (*Bereishis* 37:11), after discussing Yosef's dreams of greatness and dominance over his brothers, the Torah states, "So his brothers were jealous but his father kept the matter in mind." Rashi expounds, "Yaakov was waiting and yearning for it to happen." Many commentators explain that Yosef's awareness of his father's belief in him gave him the inner strength to hold on to his dreams.

The Take-Away

Parents' belief in their children is an exceptionally positive force. Yaakov's confidence in his son's potential greatness fueled Yosef's ascent to power in Egypt. At the moment when the temptation to err is at its greatest, when Yosef was approached by the wife of Potiphar, the image of Yaakov's face enabled his son to stay strong.

Chapter 8

Release Consistency

Slow and Steady vs. Quick and Easy

"I HAVE THE PRESS RELEASE YOU WANTED FOR YOUR *magazine,*" *the public relations director told the editor.*

"Oh, great. But I need it today because the issue is closing," the editor replied. "I'll come across town and pick it up from you."

"No need," said the PR director. "I'll fax it."

"Fax it?" the editor replied, just a bit astounded. "Well, sure, do that!"

It was 1990, and the editor considered the recently purchased fax machine in her office to be nothing but an expensive toy for the tech-obsessed publisher. But now, she had a revelation. That machine could accomplish in three minutes what would have taken her an hour.

Today, with the prevalence of email, even that three-minute wait for the fax would seem like an eternity. One universal trend that no one can deny is that life's pace is speeding up drastically. Each new piece of technology shrinks the gap between our brain and the input of the world outside us. We drum our fingers impatiently waiting 25 seconds for a song to download, when only a few years ago, gaining access to a song we liked would have required us to get in the car, drive to the store, find the right CD and stand in line to pay for it. Our idea of how long things should take is increasingly being updated.

That causes frustration. When something we want to achieve has not happened yet, our minds tend to leave out the "yet." If it isn't now, it just isn't. Period. Therefore, we think that we have failed before we've even given ourselves a chance to succeed. We want to be slim the week after we start the diet and rich three months after we open our business, and if we are not, we are ready to abandon ship.

Ron is a plumber. He worked for several years for a more experienced plumber, and then he set out on his own. He worked hard to connect with contractors in his town and was hired to install the plumbing in some new housing developments. He spends money advertising to let homeowners know about his services as well. To keep up with the workload, he has had to hire two assistants. After three years in the business, he is earning a decent amount of money, but not nearly as much as he had hoped. In addition, the hiring, scheduling, advertising, customer relations, bookkeeping and so forth are eating up his days and nights.

When his former employer offers to hire him back at a much higher salary, Ron is tempted. "I get the feeling I'm never going to make a killing in my own business. There are so many expenses and it's really such a hassle. Do you think I should take the job?" he asks.

Ron is in a quandary because he simply cannot wait as long as it will take for him to build a smooth-running, lucrative business. He is busy, exhausted and in over his head, and he just wants it to stop. In his frustration, he is ready to drop his dream of being self-employed and is willing to limit his income to the salary his former boss has offered. He doesn't take into account the fact that his business is really doing remarkably well for a three-year-old enterprise. Instead, he thinks, *I've been running on all cylinders for three years and it hasn't worked out yet. Maybe I'm on the wrong track. Maybe I'm not meant to run a business.*

But Ron is setting up a false choice for himself. His options are not limited to "eat, drink and sleep plumbing," or "give it all up and take a job." Rather, Ron can pace himself for the long run, so that he can stick with his plan long enough to reap the full rewards. That means learning to enjoy the process of building a business, rather than placing all the value on his target take-home pay.

Practically speaking, this means engaging energetically in the learning curve all ambitious goals entail. For example, if he is always late for appointments because he overbooks, he can use that difficulty to learn how to schedule himself more productively. If he finds that he is too busy with the bookkeeping and customer relations, he can use the problem to figure out exactly how much help he needs and how much revenue he must generate to make the personnel expense worthwhile. From each bump on the road, he can learn the lessons of running a successful business, so that as he expands, his skills are up to the challenge.

Another vital part of the process is establishing a balance in his life. If he insists on knocking himself out day after day to make success happen now, he is likely to burn out. His quality of life will end up on the wrong end of the seesaw, plummeting downward as his business shoots upward. Being in it for the long run means creating a sustainable lifestyle that includes all the necessities: time for family, for rest and recharging and for spiritual pursuits.

It's this appreciation of the process that we are rapidly losing in our age of instant everything. Yet most of life is a process. We spend many years raising our children before we see the adults they are to become. In our careers, we spend most of our years learning new skills and information, taking on new positions and meeting new challenges. In spiritual growth, our mission is to keep climbing the ladder, knowing fully that we can never reach the top. Slow, continuous growth is the natural way of living things. Instant is the realm of machines.

Learning to love the process removes the desperate impatience that often throws us off track. It's a transferable skill; if we master it in one area of our life, we can use it to enhance other areas as well. The opposite is also true; if we do not grasp this concept, the gap will close off many avenues of achievement.

Avi is a smart kid. He caught onto everything quickly in elementary school. He learned to read fluently, translate easily and remember what he learned. He got A's on his tests just by sitting and listening in class. His parents did not know what the other parents were talking about when they complained of long, difficult nights reviewing Chumash with their sons.

Now Avi is in a top-tier high school and the amount of material he learns each day is more than he can possibly absorb by osmosis. He feels like a failure as his grades slide and his reputation as a whiz kid fades into history.

"This yeshivah's not for me," he tells me. "Everyone thinks I'm so smart, but I'm really not. I can't keep up with the other guys."

Avi is at a crossroads. He can acknowledge that getting by without effort is not the normal state of affairs, and will not get him very far as life goes forward. If he can accept that, he can put in the time and effort needed to keep up with his peers and excel in his learning. He can stay in a top-tier yeshivah and reach the levels of achievement available in that environment.

Later in life, if he pursues a career, his habits of consistent effort will help him stay motivated as he deals with the difficulties and setbacks that inevitably arise. As a husband and father, he will have the patience to work through conflicts, understanding that he and everyone else are "works in progress."

On the other hand, he might choose to cling to his notion that if something doesn't come easily, "it's not for me." We can readily predict what that would mean, not only to his yeshivah career, but to all the situations we mentioned above. In career or business, he would be easily frustrated and inclined to keep quitting or changing course. In marriage, he would be more likely to consider divorce. As a parent, he would see the challenges of childrearing as proof that his kids are innately lacking positive qualities, rather than realizing that these qualities take time to develop. For example, he might call a child careless rather than taking the opportunity to teach the child how to be careful.

Ron and Avi are both suffering from self-doubts, losing their motivation and inspiration to be the best they can be, all because they live with the illusion that "successful" is an identity, like attractive or smart, rather than something we work toward and gain gradually. Do you share that illusion?

1. Do you seek instant success in matters like dieting, money, childrearing, learning?

2. Do you reject goals that seem to take too long to achieve? For instance, do you believe it's "not worth it" to pursue a career you would enjoy because the training takes too long?

3. Are you stuck on hold in areas of your life because the perfect option has not yet presented itself, for instance, buying a house, settling on a career path or finding a marriage partner?

4. Are you burned out, working too hard in an effort to reach success quickly?

5. Are you dissatisfied with your day-to-day life? Disappointed with your present situation?

6. Do you view people who "work their way up from the bottom" as fools?

7. Do you view people who are at the top of their fields as the norm?

8. Do you tend to switch tracks often, feeling that the thing you've been doing *just isn't for me?*

9. Do you see mistakes and setbacks as a sign that you are attempting something that can't be done?

10. When people give you advice, do you often respond, "I tried that and it didn't work"?

"Success happens where persistence and opportunity cross paths" is a motto I teach my clients. Yet more and more of us fail to stay on course long enough to meet up with the opportunities Hashem has laid out before us.

The Lock

Locked behind the "fast and easy" mind-set is a huge portion of our potential achievement in life.

• Instead of starting a career, a person remains unemployed, waiting for the $100,000 job to come his way.

• Instead of getting married, a person remains single, waiting for the person who is everything he or she desires. "Growing together" has no place in this scheme.

• Instead of pacing himself so that he can work toward his goal consistently, this person cannot take a break. He cannot go on vacation or spend time with his family, because that will slow down his progress toward making his first million.

• Instead of working for his own satisfaction, striving for goals of his own choosing, he lets the rest of the world define success and runs himself ragged trying to prove himself to the world at large.

- Instead of engaging in the joys and challenges life presents him today, he is obsessed with "making it."

We might understand logically that hard work pays off and that nothing worthwhile comes easy. These are the two clichés drummed into us from our earliest years. On the other side, however, speaking far louder and in much more alluring tones, are the millions of daily messages to the contrary: "Lose 30 pounds in 30 days." "Your child will go from F's to A's in just five weeks." "Make $5,000 a month in your spare time, right from your kitchen table." "Get your 12 daily servings of fruits and vegetables with just this one pill." And so on.

Because our minds absorb these messages and our hearts certainly hope they are true, we get trapped in a zone of frustration. We could call it the "80 percent zone," because it occupies about 80 percent of all life's experiences. The first 10 percent is the inspiration. We start something new and we're filled with excitement. Then come the complications and hard work. If we struggle faithfully and consistently through that long 80 percent, difficult stretch, we arrive at the final 10 percent, a level of pure joy and satisfaction that makes our original excitement look pale.

This is the way with everything in the world that is worth acquiring. The young couple standing under the *chuppah* certainly feels that they are at the height of happiness, and they should feel that way. That's the fuel they need to launch them into the vast, unknown territory of marriage and family life. Once they get down to "real life," the complications are too many and varied to enumerate. They might easily begin to think that the rush of joy under the *chuppah* was an illusion. However, if they work their way through the complications, they acquire something so much fuller and stronger than what they had at the beginning. That's the final 10 percent of the story.

This pattern of inspiration, struggle and then renewed, infinitely stronger inspiration is especially true in our spiritual life. As little children, we are filled with trust in Hashem, but then life gets complicated. Prayers may seem to go unanswered, mitzvos may seem to lack meaning, people may disappoint us and we may find ourselves wondering where that sense of security and trust has gone. If we meet these struggles head-on and grapple with the questions and emotions they produce, we find our answers. Then we reach a new level of connection: an unshakeable faith that embraces all our life's experiences.

In all of these matters, we lock ourselves out of the greatest reward, the final 10 percent, if we lose heart as we deal with the 80 percent. Not only do we fail to stay in the game long enough to win, but we also fail to gain all the knowledge and experience the 80 percent is there to provide for us. The 80 percent is not an obstacle between the first inspiration and the final victory: a test to be endured but better left out altogether. Rather, this is the very process necessary to prepare us for and to carry us to victory. It's how we learn how to be what we want to become.

The Why and How

Imagine an advertisement that instead says, "Here's your chance to work long and hard!" Even if the job offered a million-dollar salary, there would probably be very few applicants. We all want a life of ease, and even if we don't buy into the "miracle cure" advertisements, an easy life actually does appear to be possible. We all know of people who seem to have effortlessly slipped or accidentally tripped into success: the man who bought one house for investment and a year later owns two office buildings and an apartment complex; the girl all the teachers love; the *talmid* who soaks up everything like a sponge; the man whose father got him a plush job in his friend's law firm; the woman whose parents are supporting her and her *kollel* husband in high style in the heart of Jerusalem. Because communication today is so far reaching and fast, we know about many more people who have struck it big. They loom big in our minds as well, creating a sense that "everyone" is making millions, when in fact, these cases constitute just a small percentage of the population.

With those images in the back of our minds, the idea of slogging through years of hard work seems to be for fools. If we do not experience instant success, we quickly come to fear that we are one of those fools.

Feeding this fear is the difficulty we have in believing what we cannot yet see.

"It says make a left on Route 27, in six miles," Toby told her husband as they sped along the road. The GPS was broken, and so Toby had gotten directions online and was standing in for the ever-reliable GPS lady who usually issued directions. They were on the last leg of a six-hour trip, tired and eager to arrive.

"I think we've gone more than six miles already," the husband said. "Look, the last time we traveled on this road, we didn't pass this mall. I think we overshot our exit."

"I don't know. Maybe we just didn't notice the mall last time. Go a few more miles and let's see if we come to the exit," Toby advised.

They went a few more miles and, unable to find the exit, got off the highway and turned back in the other direction. What they didn't realize was that the exit they were seeking was just a half-mile ahead.

If Toby and her husband had known that their exit was a half-mile up the road, of course they would have kept traveling in that direction. If we knew that Hashem had our dreamed-of success waiting six months or even six years up the road, of course we, too, would stay on the road. Our problem is that we don't see it, and therefore, may not quite believe it. Ultimately, consistency is the concept of *hishtadlus:* the effort we must exert in order to meet up with the success Hashem has in store for us.

The Key

In our last chapter, we looked at the value of mentors and advisers in our lives. A very important part of their value is the vision such people can supply. In the above scenario of the couple lost on the road, the mentor would be the one who has a map. He's not just equipped with the step-by-step directions; he sees the whole lay of the land. Therefore, he can tell them that the exit is coming up. Having people in our lives who have a clear vision of where we are heading and what it takes to get there can help us tap into the determination we need to stay the course.

As important as it is to know and believe that "we'll get there," it's equally important to realize that all our seemingly unproductive effort — all the miles we travel before we see the exit — is *getting* us there. No effort is wasted, even if success seems to elude us. As one person puts it, "I never lose; I either win or I learn." It's the learning that makes the ultimate success a strong and lasting one.

This is the lesson of Chinese bamboo. When a farmer first plants this species of bamboo, he goes through an entire growing season seeing nothing at all sprout. Nevertheless, he must keep watering, fertilizing and weeding. When the next growing season arrives, he once again sees nothing for his efforts. A third season passes as well, and the bamboo appears to be nothing but a failed crop. Nevertheless, the farmer keeps tending it. Finally, in the fourth season, the bamboo sprouts and grows in a few months to a height of 10 feet. The elaborate, mighty root structure it developed during the previous three years gives it the base it needs to shoot up faster than any other species. While nothing seemed to be happening, plenty was happening: the plant was forming its root structure, laying the groundwork for fantastic growth. Because the farmer respected the process, he profited from his labors.

Another key to developing consistency is to acknowledge it is an amazingly powerful force. The fable of the tortoise and the hare illustrates our cultural bias against "slow and steady" and tries to upend that bias. The hare is quick and agile, smart and overconfident. The tortoise, on the other hand, is quiet, plodding and humble. To our eyes, the hare makes a much more attractive hero. That's what we want to be: the smart guy who leaves his competition in the dust and arrives at the finish line having barely broken a sweat. We don't see the tortoise as a high-achieving "alpha-male." Yet in the fable and in life, he is. The strength required to keep on going day after day, sticking with our plans and working through our problems, keeping a balance of work, family and spirituality in our lives, displays enormous personal power. Best of all, it's what works.

A study by the psychologist Eric Anderson illustrates that consistency is not only the key to achievement, but it is also the key to world-class greatness. By tracking the habits of people who are masters in their fields of endeavor, including famous athletes, musicians and chess champions, he finds that those who make it to the top do so by sheer force of repetition. His study shows that greatness doesn't come from unusual talent or good luck; it comes from 20 hours per week of "deliberate practice" – real effort and challenge – over a period of 10 years, or a total of 10,000 hours of practice. He posits that we can master anything to which we apply ourselves for that amount of time.

If you still doubt the power of consistency, here is a graphic illustration of what "stick-to-itiveness" will accomplish. It's called "A Penny Doubled," and it illustrates what happens when we choose consistent effort over immediate gain. Imagine that someone asks you, "Would you rather I give you a million dollars right now, or a penny today, which I will double every day for 31 days?" Most people would quickly surmise that a penny today cannot possibly morph into anything valuable over the course of 31 days. But the graph below — and simple mathematics — tells a different story.

Day 1:	$0.01
Day 2:	$0.02
Day 3:	$0.04
Day 4:	$0.08
Day 5:	$0.16
Day 6:	$0.32
Day 7:	$0.64
Day 8:	$1.28
Day 9:	$2.56
Day 10:	$5.12
Day 11:	$10.24
Day 12:	$20.48
Day 13:	$40.96
Day 14:	$81.92
Day 15:	$163.84
Day 16:	$327.68
Day 17:	$655.36
Day 18:	$1,310.72
Day 19:	$2,621.44
Day 20:	$5,242.88
Day 21 :	$10,485.76
Day 22:	$20,971.52
Day 23:	$41,943.04
Day 24:	$83,886.08
Day 25:	$167,772.16
Day 26:	$335,544.32
Day 27:	$671,088.64
Day 28:	$1,342,177.28
Day 29:	$2,684,354.56
Day 30:	$5,368,709.12
Day 31:	$10,737,418.24

If you look at this graph not just from the mathematical perspective, but from the psychological, you can quickly understand the strength it takes to stay on course. The person who chooses the penny doubled, on day 15, halfway through the month, doesn't have $200.00. Even on day 26, he has still received only slightly more than one-third of the million dollars he could have had on day one — and there are only five days to go! He should be kicking himself for turning down the million. However, he keeps on doing the same thing every day, day after day, and when the 31 days are over, the wisdom of his choice is brilliantly clear.

In life, as in the chart, the effort we invest every day doesn't just add one more shot of effort. It doubles yesterday's achievements: the lessons we learned as we tried, failed, adjusted and tried again. This is the journey of life. If we face it like small children who sit restlessly, wondering, "Are we there yet?" then we miss the point, because we get the most out of the destination only if we absorb the lessons that are there for us along the road. Every successful person will say that he got where he is only by engaging in the long process of trial and error, growth and progress. Even though such people have found themselves to be on the wrong track, they have profited from the journey, for perhaps it was on that "wrong track" that they met the person who connected them with the winning idea, or inspired them to try something different. No effort is wasted if we embrace the process with energy and optimism. With a change in perspective, we can not only inspire ourselves with great goals and visions for our lives; we can feel the joy each and every day of doing what we must to get there. Here are some ways to do that:

Unlock Consistency

Inspiration

1. Ease up on your mental time frame. Realize that your goals might take you 10 years rather than 10 weeks, and feel comfortable with that.

2. Feel content with your life today, including a balance of family, spiritual pursuits, social involvement and work.

3. Allow yourself to adopt a one-step-at-a-time approach to your goals. Feel comfortable saying to yourself, *First I'll do this, and then I'll do the next thing,* without fear that if you leave something for "next" it will never get done or that you cannot succeed unless everything happens at once. For instance, a student who has a goal of improving her grades might need to choose one or two subjects on which she will focus, deciding that once she has gotten a better grasp of those subjects, she will take on another. If she feels defeated because she is still seeing some C's on her report card, she will give up. To ultimately succeed, she must tell herself, *I'm getting there, but I can't expect to do everything at once.*

This step helps to develop a mind-set that appreciates the value of the process, rather than focusing on immediate results. It also includes admitting room for failure in our lives, seeing it, too, as a valuable part of the process of achieving success.

Logic

4. Understand that the mirage of the instant result is for the masses and not for intelligent, experienced people. It is "fool's gold" that traps people who suspend their critical thinking in pursuit of an easy path.

5. Consider the emotional and spiritual price of life in the fast lane. Even if you do succeed in making your first million in two months, you have set yourself on a road that has no room for family, spiritual growth or true friendship.

6. Assess your progress toward your goals only at specific times you have set in advance. So much damage comes from taking an accounting too soon, as we demonstrated

in the "penny doubled" chart. While you may indeed discover that you are on the wrong track — perhaps your business idea is not a winning one, or you're not cut out for a particular career you've chosen, or the new diet you're trying doesn't actually work — you have to ensure that you give yourself enough time to succeed. Set up a time when you will evaluate your situation and until that time, don't look back, don't look down, just keep moving forward.

Action

7. Get started on a five-year plan. Decide on a goal or goals you would like to reach in the long term, and begin working toward your goals today.

8. Use the resources you already have to accomplish what you can now accomplish, even if it doesn't measure up to what you hope to achieve in the future. For example, if you are a young mother who envisions a household in which all the children will pitch in with the chores, start with the children you have now, at the ages they are now, helping them now to do whatever they are capable of doing. If you are a boy who dreams of being a great learner some day, start now with the material you are learning now, and put in as much extra effort as you can realistically put in now. Even if your goal is simply, "I want to be rich," start now with the budget you have now to dress for success and carry yourself with confidence.

9. Keep learning. Take courses that can help you advance your plan, and meet people who have traveled the road you are traveling.

10. Let Hashem set the clock. Stay active and in forward motion knowing that when the time is right, and only then, Hashem will show you the opportunity that is there

for each of us. By doing this, you will keep anxiety and frustration at bay, maintain your energy and live each day knowing that even if you haven't gotten there yet, you're getting there.

Achievement and consistency go hand-in-hand, as the Torah illustrates.

The Gemara (*Taanis* 4a) compares a young Torah scholar to seeds under a hard clod of earth. "Once he has sprouted, he soon shoots forth."

The Take-Away

When a seed is buried underground, it seems as if there is nothing happening. Likewise, when a boy begins learning Torah, he may have little to show for his effort. But just as the seed's shoot is developing underground the whole time, so the boy's grasp of Torah is quietly developing in his mind. Finally, it sprouts forth and from there, it begins to blossom and grow. Thus, just as the gardener keeps watering and nourishing the seed every day, even though all he sees is hard earth, the teacher must consistently nurture the student. In both cases, the consistent effort enables the "first sprout" to break through.

The Gemara (*Chullin* 105a) records that R' Shmuel said, "As vinegar is compared to wine, I am compared to my father, for my father used to inspect his property twice a day, but I do so only once a day." R' Shmuel declared, "He who inspects his property daily will find an *istira* (half a *zuz*)."

R' Assi used to inspect his property daily. He exclaimed, "Where are all those *istiras* of R' Shmuel?" One day he saw that a pipe had burst on his land. He took off his coat, rolled it up and stuffed it into a hole. He exclaimed, "Now I have found all those *istiras* of R' Shmuel."

The Take-Away

R' Assi prevented great damage to his property by being there to see that a repair was necessary. Of course, had he not been in the habit of coming every day to inspect, he would not likely have been there on the day when the pipe burst. Doing the right thing over and over again, regularly, every time, may not lead to quick, fabulous achievement, but it is the guaranteed route to lasting success. As one person expressed it, "99 percent of success is being there."

In *Sefer Darkei Noam*, Rav Avrahom Pam, *zt'l*, in the name of the Chofetz Chaim, discusses the census taken in *Parashas Pinchas* (*Bamidbar* 24:41-43). There we learn that the tribe of Binyamin had 45,600 and Dan had 64,400. Dan was the second largest tribe after Yehudah, which had 76,500. What made Dan's population noteworthy was that it started with the sole male offspring of Dan, son of Yaakov. Over time, that one child who was profoundly hearing-impaired became the founder of one of the most populous tribes.

The Take-Away

What turned Dan from a lone child into a great tribe? Only time and consistency. Each generation did its part, marrying, raising children in the ways of their fathers, marrying off their children and so on. Many major businesses start in someone's basement. Many great organizations start with a couple of friends and a worthy cause. What turns these small beginnings into great accomplishments is consistent effort over time.

 The Gemara (*Yevamos* 62b) tells us that Rabbi Akiva had 24,000 students, all of whom died in a plague. Rather than give up in the face of such devastation, he began again, this time with five students. Those five students became the foundation of the Talmud we learn today, leaving a far-greater impact on the world than the entire 24,000 who had perished.

The Take-Away

For Rabbi Akiva, the goal was not the size of his academy. Rather, it was the dissemination of Torah. He went about this goal the same way, whether he was leading 24,000 students or five. With consistent effort over time, he continued along the path he had started and ultimately achieved everything he could have hoped to achieve. In the same way, someone who is consistent and methodical in his handling of a small business will see it grow into a large business. Someone who is consistent and methodical learning fifth-grade Mishnayos will find success learning advanced-level Gemara.

Chapter 9
Step Nine

Release
Forgiveness

Letting Go of Anger vs. Bitterness and Blame

WHEN ELIEZER WALKED INTO MY OFFICE, HE WAS THE picture of a "put-together guy": neat, well dressed, poised and confident. I could almost hear him saying to himself, "What am I doing here? Let me just get this over with and get out."

He had come at the urging of an older friend who felt that Eliezer, now 29, was blocking his own path to the chuppah. But as the young man promptly informed me, "I really don't belong here. I don't need therapy. Being an older single is not a mental illness."

As I spoke to Eliezer, what emerged was a deep, roiling anger that cast a shadow over the entire shidduch process. Seven years earlier, at 22, he had been open and excited about the prospect of getting married. The

second girl he met was, in his opinion, his true soul
mate. After several meetings, he was ready to become
engaged. Then, without any reasonable explanation,
the girl withdrew. "She feels it's not for her," the shad-
chan had told Eliezer's parents. No further informa-
tion was forthcoming.

Eliezer was not just hurt. He was furious. By nature a
reserved person, he had let his guard down for this girl;
he had allowed himself to become excited and to share
his excitement. Now he felt like a fool. He would never
let it happen again. Since then, every girl he met caught
his edge of distrust and cynicism, and not surprisingly,
none of them wanted to buy into a lifetime of it.

For Eliezer, the rejection he experienced was not just a disappointment, not just a loss; it was a humiliation, an affront
worthy of a tightly held grudge. The girl who had broken off
with him had long since married. Eliezer's anger didn't hurt her.
It didn't even touch her. Instead, it ruined his own life: his own
prospects for happiness. As one aphorism goes, "Being angry
is like taking poison and expecting it to kill the other person."

Not only is anger a poison, but it is a slow-acting, time-release
formula that does its damage for years or even decades after the
initial affront takes place. Because it is an emotion, it resides in
the limbic system of the brain, the seat of emotion. As we will
learn in the Appendix, the emotional side of the brain has no
sense of time. It can make us cry over a loss, smile over a happy
memory or bristle over an insult, even if those events occurred
30 years ago. Our logic does not factor into these emotional
reactions. Does the insult matter anymore? Who cares whether
it matters? We're still mad!

Nine-year-old Kaila asked her cousin Sara to come to her
house for Shabbos. Sara said "no," making an excuse about a
friend's Shabbos-afternoon birthday party. No one ever came

for Shabbos. No one even came just to play, or do homework, and Kaila knew why.

Her mother had a quick temper and no reservations about displaying it in front of whoever happened to be in the house. It frightened Kaila's friends. In fact, it frightened Kaila and her siblings as well. They always felt as if they were standing outdoors as a thunderstorm loomed on the horizon. Would it strike? Would they have to bear the harsh winds, crashing thunderclaps and torrents of rain? Or would it blow off in another direction and leave them to play happily in the sun? The children knew one thing: stay out of Mommy's way.

For the mother, however, the exhaustion and non-stop nature of her daily obligations was too much to handle. She knew that if she screamed, the kids would listen. She also knew that it hurt them, but what else could she do? There was simply no time and energy to come up with creative parenting strategies. Still, she wished there was more love and warmth in her home.

Because the vast majority of people want to give and receive love, anger is not usually a strategy of choice. More often, it is the default mode of people who have no idea how to otherwise deal with a situation. They are like people trapped in a closet. All they can do is kick and scream, hoping that somehow, that will help them get out. It gives them a feeling of power, of doing something vigorous and proactive while they are essentially accomplishing nothing to repair the underlying problem that put them in the closet in the first place. Sometimes what seems like a terrible angry streak is just a lack of problem-solving skills, and once those skills are acquired, the "intractable" trait goes away.

Kaila's cousin Sara arrives for a Shabbos visit. It is 2 o'clock on a Friday afternoon. Kaila and her siblings had just finished helping their mother clean the living room and set the table. "We have to be quiet until 2:30," Kaila told her cousin softly. "My mommy is taking a nap."

In a short while, Kaila's mother emerged from her room. "That was just what I needed," she said. "Want to come with me to pick out some Shabbos flowers?" she asked the girls. "You can help with the twins." The girls helped put the twin toddlers into their car seats and went off with Kaila's mother to do the last pre-Shabbos errand.

In the case of Kaila's mother, soliciting help from her children, delegating tasks and carving out some time for an occasional break in the action was all that was needed to turn her from an angry tyrant into a warm, involved mother. With that change, the family's children were able to confidently invite friends into their home. They were able to feel secure in their surroundings rather than living in fear of impending storms. The love and warmth the mother longed to share with her family materialized. It was a different life for everyone.

But what about Eliezer? What could he do to shed the anger that was standing in the way of his future? There was no strategy that could ensure that he would not be disappointed again. He could not change what happened, and therefore, the only way to move past it was to forgive the hurt. By expunging the bitterness to which he was still clinging, he could approach other marriage prospects with a fresh perspective. A cloud of anger would not longer cast its shadow on each and every member of the female gender.

The result of anger, whether it is in reaction to a specific situation or is a pervasive personality trait, is misery. Anger turns a workplace into a daily nightmare, a shul or community into a whirlpool of gossip and resentment and the family tree into generations of divisiveness and dysfunction. Physically, it wrecks the person who harbors it. It creates a constant state of stress, which spins out a seemingly endless list of human infirmities.

But we don't have to be angry: even if someone does us a wrong turn; even if life hands us a bad deal; even if the only strategy we ever learned was to strike back and make others suffer for their transgressions against us. Like the person stuck in the closet screaming and kicking, we can expend every bit of ourselves in anger, or we can calm down, let go of the desperation and use our minds, talents and abilities to find the way to freedom.

The Lock

If forgiving others is such a cure-all, we might wonder why people find it so difficult to do. Who wants to keep poison pumping into his system? Who wants high blood pressure, headaches and insomnia? Who wants loneliness? Obviously, if the symptoms of anger are so debilitating, many people must consider the cure to be even riskier and more painful.

Often, those perceived risks come from a misunderstanding of what forgiveness signifies. Do you harbor some of these false ideas? Ask yourself:

1. Do I believe that forgiving someone's misdeeds gives them permission to do it again?

2. Do I think the message of forgiveness is, "I don't mind what you did"?

3. Do I see anger as an expression of power?

4. Do I feel that by forgiving the other person, I am admitting that I was wrong?

5. Do I fear that if I do not blame others for the challenges in my life, I will have to blame and be angry at myself?

6. Do I believe that acknowledging others' positive traits or actions means that I endorse their negative traits or actions?

7. Do I believe that mistakes are inexcusable? Can I listen to another side of an argument?

8. Do I rehearse grievances in my mind, going back over instances that hurt me even if they happened many years ago?

9. Do I feel that I am making myself weak or vulnerable by communicating my painful feelings directly to someone who has hurt me?

10. Do I believe that everyone has some enemies? Do I have long-held grudges against some people?

Forgiveness is not surrender. Nor is it a confession of wrong-doing on our part or an absolution of the damage someone has done us. Even when we let go of our anger, we can still know that we are right. We can still seek restitution if it is due to us. We can certainly go to whatever lengths are necessary to ensure that we are not damaged again in the same way by the same person. What we *cannot* do if we want to stay healthy, functional, effective and optimistic is to allow our angry feelings to fester. With forgiveness, we learn whatever there is to be learned from a painful situation and we move forward, wiser and more experienced than before. Without forgiveness, we are stuck in place, reliving our pain and expending our energy dealing with the past.

How and Why

Since no one would logically choose to live in a bubble of pain and negativity, there must be forces at work in our lives that make anger appear to be a reasonable adaptation. Physiologically, when people are confronted with a threat, they undergo what biologists call the "fight, flight or freeze" response. We feel a massive surge of adrenalin that gives us the boost of strength we need to fight off the threat or, in the alternative, the speed we need to flee from it. This is a survival tool given to every species. A wasp under attack will fly away if it can, and if not, it will sting. A rabbit being stalked by a hawk will instantly choose flight and run with lightning speed to its hole. A person under physical attack may fight back or he, too, may run. Sometimes, our fear is so great that we freeze like the wide-eyed "deer in the headlights."

However, unless there is an actual physical threat or war situation, a civilized human being has very little call for a physical response. Nevertheless, even when we feel under attack emotionally, we experience the fight, flight or freeze response. We feel our hearts beating fast and our muscles clenching, but the surge of energy has no outlet. We are physically ready for battle but mentally holding onto our elevated, human selves.

In this view, it might seem that red-faced, heart-thumping anger is the only possible response to emotional attack. However, people who are troubled by anger are not trapped by the physical response over which they have no power. The pitfall lies in our free choice to view something as a threat. For instance, an irate parent tells his child's teacher, "You don't know how to teach! My son has gotten A's with every other teacher he's had." If the teacher equates parent criticism with an attack, the teacher's blood will begin to boil. If he views it instead as the outcry of a parent who is worried about his child, there is no attack. Therefore, there's no need for "fight, flight or freeze." Unless someone has the proverbial "gun to his head," a person actually has a choice of whether or not to register someone else's actions or words as aggression.

If we grow up in an atmosphere where grudges and slights are part of the landscape, our idea of a fight-or-flight-worthy threat might include such non-fatal assaults as being overlooked for a wedding invitation, being passed over for a job promotion, having our politics or religious views called into question, not getting our preference for the naming of a baby, losing money to someone, being rejected by a school, turned down for a *shidduch* and so forth.

While these "assaults" cannot physically harm us, they threaten us in a way that, for some people, presents the even-greater peril of undermining their self-image. The adrenalin starts pumping, self-control flies away and anger takes over. It may emerge in a volcanic outburst, a slow simmer or a quiet, glacial grudge.

Some people have never learned any other way. They never learned how to say to another person, "What you did hurt me," or to sanely argue their position or calmly and firmly demand their due. In their lives, especially as children, anger and hurt were the inevitable, natural consequence of something going wrong. If there was an unpaid bill, a neglected chore, a broken vase, a bad grade, a burned dinner, anger was sure to follow. We see this in families where every mishap arouses the cry, "Who did this?"

Another pull that anger exerts over people is that, at least temporarily, it feels good. Living in a culture that values control and reserve, we may not find the proper outlets for high emotion. Men, especially, tend to hold back the shrieks of joy or tears of sadness that women more comfortably express. Even women, however, are often held back because they don't want to draw attention to themselves or appear to be odd or "over the top" in any way. Because so many people keep their emotions on such a tight leash, they begin to feel dead and come to believe that they can no longer feel anything. When they blow up in anger, they suddenly feel alive. The pumping adrenalin and heightened emotions are as satisfying as a hard game of basketball or a frantic whirl of dancing at a wedding. Additionally, for men especially, a reputation for ferociousness can sometimes be seen as an indication of strength.

No matter how we explain anger, however, it makes a terrible traveling companion in life. It's hard to get anywhere when we carry along an ever-expandable knapsack of woes that we keep on stuffing with all the insults, injuries, conflicts and mistakes we encounter. We don't even realize how heavy this burden is until we finally find the courage to lay it down and leave it behind. Once we take that step, we find ourselves suddenly light and free, suddenly infused with optimism that we can get where we want to go. Forgiveness is the key.

The Key

Chana Goldstein had a dilemma. She and her husband were making a bar mitzvah for their oldest son, Yaakov. All the preparations were going along smoothly and the family was thrilled to be reaching this milestone in their lives, but Chana was in turmoil. Her mother, Baila, made all the family's simchahs difficult.

"I don't know what to do about my mother," she told me. "She has six sisters, and I'm close to them all. But my mother is the type that gets insulted and she stops talking to people. She hasn't spoken to my aunt Hadassah in about seven years, since right before my father passed away. Anyway, she told me that if I invite my aunt, she's not coming. Now how can I not invite my aunt? She'll be devastated. But how can I not have my mother there?"

As we discussed the situation, Mrs. Goldstein realized that the problem was really her mother's. The family would invite everyone they felt should be invited, and her mother would do what she felt she needed to do.

Ultimately, the grandmother and the aunt both showed up at the simchah hall. Hadassah cautiously approached Baila, and to her surprise, Baila didn't turn her back or walk away. Hadassah sensed that this was an opportunity to end the feud. She told her sister that she missed her and was sorry for saying something that had hurt Baila's feelings.

"My mother felt my aunt's sincerity, so she forgave her and they hugged and the whole family was on cloud nine," Mrs. Goldstein later told me. "After that, my mother was the social butterfly. She sat with her sisters and they laughed and talked all night. Before she left, she gave me a big hug and whispered, "Thanks for not listening to me.""

It turned out that the fight between the sisters had been about the medical care that Baila's husband was receiving shortly before his demise. Hadassah voiced some doubts about the doctor they were using and Baila took great exception. She interpreted her sister's remarks as an accusation that she wasn't taking proper care of her husband, and when her husband passed away, that thought gave her no peace. Baila's way of dealing with such matters, as her daughter commented, was to declare a feud.

Because of the feud, Baila had absented herself from many family *simchahs* and exacerbated the loneliness of widowhood many times over. But in the end, she chose to forgive. She heard her sister's conciliatory words and chose to accept them. Having the warmth and love of her sisters finally became more important than having a righteous grievance.

Forgiving is in some ways like driving defensively. We may have the right of way, but what good does that do us if asserting that right will lead us into disaster? For instance, Hadassah may have said something to Baila that really was insensitive. Had she given the matter a bit more thought, she would have realized that there was nothing to be gained by casting doubt in Baila's mind regarding the difficult choices that were made in treating her husband's terminal condition. She would have realized that this was the wrong time to raise questions and doubts. Baila may well have had the right of way, but in exercising it, she drove herself headlong into isolation and bitterness.

In order to forgive, we have to drop our insistence on being declared right. Whether others think we are right or wrong, we can still say to the other person, "I am no longer angry at you." The fact that we have been wronged does not mean that we must be stuck with our anger until the other party sees things our way.

To get to this point, we need a certain sense of security within ourselves. Baila's fears about her husband's condition, his impending death and the terrible loss that loomed in front of her made her tremendously vulnerable to anything that seemed like an attack. She was like someone with a severely compromised immune system; if someone sneezes near her, she feels that they're killing her. In addition, we always react strongly when someone hits a chord of uncomfortable truth or a hidden fear. Because they are verbalizing thoughts that we are trying hard not to confront, we react with rejection and fury. Until we face these buried fears and work our way through them, we may not be able to shed our anger at the person who unearthed them.

Sometimes, the conflict that causes anger really does involve damage and restitution. We know that in the Jewish laws of repentance, a person must try to rectify the damage and seek forgiveness from the victim before he can earn Hashem's forgiveness. Judaism does not provide instant absolution for unredressed wrongs. However, even in these cases, which often require third-party mediation, anger does not have to be part of the equation. We do not have to fear that by letting go of our anger, we are giving up our principles. In fact, whenever someone says, "It's not about me. It's the principle of the thing," we can be almost positive that it's about him.

When we find the inner security to wean ourselves from anger, we dispel a thick cloud of confusion from our lives. What is revealed behind that cloud is an awareness of Hashem as He engineers our lives to provide us with ways to learn what we must and grow into the people we can become. Forgiveness enables us to accept the mistakes, insults and damages others inflict on us and imprint on ourselves the knowledge that we do not control the world. Often, we learn many other useful lessons as well.

"I'm quitting law," Reuven told me. "I'm not cut out for it. I can't believe what my friend Zevy did to me. He made a fool out of me in front of the judge. He used me as his lawyer just because I'm new at it and my fees are cheap, and he knew he could run me around. And now I look like an ignoramus."

Reuven had agreed to represent his old friend, Zevy, at a hearing to formalize an agreement Zevy had signed with his former business partner, Jack. The split-up had been full of acrimony. Both parties had spent a fortune on legal advice, and now, Zevy had to content himself with having his inexperienced friend Reuven handle the consent hearing.

"All the way to court, Zevy was telling me about what a genius his last lawyer was and how he managed to bring things up in front of the judge, just to get it on the record." Reuven recalled. "He wanted me to ask Jack a bunch of questions that don't belong in this kind of a hearing. I had never gone to court before, so I just figured maybe that's how things are actually done. Maybe the rules aren't really so set in stone. So when it was time to question Jack, I started asking about all this stuff that was already settled. The judge looked at me and said, 'If you want a trial, we'll have to reschedule. This is not a trial.' I felt like a complete idiot. I'm so furious at Zevy. He really used me."

Going back over the story, Reuven realized that, out of his own insecurity, he had allowed Zevy to call the shots. He had abandoned his professional judgment and tried instead to satisfy his friend and live up to his friend's idea of what a sharp lawyer should do. "All right," he concluded. "It was a lesson. Don't let the client run the show, even if he's your friend. Zevy was nervous about the split-up so of course he was trying to get every advantage he could. I can't let clients drag me into their emotions."

Had Reuven focused instead on how badly he was wronged, he would have missed a lesson that ended up helping him with every client he subsequently served. He learned to filter out the desperation and emotion so that he could advise them intelligently and handle their cases in a methodical, effective way. He learned to trust his own judgment or, when he really had doubts, to seek advice of a more experienced lawyer so that he didn't react out of insecurity. It didn't take long for him to forgive Zevy's misdirected pressure and credit him instead with a crucial lesson in the handling of clients.

Most importantly, and essential to the "key" of forgiveness, Reuven forgave himself. He realized that an inexperienced attorney is guaranteed to make mistakes. Because anger at others is so often displaced anger at ourselves, forgiving ourselves enables us to forgive others as well.

What if Reuven had not been able to recognize his own role in the courtroom mishap? What if it was just too much for him to acknowledge and forgive himself for his foolishness? In that case, he would have been locked into the view that Zevy caused his troubles. He would have been forced to maintain his grudge against Zevy; he would lose a friendship and miss out on a priceless piece of career wisdom. If we can't forgive ourselves, we can't accept responsibility either, because the downside — eternal self-condemnation — is too high a price to pay. In fact, at the core of many long-held grudges is a person's own guilty grudge against himself.

When we refuse to forgive a person, we are essentially tossing them out of our lives like yesterday's trash. We are saying that they have no redeeming value to us; whatever they might have to offer is totally negated by the wrong they did.

Efraim married Rosy, not her parents. Soon after the chuppah — the next day in fact — it became clear to him that Rosy and her parents were a package deal. Her mother texted the couple incessantly during their entire first week together, apparently worried about her daughter's happiness and adjustment to her new status in life. And that was just the beginning. When the couple arrived at my office, already three years into their marriage, the issues had mounted up to the stratosphere.

"*Everything would be great between us,*" *Ephraim asserted,* "*if her parents just stayed out of our lives. They have something to say about everything I do. They don't like my job, they think I should go back to school, they think our apartment is too expensive and our car uses too much gas and that*

*I don't help enough with the kids and that's just the short
list of complaints."*

*The worst part of the situation was that Rosy still needed
her parents' approval. Therefore, she echoed whatever they
said, hoping to get Ephraim to shape up and become a son-
in-law of whom her parents would be proud. As a result of
Ephraim's resentment of his in-laws' interference, he was
beginning to hate them.*

*There were many issues to work through in this marriage.
Ephraim's anger arose from many root causes that needed
to be addressed. Nevertheless, the anger itself needed to be
relieved, because it was causing conflict and friction for the
couple. To help deflate his anger, we worked on giving Ephraim
a fuller picture of his in-laws: What was the purpose behind
their meddling? Was it evil, or misguided helpfulness? Were
the parents nothing but a burden, or did they provide some
positive resources for the couple? Were they loving toward
their grandchildren? Did they value a close-knit family?*

As Ephraim discovered through this fuller perception of his
in-laws, they were much more than their annoying traits. Those
traits indeed had to be dealt with, mostly by reconfiguring Rosy's
relationship with her parents. Ephraim began to see that there
was a lot of love and good intention in his in-laws' overbearing
approach. When he saw them as whole people, he was able to
stop being angry. They were good people doing some foolish
things. How to deal with those foolish things was a problem for
the couple to solve, but not a reason to hate two people who
essentially, after all, loved and cared for them.

As Ephraim learned, when we try to see things from the other
person's perspective, our understanding usually opens a channel
through which our anger flows away. The fact that the person
has flaws proves nothing other than that he, too, is human.
While we feel an obligation to hate real evil, we do not have to
hate mistakes, misjudgments, misstatements or even mischief. If

we can somehow put ourselves in the other person's place and imagine how he might have come to say or do that which has offended us, we can usually find the motivation to forgive.

Perhaps the most vital step in forgiving others is recognizing where we may have contributed to our problem and forgiving ourselves. In the above situation, Ephraim was angry at his in-laws for their meddling, but angrier at himself for not standing up to them calmly and firmly. He realized that he bore the responsibility for having never once said to them, "We really appreciate all your love and concern. But we're married now, and we have to make our own decisions about what's right for us. I hope you'll be proud of us." Likewise, he had never told his wife, "I know you respect your parents and you want to please them, but you and I are the only ones who have a vote in our decisions."

Instead of firmly asserting his desire for reasonable boundaries in his marriage, he let his resentment build to volcanic proportions and ended up acting and speaking in ways that laid even more guilt upon the heap. In therapy, I often ask clients who are carrying a grudge to tell me why they are angry at themselves. They never fail to come up with an answer.

The negativity in life will not weigh us down if we do not insist on holding onto it and taking it with us wherever we go. Once we understand that anger is not strength and forgiveness is not defeat, we can fearlessly release our grasp on the gripes and grievances that drag us down. With forgiveness, we can plunge forward at full throttle, fueled by positive energy and guided by the lessons learned along the way. Here are 10 ways to start the process:

Unlock Forgiveness

Inspiration

1. Imagine your life without anger. Picture a scene of utter serenity. It might be the seashore, the countryside, the

night sky or anything you find peace inducing. Picture it vividly and keep that picture in a mental "file" to pull out when you feel yourself becoming agitated.

2. Think of a time when you "blew your top" at someone. Did you notice the facial expression of that person? Picture the look of hurt or fear on that person's face and realize that you caused this pain with your anger.

Logic

3. What is your part in the grievance you have against someone else? Even if you bear only 10 percent of the responsibility for the situation, identify that 10 percent.

4. Think of a situation in your life that stirs a lot of angry feelings. Has your anger accomplished anything to remedy the situation thus far? Have you ever found anger to be a useful tool in improving a situation?

A couple was seeking some parenting advice. The mother complained that the father often lost his temper with the children. She preferred a softer approach, but he insisted that anger was necessary to impress upon the children the seriousness of their infractions. "Kids need us to set limits and let them know what's acceptable and what's not," the father said.

"That's absolutely true," the mother agreed. "But if it worked, why are you still yelling at them about the same things? Why is Rivky still not putting away her schoolbooks and why is Dovid still not getting his homework done after supper? Whether the yelling is right or wrong, it doesn't work!"

5. Is there someone against whom you hold a grudge? Think about the ways in which this anger affects *your* life. Who is suffering more, you or the object of your anger? Even

if the other party is suffering more, is your own suffering helping you in any way?

6. Think about something you have done that made someone angry at you. Why did you do it? What was your intention? How did you feel when you realized that another person was hurt or offended by what you did? Can you apply those same questions to someone who has angered you? Is it possible, perhaps even likely, that he or she also has an explanation and also feels remorse?

7. When people disappoint us or oppose us, we often take it as a personal attack and respond in anger. Think of situations in which someone might be your adversary in a particular situation without being your personal enemy. For instance, you may be turned down for a job, but that does not mean the boss dislikes you. Someone might negotiate a business deal with you that leaves you with less than you hoped for, but that does not mean the other side is trying to cheat you. In a social situation, someone might turn to greet another friend, but that does not mean she is trying to ignore you. Try to depersonalize such situations that may exist in your life and eliminate the "fight, flight or freeze" response from them.

Actions

8. Make a list of 10 things that make you angry. Write down one idea next to each one that counteracts the anger. For instance, you might list "people who keep me waiting" as one of your anger issues. Next to it, you might write, "Sometimes I keep people waiting for reasons that can't be helped. Maybe the others also have a good reason." In some communities, you might just have to deal with the fact that lateness is "normal." Your counteracting idea might be "I can't expect everyone to change their standards to my standard."

9. Rehearse your reaction to a common anger-provoking scenario in your life. If it's something that happens regularly, you can prepare yourself with a non-angry response and thereby greatly cut down on the amount of anger in your life. For instance, if you always fight with your child over getting up in the morning for school, you can work out a strategy to deal with that one issue and every morning, you will reap the benefit.

10. Forgive someone. Is there someone in your life against whom you are holding a grudge? Is there someone you dislike because of something he said or did to you? Let go of your anger against that person. If you have been treating that person coldly, make a friendly overture in whatever way is appropriate to the type of relationship. Do this three times and the relationship will be normalized, and most likely, stronger than before.

11. Seek forgiveness. If you have wronged someone else, first admit it to yourself and forgive yourself. You made a mistake as all human beings do. Now get in touch with that person and tell him that you regret what happened and want to apologize.

Forgiveness is a fundamental Jewish concept. We all know that we could not exist for even a day without the benefit of Hashem's forgiveness and yet, many people find it difficult to let go of their anger and grievances against others. The Torah teaches us that in truth, grudges do the most harm to the people who harbor them.

The Gemara (*Megillah* 28a) delves into the secret to a long life. R' Nechunyah ben HaKanah tells R' Akiva that one of his secrets was to never insist on retribution when wronged. Rabbah teaches that those who waive their right to retribution have their sins forgiven, and thus, the sins that might have shortened R' Nechunyah's life were overlooked. R' Nechunyah gives his students his recipe for long life: "Never in my life have I sought respect through the degradation of my fellow, nor has the curse of my fellow gone up with me upon my bed, and I have been generous with my money. R' Z'eira answers the same question with a list of five principles, among which is: "Never in my life have I been harsh with my household."

The Take-Away

The more we let go of our insistence on honor and principle, the more we turn over the judicial robes and gavel to Hashem, the more peace we have in our lives. Like R' Nechunyah, we can sleep in peace, knowing we have caused harm to no one and helped everyone we could help. As R' Z'eira points out, this is especially important within our own homes, where some people tend to let down their guard against temper and harsh criticism.

The *Reishis Chachmah* (4:10) cites, "We learned in *Avos d'Reb Nosson* (*Perek* 4) that Reb Yehoshua says, 'An evil eye, the evil inclination and hatred of other people remove a person from this world and from the next world. Whoever hates his friends, Hashem uproots from this world, as we see in Sodom, where the people hated one another.'"

The Take-Away

A person who hates his "friends" is someone with an "evil eye," someone who sees the negative and the faults in everyone. People who live like this have no peace or happiness in this world, and because of all the pain they sow in their lifetimes, their reward in the next world dissipates as well.

How do we know whether Hashem takes pleasure in us? *Pirkei Avos* (3:10) offers a litmus test. Rabbi Chanina ben Dosa says "A person in whom people take pleasure, Hashem takes pleasure. And those in whom people do not take pleasure, Hashem does not take pleasure."

The Take-Away

People work on many goals in their lives: wealth, health, *chesed* projects, Torah learning, running a home and so forth. Yet none of those goals are chosen as the key to Divine favor. However, if we meet the goal of making our relationships with others pleasant and positive we can be certain that Hashem is smiling down on us.

What did the great *talmidei chacham* of Kelm seek to improve during the month of Elul in preparation for the upcoming judgment of Rosh Hashanah? In the *sefer Kesuvim of the Saba of Kelm* (p. 9) the Alter of Kelm explains that the primary purpose of Rosh Hashanah is for the Jewish people to reconfirm Hashem as their King. Since a king is not a king without a nation, the unity of the Jewish people is the essential first step to Rosh Hashanah prayers. Therefore, the yeshivah worked on the mitzvah of loving one's fellow Jew, so that rifts could be healed and the nation could stand united. So vital was this message that throughout the month of Elul, a sign was placed on the door relating this concept.

The Take-Away

The judgment of Rosh Hashanah determines our year, and the way we relate to each other determines that judgment. At their high level of learning and *avodas Hashem*, the yeshivah *talmidim* could have prepared for Rosh Hashanah in many ways. They could have taken on many stringencies for Elul, and yet the task that stood out as most important was to let go of anger and stand together with their fellow Jews.

Sometimes anger festers because people mistakenly believe that the "high road" is to say nothing. However, the Rambam (*Hilchos Dei'os* 6:6) warns that when a person is wronged, he "should not remain silent and despise him....Rather, he is commanded to make the matter known and ask him, 'Why did you do this to me?' If the wrongdoer asks for forgiveness, the wronged party should give it."

The Take-Away

There's no virtue in nursing a grievance. If a person thinks he is wronged and says nothing for a short time to see if the issue will perhaps seem unimportant in hindsight, that strategy may indeed be beneficial. However, if the wronged party simply keeps a hurt bottled up inside, that negativity will certainly leak out countless times and damage the relationship. Furthermore, the grudge will fester and inflate to great proportions, when it may have been dispelled in one honest conversation.

The Rambam further teaches (Halachah 8) the proper way to bring up a grievance against another person. He must speak in a way that does not cause the other person embarrassment, especially in public, because "Our Sages say, 'A person who embarrasses a colleague in public does not have a share in the World to Come.'"

The Take-Away

Assuming that a person's purpose in airing a grievance is to lay it to rest, there is no purpose served by a harsh reproach. It won't be accepted by the other party because when people are attacked, their instant response is to defend themselves. If a person feels that he will not be able to handle a face-to-face exchange, he may be better off putting his message into writing. In any mode, words of reproach should be as soft and respectful as possible.

Chapter 10
Step Ten

Release Your Influence

Leading vs. Dominating

YOSEF REISS WAS THE PRINCIPAL OF A STRUGGLING *yeshivah elementary school The rebbeim and teachers lived in fear of his disapproval. From the day he assumed the position, he told his staff that his goal was to make the school "second to none." He believed that each teacher should be held accountable for the progress of his students, and to keep tabs on that progress, Rabbi Reiss demanded constant testing and exhaustive record-keeping. He strode the corridors each day, dropping in unannounced to observe and critique the teachers' effectiveness. By the end of the school year, one-half of the teaching staff had informed the school administrator that they would not be returning.*

"I can't understand why I got fired," Rabbi Reiss told me. "I had that school running like clockwork. We had the highest standards of any yeshivah in town. And my rebbeim and teachers were finally being forced to perform like professionals. I guess when they told me they wanted me to upgrade the school's reputation, they didn't really mean what they said."

Rabbi Reiss was hired to elevate the level of education and the standing of his yeshivah. He was placed in a leadership position with 280 students, 4 pre-school teachers, 8 *rebbeim*, 16 part-time secular-studies teachers, a secretary and a custodian all under his authority. It was his job to forge that group into a winning team. He took that charge seriously and put his best efforts into making policies that would push his "team" to the next level. Where did he go wrong?

Rabbi Reiss mistakenly equated leadership with monarchy. Had he conceived of his job as serving the school rather than ruling the school, his strategy would have been much different. He would have sought the involvement of his teachers and staff in ways to upgrade the level of instruction. He would have done whatever he could to inspire and motivate the entire school to strive for a common goal. His message would have been "Let's help each other climb as high as we possibly can" rather than "Do what I say or else."

Rabbi Reiss was in the perfect position to influence an entire miniworld of Torah learning. He could have helped his *rebbeim* and teachers grow professionally. Instead, he scrutinized their in-class performance looking for their flaws. He could have inspired them to feel loyalty to the school and love of their jobs. Instead, he made them dread their work and look for the nearest exit. He could have nurtured the talents of his staff and students. Instead, he stomped upon them heavily with his authority, giving them no room to grow and blossom.

How did he go so phenomenally wrong? He did it by making his authority the top priority, rather than focusing on the greater good of the yeshivah. Rabbi Reiss truly did have a lot to offer in experience and knowledge, but he was not able to use his assets for their higher purpose because he alienated the very people he needed to reach. He lost his chance to influence and build his corner of the world, all because he sought to rule it instead.

His mistake was not in expecting his staff to work hard. To ramp up the stature of his school, hard work was necessary. The principal's mistake was in applying relentless pressure in order to elicit that hard work from his staff. Instead of trying to inspire their enthusiasm and energy, he sought to force it.

He might have learned a lot from another great leader, Mrs. Esti Lerner. She is the CEO and mother of the Lerner household, an "institution" that houses, feeds and educates 10 children. It's a successful, happy institution because Mrs. Lerner and her husband have developed the X-ray vision they need to see the strengths inside each of their children. For instance, the oldest girl doesn't have the personality to be a "junior mother" as many eldest daughters of large families tend to become. The next daughter, however, loves that role, and so she is more often asked to help with the younger children. Nevertheless, the older daughter does have a valuable strong point. She loves to cook; twice a week, she makes the family's dinner. The children who have a lot of physical energy are encouraged to play sports and go biking; they also help their father with house repairs and yard work.

Watching the Lerner family in action, Rabbi Reiss could learn the art of true leadership: using our strengths and abilities to nurture those around us so that everyone, including ourselves, grows and flourishes. Teaching, encouraging, guiding, serving, complimenting and empathizing: these are the hallmarks of true leaders. These are the traits that enable us to use our strengths for a higher purpose, and to give back to the world from the wealth of wisdom, talents and abilities we have gained over the years.

As we have made our way through the previous chapters, we've worked on unlocking the powers that lie latent within us. We've spent a great deal of energy trying to unleash the talents and passions Hashem has planted within us so that we can become all we are meant to be. But then what? Why is it important to become all we can be? It's important because we have a role to play in Creation, and we can't play that role effectively unless we know who we are and what we have to offer. Therefore, the last step in the process of living a fully vibrant life is to learn how to create a vibrant world around us. When we bring out the best in others, we create a biosphere of self-sustaining growth. We, they and our world just keep getting better.

Clearly, "leadership qualities" are not just for CEOs. Each person is a leader to others. Even a fourth grader may play a leadership role to a second grader. Parents are surely leaders of their families; grandparents, older siblings, neighbors — all of us — have the ability to influence the world around us and lift it to a higher level. We each have the tremendous potential to leave a lasting, positive imprint on this world, as long as we do not fall into the trap of misconstruing our role. How do *you* define a leader?

1. Does a leader always know what to do?

2. Can an effective leader entertain doubts about his course of action?

3. Is a leader adept at delegating responsibilities?

4. Does a leader take on tasks that are beneath his status?

5. Does a leader make certain to publicize his achievements?

6. How much credit should a leader take for accomplishments others have achieved under his guidance?

7. Should a leader hold himself above those he leads?

8. How important is it for a leader to maintain his position against opposition?

9. Does a leader lose status by admitting a mistake?

10. Must a leader strive to keep others tied to him and his team?

Tova was a willful, difficult little girl. Her favorite mantra was "I can't wait until I'm a mommy and I can do whatever I want!" Naturally, when she finally arrived at that station in life, she realized that she was busier and bound more than ever to the demands of others. Her children's and husband's needs were a continual source of resentment. "Why can't they just leave me alone?" she silently screamed.

Many of us somehow maintain the illusion into adulthood that leadership means being in total control of our world. If we take the simple lesson learned by Tova, however, we quickly realize that leaders usually work hard, serve others' needs and constantly discover what they *don't* know. A good boss works harder than his employees. A good *rav* sees himself as a servant to his community, even as they accord him deference and respect. A good doctor is always learning new methods and questioning old assumptions.

When we discover the difference between leading and controlling, we open ourselves to the infinite possibilities that real collaboration can generate. By accepting input from others, we are able to transcend our limitations and create something so much bigger and richer than we could ever create all on our own.

The Lock

Locked behind the need to dominate, we lose our openness to learning as well as our chance to teach. We may become tough and cynical, believing that no one else knows how to do things right. We become the type of leader who makes sure that *every* step of *every* process is thoroughly monitored and criticized to ensure "quality control." Sometimes this stems from an overly competitive personality: if we give credit to someone else's idea or achievement, we experience it as a loss for ourselves.

When the Baumgartens decided to shop for a new car, their oldest son, Yehoshua, made up his mind to investigate consumer information to find out which model would be the best value. The father, Chaim, was a longtime car enthusiast who had once worked as an auto mechanic. After doing exhaustive research, Yehoshua told his father, "I looked at all the consumer reports and I think I found the kind of car we should buy."

"Shua, I don't need that," Chaim told his son. "I know cars. We're getting a Honda and that's that."

"But Daddy, did you compare the gas mileage and the repair rate? I saw that the Hondas are...."

"Don't drive me crazy with all this," Chaim cut him off. "I know cars and I know what to get. When you buy your own car, you can decide what to get."

If we examine this situation for a moment, we see that Chaim, rather than nurturing his son's desire to offer valuable information for the family to use on a major purchase, stomped it out like a little brush-fire. Why? What would have been so difficult about hearing his son out and considering his input? One highly transparent motive was Chaim's desire to protect his authority, which he perceived as threatened by Yehoshua's involvement. In Chaim's competitive view, if Yehoshua was right, then Yehoshua won and Chaim lost.

Had Chaim instead acted as a true leader, he might even have requested that Yehoshua do the research, just to give him the satisfaction of using his research skills for the benefit of the family. Certainly, once the research was done, he would have shown appreciation for his son's concern and opened his mind to the possibility that despite his car expertise, he might not have all the answers. In the end, of course, he would make the decision about which car to buy, but Yehoshua would have felt like a valued member of the "team" rather than a kid who didn't know his place.

For some people, authoritarianism is the very definition of leadership. To such a person, being in charge means giving orders, issuing edicts and making decisions that others must accept. This model doesn't allow room to admit error. It requires an infallible leader, because and if we show fallibility, how can we demand total obedience? If we admit that we sometimes make mistakes, we invite others to question our decisions on the grounds that perhaps we are making another mistake. Because we cannot admit mistakes, we not only stunt other people's growth, but we stunt our own.

In contrast, a true leader feels free to admit his mistakes. He is even willing to share stories of his past mistakes with others so that they can benefit from his learning experiences. He knows how to turn the page and start fresh, bolstered, rather than weighed down, by what he has learned through trial and error.

A controlling leadership style locks us into a life of strife and locks us out of the kind of success and achievement we hope to realize. Like Rabbi Reiss in the opening story, most people do not dominate and control in order to make others miserable. Rather, they believe they are working toward a good cause and that, unfortunately, those who are not willing to go with their program will just have to suffer the consequences. That's why Rabbi Reiss could not understand why he was fired. He thought he was doing a great job. He thought his demands were reasonable and the teachers who didn't like it were simply not professional enough for his upgraded yeshivah.

Because of his perspective, the yeshivah he hoped to build became a battleground. His teachers complained constantly to him and to each other. They balked at every new procedure he introduced, even when they made sense, because he had set himself up as their adversary. Thus, ironically, the need and desire to control a situation is often precisely what causes us to lose control. The result the leader envisions fails to materialize and conflict takes its place.

The Why and How

If the results of authoritarian control are so dismal, we might justifiably wonder why this mind-set is so widespread. We can plainly see that the most successful people are those who build others through positive energy and motivation, and yet for some reason, we continue to see force as the only truly effective means to move our world in the direction we desire. The roots of the problem lie in one of the most elementary leadership roles in existence: the parent-child relationship. Parenting books fill the shelves, and the vast majority of those pages are packed with advice on getting children to cooperate and obey. How do we get them to eat healthy food, do their homework, help with household chores, go to bed on time and behave in a civilized way if they don't want to do so?

No matter what technique a particular book advises, the one method that is consistently discredited is force. The larger, stronger parents, the ones who hold the child's very life in their hands, are warned not to yell, threaten or use physical force to win a battle of wills with a child.

The reason so much ink is utilized on this subject is because when we cannot bend others to our will, our instinctive reaction is to use force and coercion. If we can't get a door open, we push harder. Likewise, if we can't get a child to go to bed, we push harder. In addition, many people instinctively try to prevent opposition in the first place by stating their demands in a way that leaves no room for argument. Give an order loud and clear, they believe, and no one will dare question it.

If people do not develop other tools besides force, they are left with this default mode as their only means to manage others. If we grow up with parents who rule by fear, we are apt to accept that as a legitimate method. Unfortunately, this dynamic presents a perfect example of losing control by asserting too much control. Children raised this way may defer to their parents for awhile, but inevitably, they can no longer be controlled. They arrive at a size, age or stage in life when they can no longer be intimidated. If their parents have not developed a relationship in which their influence is valued, then the parents' guiding role in their children's lives is essentially over. Another motivation for striving to dominate is "payback time." The experienced doctor might berate a young intern harshly, thinking, *I had to take it when I was an intern, and now he has to take it.* Parents sometimes deny their children something for no other reason than, "I didn't have that when I was a child and I grew up just fine."

The need for status also feeds into a dominating leadership style. Everyone needs to feel important, to see himself as the master rather than the servant. How do we carve out and protect that role for ourselves in our own personal worlds? Many people believe that having the power to command others is what confers the title of "important person" upon them. They spend their energy clawing their way up the chain of command and keeping down anyone who might try to rise above them. We see this often as people move up along the hierarchy of the workplace:

When Meir was a salesman in his company, he had a great relationship with his co-workers. Ever since he was promoted to sales manager, however, he feels that everyone hates him. "I have to make sure that they realize that now I'm their boss," he explains. "And they resent it."

As he explored the details of how he enforced his new authority, he realized that it was not his promotion that his former co-workers resented. It was the new, imperious attitude he had adopted, the arbitrary demands he made and the complete disappearance of warmth and humor in his relationship with them. Once Meir began to see his role as a team

builder rather than a general, he was able to create a positive
workplace for himself and his salesmen.

Even in the universe of family relationships, the status-
conscious individual alienates other family members. "Because
I'm your father and I said so" might ultimately be the right answer
to a child's resistance, but if it's the answer to every question,
the father-child relationship is bound to unravel. As a result, the
father loses his opportunity to influence his child.

In reality, status, as little Tova discovered in the story above,
is defined more by the word "servant" than "master." Leadership roles do carry with them a measure of authority and power;
however, those attributes are meant to be used in service to the
greater good. We see the paradigm of this model of leadership
throughout the Torah. From Avraham, Yitzchak and Yaakov to
Moshe and King David, the Jewish people's leaders get their job
training by tending sheep. By caring for the flock, fulfilling its
needs and keeping an account of each sheep and its well-being,
they learned to lead their nation.

Throughout our history, this example has set the standard for
great leaders of the Torah world. They are not too important to
raise money for a person in need or to give heed to the woes
of an orphaned child. Their status earns them neither riches nor
leisure time nor protection from criticism. In fact, it usually limits their income, requires a superhuman dedication of time and
opens them up to the criticism of everyone capable of having
an opinion. They do not grasp power; rather, those who they
serve and lead confer it upon them. People want to be part of
their flock.

Like many other issues we've discussed, self-esteem plays a
major role in the ability to lead effectively. If we're afraid to let
someone else have their say, it is often because we are afraid
that he will be right and we will be wrong. When our self-image
is a wobbly house of cards, being wrong knocks it down. It is
too stiff a wind for our inadequate inner structure to withstand.

On the other hand, someone with a strong, sturdy sense of self still feels valuable even when he is wrong. In fact, he wants to be truly right, and so he listens to other opinions in order to objectively weigh his ideas and actions. He values and acknowledges all good ideas and all contributions to his cause because he doesn't need to bolster himself up by keeping others down. When he is wrong, he can comfortably admit his error and apologize without fearing for his position. He realizes that his willingness to admit error actually enhances his position, earning him the trust of those he seeks to lead.

There's a world around us that needs what we have to offer. Whether we want it or not, whether we realize it or not, our influence is making an impact everywhere we go. But what kind of impact do we have? How do others feel when they are in our presence? How do they feel when they think about us? What kind of atmosphere do we create around ourselves? By unlocking our leadership qualities, we can rise to our highest selves, and bring everyone in our lives along with us.

The Key

When we seek to control rather than to lead, we are forgetting one important fact: we will never get our hands on the steering wheel. Hashem is occupying that position, and there is no room for two in the driver's seat. This fundamental realization that Hashem is in control relieves us of the role of Supreme Commander, leaving us instead to simply do the best we can with what we have. We are no longer fighting the opposition; we are building the coalition.

This approach has many practical benefits. The first is that people are more apt to listen to what we have to say when they do not feel coerced or attacked. The first step in influencing others is listening to them so that we can see things through their eyes. We can't move a person from Point A to Point B if we don't even know where they are standing. For instance, if we want to influence a child to become a better student, we have to try to see the school experience through that child's eyes. What are the challenges? What stands in his way of achievement? What does he find enjoyable about school?

Basic communication skills require us to listen with an open mind to other people's input, carefully avoiding the temptation to frame our response while they are still speaking. If we do this, then the other party feels that we are sincerely interested in his point of view. He, in turn, is more willing to hear our point of view. Instead of two people expending their energy defending their positions, a real exchange of ideas can take place.

Even with the best communications, a person in charge will sometimes have to make decisions that others may not like. Yet when everyone feels that there's a united goal and a greater cause, they can usually accept such a decision.

Likewise, a leader will sometimes have to correct others. If his approach is "You did something wrong and now you have to pay," the correction will arouse resentment. His anger reveals the fact that in his view, the worst thing anyone can do is disappoint or disobey him. The impact of the mistake on the greater goal becomes secondary.

Moshe's assistant was having a crazy day. The phone did not stop ringing, and meanwhile, he was trying to compile a price quote for a potential customer. The constant distraction of the phone led to an error and the quote came in very low. The customer hired the company based on the erroneous quote, and now, Moshe was left with an obligation to provide services at less than his cost.

"I've told you a thousand times to let the phone go to voice mail when you're working on a quote," he shouted at his assistant. "If you can't do things right, you're of no use to me. Your mistake is costing this company $1,200! Why should I put up with that?"

What the assistant learned from this episode is that when he makes a mistake, his boss is mad and his job is in jeopardy. What he did not learn was any way to handle the overflow of work and avoid the mistakes that the constant distractions could cause. What if instead of making the error into a personal affront, Moshe had used real leadership skills?

"We've got a serious problem here," Moshe told his assistant. "You know that quote you gave our new customer? There was a mistake in it."

"Oh, no. How big a mistake was it?"

"You were $1,200 off....in the customer's favor."

"Oy, I'm really sorry. That's a really huge mistake. Is there any way to fix it?"

"Not really. We have to keep our end of the bargain. But let's look and see how this happened. Do you have any idea what went wrong?"

"I just know that there's too many things flying at once. When I do these quotes, I really need to concentrate, and even if I don't pick up the phone, the ringing and the messages get my attention. Then there's all the people coming in and out of my office with questions. And it's also a problem when the customer is pressuring me to have the quote right away. Then I end up not having enough time to check it over properly."

The result of this conversation between Moshe and his assistant will be a strategy to address the problems the assistant has described. The only message the men are transmitting to each other is that the business — their mutual greater cause — has suffered a setback, and together they must find a way to avoid a repeat of the problem. In this scenario, it almost doesn't matter who is the boss.

As we grow older and wiser, our leadership potential grows. The skills, experience and understanding we acquire throughout our lives can be the most valuable gifts we offer to others. A true leader possesses a generous spirit that wants to see others succeed and even exceed his own achievements. A *rebbi* has no greater satisfaction than a *talmid* whose reputation outpaces his own. Parents glory in their children's successes and professionals delight in pointing out a star and saying, "I helped him get started." We know that our time on the stage is limited, but when we know how to lead, we can be assured that our influence will endure.

That is why teaching others is an essential key to developing ourselves as leaders. Once again, healthy self-esteem is a vital factor, for it enables us to advance others' progress without the worry that their ascent up the ladder will leave us feeling comparatively low. A good teacher teaches for the sake of his students. His success is not diminished by the student's achievements; just the opposite is true. The better his students do, the more successful the teacher feels. Even when someone trains a professional or helps launch a business that will later compete with him, there is no disadvantage in the view of a real leader. He is secure that everyone will have the due portion of success that Hashem allots him.

As many people quickly discover, teaching others is one of the most powerful ways of enhancing our own talents. When we know we are setting an example, we try to be a worthy role model. When we know we must answer questions, we try to clarify our own thinking. As we generously give of ourselves to nurture others, we reap the benefits. The key is to realize that by strengthening the people in our world, we lose nothing and gain a stronger world for ourselves and everyone in our lives.

We can't tap into these benefits if our idea of teaching is to pontificate, interfere, nag or browbeat others into accepting our superior knowledge. Teaching has to arise from the desire to help the other person. When we show people that we want to help them by perceiving their needs and making efforts on their behalf, we draw their love and loyalty.

Ezriel was in charge of getting his children into bed each night. He complained that it was a draining and chaotic scene, especially with his perpetually contrary 9-year-old. I suggested that he make some special time to sit down and talk with that child and see if there was something bothering him. Ezriel followed my advice and elicited from his son a list of "big problems" that made him unhappy. They were indeed major challenges: he felt he had no close friends, he disliked his classes, other boys teased him and his health-conscious parents never gave him a good snack to bring to school.

"I asked him which of those problems he wanted to talk about right now so that maybe we could come up with a solution. Of all things, he wanted to talk about the snack situation. I told him that I could see it might be hard to watch other kids eating snacks that look so good, so we agreed that once a week he could bring in a snack of his choosing. After that, he became so cooperative about going to bed that he even got the other kids to cooperate."

The battle of wills over bedtime is a well-known ritual to many parents. In this case, Ezriel was able to call off the battle and gain cooperation by showing his son that he wanted to help him. Once the child experienced the father's care and concern, and saw that the father took his troubles seriously enough to discuss and problem-solve, he was on board. He felt his father was on his side and therefore, he took his father's side in getting everyone else to cooperate.

To lead, we must allow our strengths and talents to overflow their boundaries and nurture those around us. We must believe that what we have is worth sharing, and that we will not be depleted one iota by sharing it. When we unlock our strengths and then use them to make a positive imprint in the world, we are using our lives as they are meant to be used. Here are some ways to unlock your influence:

Unlock Leadership

Inspiration

1. Develop a sense of how people feel when they are around you. Do they feel acknowledged, encouraged, energized? If so, recognize that you are already a leader.

2. Recall times when your advice has been sought and followed. Feel the satisfaction of having helped someone. See yourself as that person who others turn to for advice, someone whose wisdom, strength and experience are abundant enough to share with others.

3. Feel the love and caring you have for the people in your life, and the gentle power you can use to softly, consistently prod others to take one small step forward.

Logic

4. Think about your style of leadership. How much do you try to assert control and dominate others? How much do you recognize Hashem's control of every situation?

5. Build a team. Engage others' strengths and solicit their ideas. Ask, what do you think? How would you solve this problem?

6. Signal to others that you are approachable. Thank them for their input and listen sincerely to their ideas and even their complaints.

7. Think about people who wield their power aggressively. Even if they seem successful, do they seem happy? Do they have peace, friendship and balance in their lives? Realize that this kind of power destroys a person from within by causing a life of loneliness and anxiety.

Actions

8. Lead by example rather than by command and edict. Work toward building the types of traits and habits you want others to exhibit, and as you strengthen yourself, you will strengthen others.

9. When you have the opportunity to let others take credit for an accomplishment or a good idea, do it. You'll be building others up and encouraging them to continue to offer what they can.

10. Pass it on: Repay the help others gave you in getting started and developing your personal assets by doing the same for those who are starting out now. Give them the benefit of your experience by mentoring or teaching others.

Tyrannical leadership methods are often thought to be the "old-fashioned way" which, when all is said and done, works better than modern, egalitarian methods. We discover, however, that the truly "old-fashioned" style of the Torah's leaders, while exercising all the necessary authority, was devoid of arrogance and bluster.

Moshe was the Jewish people's penultimate leader whose word was law. Nevertheless, he was also the most humble of all men. The Torah records an instance (*Vayikra* 10:20) in which Moshe questions Aharon's sons, Elazar and Issamar, as to why they did not eat the meat of the offering as they were commanded to do. Aharon explains that they were not permitted to eat because of the laws of mourning, which they were observing upon the deaths of their two brothers. The Torah says, "Moshe heard and he approved." The *Leket*

Bahir expounds on this verse, saying that Moshe admitted his mistake "with his full mouth" and was happy for the clarity that the correction gave him. While other leaders might have debated the point or defended their position, Moshe stated simply that he had heard the halachah but had forgotten it.

The Take-Away

We learn from Moshe that a true leader is one who can admit to a mistake. The greater the person, the less arrogance and defensiveness he employs to protect his position. He wants to do his job and do it right, and that is more important than appearing invincible.

The Gemara teaches many times that the reason David Hamelech's reign endured and Shaul Hamelech's did not was because of David Hamelech's ability to admit his mistakes without excuse or justification. This type of humility is one of the criteria for leadership in *Klal Yisrael*.

In *Parashas Vayishlach* (*Bereishis* 32:11) Yaakov prays to be saved from his brother Esav, who was approaching with an army. He tells Hashem, "I have been diminished by all the kindness and all the truth You have done to me." Yaakov certainly knew that he had endured and passed many tests, yet he focused on the debt of gratitude he owed Hashem and, Rashi explains, he wondered if perhaps his merits had been depleted. His gratitude for all he had been given far outweighed his sense of entitlement to Hashem's help.

The Take-Away

We see that the greatest people in our history were motivated by gratitude and the desire to serve Hashem and *Klal Yisrael*; status-seeking and self-aggrandizement had no role to play in their lofty missions. We can therefore clearly see that such traits have no place at all in our own, far-less earthshaking tasks in life. True leaders do not focus on what they have done for the world, but rather, they are humbled by what Hashem and their fellow Jews have done for them.

Leadership is one area of life in which age and experience are a precious asset. In the story of the young King Yehoash (*Melachim II* 12:3), the verse tells us that "Yehoash did what was proper in the eyes of Hashem all his days that Yehoyada the Kohen taught him." Yehoyada was the Kohen Gadol and the king's uncle, and he trained and educated the child king in the proper ways, Rashi explains.

The Take-Away

This brief verse illustrates the crucial value of a wise teacher. Those who are older and perhaps out of date with the latest thinking and technology might feel they have little to offer, but in fact, the perspectives and wisdom brought by experience can have a profound impact on others.

Alive!

A leader who is motivated by arrogance can actually lose everything, as R' Nachman teaches (*Sanhedrin* 101b). He declares that "The arrogance that possessed Yeravam drove him out of the world." Yerovoam was the king of the Ten Tribes of Israel, and he could not abide the fact that Rechavam, the king of Yehudah, possessed the sole right to sit in the court of the *Beis HaMikdash* when people came to bring their offerings. He therefore set up golden calves in two locations in his kingdom and commanded his subjects to bring their offerings there, rather than making the lengthy journey to Jerusalem. Thus he brought the masses of Jews to commit the cardinal sin of idol worship.

But even then, Hashem gave him a chance to repent, telling him that if he would do so, he would walk together with Hashem and David Hamelech in Gan Eden. Yeravam asked who would walk at the head, and when Hashem replied, "The son of Yishai (David)," Yeravam rejected the offer.

The Take-Away

In Yeravam's world, there was room at the top for only one person, and in his arrogance, he felt that it had to be him. Arrogance blinds a person to what is best for others and for himself as well. Therefore, it is really the antithesis of leadership, the exact opposite of the quality a person needs to win the trust of others. No one wants to follow a blind leader.

Chapter 11

Three Case Studies

The following three case studies give the reader an insight into how the ILA system (see Appendix) and the concepts in the previous chapters work together to help people overcome their barriers to success. In deference to the confidentiality of my clients, I have altered the details of the situations so that the individuals involved are not identifiable. The underlying issues they faced and the strategies we used to address those issues, however, are true and accurate.

I would like to note, however, that these studies do not provide a complete explanation of the complicated process of addressing subconscious issues. Since those therapeutic methods require a great deal of background and explanation, we have not addressed much of that aspect of treatment in the case studies portrayed here.

Case Study #1: Trapped in Perfectionism

Herschel Greenbaum, 39, a highly successful businessman, was plagued by anxiety. When he first arrived in my office, he told me that he was subject to panic attacks. He described the classic symptoms: his heart would race, he would break out in a sweat and the room would start spinning. His doctor wanted to put him on anti-anxiety medication, but Herschel had balked.

Along with the panic attacks, Herschel's anxiety expressed itself in many other ways that eroded his relationships with family and kept him from developing close friendships. He was extremely secretive, so much so that he would not even disclose to others what type of business he was in. He felt certain that if he let others know how he was making his fortune, they would steal his idea and begin competing with him. Therefore, he only did business with people outside his community.

He also kept his wife in the dark about everything that was important to him. She had no idea how much money he made because he feared that if she had access to that information, she would insist on spending more. He was especially careful not to disclose any fears, weaknesses or doubts to his wife, lest she think of him as weak. In fact, he came to therapy for a full year before he found the courage to tell her that he was doing so.

Another closely held secret in Herschel's life was that he had earned a law degree. He had a quick, logical mind and had always loved to learn, but he trembled at the thought of anyone asking him a legal question. What if he didn't know an answer, or gave someone the wrong answer? What if someone didn't like his answer? Rather than risking any of these seemingly crippling situations, he kept his intellectual ability a secret. For all anyone knew, Herschel was a down-to-earth, action-oriented man who had no interest in the world of theories and ideas.

With his closed-off emotions and massive anxieties, Herschel barely functioned as a husband and father. At 39, he was financially successful and emotionally miserable. He could not envision a happy life.

Here we will briefly outline the ILA system explained fully in the Appendix. Using this system, a person rates himself in three areas: inspiration (his enthusiasm and emotional vitality), logic (knowledge and intellect) and action (ability to get things done). The rating scale goes from 1, the lowest, to 10, the highest. These numbers are multiplied to get an overall "life satisfaction" score. Therefore, the perfect life — 10x10x10 — would render a score of 1,000. We assume that the average in any one area is 5; at that level, a person is functioning well but not excelling. When a person has a score below 5 in any one area, his deficit is noticeable to himself and others. Likewise, if he scores 6 or above, he feels that this is an area of strength and others perceive his strength as well.

If we were to evaluate Herschel's quality of life using the ILA formula, we would rate his inspiration as 2. He kept his inner self locked so securely within a lead vault of fears and misconceptions that he was barely acquainted with it. With no understanding of what his real strengths and passions were, he had no way to utilize these assets to ignite a passion for life. His heart was not in it; he didn't even know where his heart was.

On the other hand, his logic and action were both above average, held back only by his fears. He was shrewd and adept at assessing a situation, especially in business. He knew what he was doing and whatever he did not know, he learned from experience. Thus, his logic could be rated an 8. Likewise, Herschel was a man of action. His emotional numbness gave him one great advantage; he would forge ahead with his plans without hesitation, just as someone without feeling in his hand might not hesitate to touch a flame. In the realm of action, he rated about an 8. Thus Herschel's overall rating, 2x8x8, was 128 out of a potential 1,000. This mere fragment of the total expressed the great deficit in Herschel's satisfaction with life. Two great strengths were almost completely undone by one gaping void: inspiration.

Therefore, we began therapy in the area of his inspiration/ emotions, trying to discover the subconscious messages that gave rise to his fears. I asked him to listen to his anxiety, to hear what his mind was telling him when he felt a wave of fear. The message he heard was "You must be perfect." It was the message instilled in him by his mother, who was tremendously protective of her social standing in a successful family. She did not admit to any cracks in her mask of perfection, nor did she accept any flaws in her family members. She saw everyone outside the family as a potential competitor for status.

The inner program of perfectionism ran Herschel's life. Because of it, he dreaded doing anything that might attract scrutiny. He stayed out of the limelight and labored mightily to look, talk and act like everyone else, insisting that his wife and children do the same. In fact, my radio show on the subject of perfectionism was the catalyst for him coming to see me. He recognized himself in the mind-set I described and the stultified life a perfectionist nature spawns. Using the keys in Chapter 2 (Unlock Self-Acceptance),[1] we worked on freeing him from the demands of perfectionism, enabling him to see that he could make mistakes and admit mistakes without losing any of his status in business, family or his community.

Herschel's fear of disclosing his law degree and his overall intellectual ability was another manifestation of his terror of being less than perfect. To become comfortable with this aspect of himself and begin capitalizing on it as a personal asset, he

---

1. In this chapter, we learned to recognize that perfection is an unreachable ideal that keeps people in a state of dissatisfaction with themselves and others. It also prevents people from doing things they are not good at for fear of making mistakes.

had to learn to accept his status as a beginner in a new field. We used the keys in Chapter 3 (Unlock New Beginnings)[2] to reframe his perceptions. Instead of seeing his beginner status as a threat to his self-image, he learned to see it as a source of excitement and renewal. He recalled the nervousness that accompanied every new adventure in his life, from walking to the *chuppah* to bringing home his first child to opening his business, and how each aroused the same shaky, stomach-churning anxiety. Realizing that this feeling meant life, growth and progress, he came to accept it.

At the same time, we worked on Herschel's acceptance of himself as an individual. His defensive strategy of hiding within the crowd, doing what everyone else was doing and espousing everyone else's opinions had played a major role in closing him off from his inborn talents, interests and inclinations. Using the keys in Chapter 4 (Unlock Your Free Choice),[3] we re-connected Herschel to the things in life that excited him. His defenses were so strong that this effort was a bit like drilling for oil under bedrock; he insisted that nothing mattered to him but being successful and doing the right thing. Only after a great deal of persistent digging did he hit the buried treasure of his true personal strengths.

As we brought all these thought patterns to light and worked on releasing Herschel from their crippling limitations, we would sometimes find ourselves reverting to his old, perfectionist beliefs. Even as he experienced the release, the revival and the calm of his new perspectives, something inside him nagged. *You're just lying to yourself. You can't cut it, so now you're*

---

2. Learning to appreciate and even enjoy the thrill of starting something new, with all its unpredictability and potential for error, is a vital skill for living a life of vitality and growth.

3. This chapter discusses the importance of recognizing our own goals and hopes and actualizing them when possible, or finding a realistic way to bring into our lives some of the joy they stir within us.

pretending that it's just as good to be mediocre. You're giving yourself excuses.

The problem was that Herschel needed to forgive himself. He needed to let go of the guilt he was feeling about abandoning the standard of perfection. He also needed to forgive others, whose mistakes and flaws he viewed with disapproval. Finally, he needed to forgive his mother, whose highly conditional love had created the entire warped framework of his life. As we employed the keys of Chapter 9 (Unlock Forgiveness),[4] Herschel gradually learned to release the past and enjoy the freedom to move forward in life unencumbered by guilt and anger.

After many months of therapy, Herschel came to the point where he was able to share with his children some of his mistakes and struggles. He learned to empathize with their shortcomings. At one point, his son complained that he was having a test the next day and didn't know the material. Formerly, Herschel's response would have been, "What do you mean, you don't know it? Sit down and study it until you do!" But because Herschel could now accept imperfection, he asked his son, "What do you think you need to do well? Would it help if I review it with you?" The son welcomed his father's help and Herschel was able to give his son confidence to succeed.

Since Herschel only knew himself as a hard-headed business-man, we worked on identifying his natures (Chapter 6, Unlock Your Natures).[5] He realized that his vulnerability to criticism was a sign of a sensitive nature. He cared about what others thought and said, which demonstrated a warmer, more emotional nature than he had ever acknowledged.

We also explored Herschel's need to set limits in his life, to keep his business life from overflowing into his family time and to

4. In this chapter, we learn about the self-destructive nature of anger and discuss ways to avoid it, dispel it and forgive those who arouse our anger.

5. This chapter outlines 18 different natures and guides the reader to recognize the composite of natures that define his personality.

apportion time for his pursuit of Torah learning, which he valued very much. He needed to put his life into balance so that his entire identity was not invested in his business, which like any business, could conceivably run into trouble. With that balance, potential losses in business would not seem so completely annihilating.

Throughout this process, we worked on Herschel's self-esteem (Chapter 1, Unlock Your Self-Esteem).[6] No one would have imagined that this hard-driving, successful businessman lacked self-esteem, but that was exactly what his massive fear of failure indicated. Using the keys to inspiration, he was able to list 35 things he could count as positive attributes, and I had him read this list out loud to himself several times each day.

A key part of the process of helping Herschel was to gradually build up his courage to face and accept failure. I had asked him what his panic attacks were saying to him, and now I asked him what he wanted to say to his panic attacks. "I wish I could tell everyone, 'I'm not perfect. Accept me as I am.'" I asked him to imagine saying those words and feeling absolutely safe in saying them. No one attacks him, no one is outraged, no one throws rotten tomatoes at him. Everyone just nods and says, "O.K., so what? No one's perfect." I guided him to hold on to this image and vividly live it in his mind. He did this many times, not just imagining the image but actually wallowing in it, soaking it up and letting it permeate his mind.

Nearly a year into our therapy, Herschel lost a big customer. He knew that this was just the kind of episode that, in the past, would have thrown him into a bout of almost unbearable anxiety. Instead, he put the situation into perspective. The customer was new, and was using Herschel's services on a trial basis; it was a given that it might not work out. Meanwhile, he noted that business with another customer had been growing, which would mitigate the loss. He moved past the episode with ease.

---

6. In this chapter we explore the roots of self-esteem, its impact on success and emotional health, and ways to build and maintain it throughout life.

During the first year that Herschel was in therapy, he gradually drew his wife into a more meaningful role in his life. He began sharing more with her about his business and listening with more interest and empathy to her concerns.

Meanwhile, Herschel's anxiety attacks have disappeared. He was able to entirely avoid medication. His "Inspiration" rating has gone from 1 to somewhere well above average, perhaps all the way to 8. He has worked hard to crack through the barriers and come to appreciate all he has to offer as an individual with talents, ideas and strengths that are not the same as everyone else's, but rather, unique to him. Because he has released himself from the trap of perfection, he feels free to let his nature and abilities free into the world to benefit others. He can deal with someone thinking he is different or thinking he is wrong.

The improvement in his inspiration level has spilled over to the logic and action aspects as well. Because he no longer fears letting others know about his law degree, he has become involved in researching zoning laws to advise a local school about options for a new location. His mind is engaged in an area he enjoys, and he continues to learn more as he does his research. This involvement has also enabled him to expand his network of friends and contacts in his community, helping him feel more connected to others.

At the same time, he has begun talking to people about his business now that he has lost his morbid fear of competition. As a result, his business opportunities have expanded. Both his Logic and Action have ticked upward to at least 9. By working with his subconscious, mostly to free him from the perfectionist trap, we have turned an ILA score of 128 into 8x9x9, 648. He no longer feels as if he is struggling to just get through the day without making a mistake. He enjoys the connections he has made in his business and now feels like a valuable part of the business community. He enjoys using his legal mind to help the community and finds the questions others ask him to be stimulating and challenging rather than terrifying. Best of all, his level of stress has plummeted, and his wife and children are the happy beneficiaries. Herschel has a newly opened wellspring of emotional energy to give them. A gifted, intelligent young man is living a life filled with challenge, satisfaction and joy.

Case Study #2: A Depressed Teen

Moving Out and Moving Up

Zalman, a married man in his late 20s, called my office one day to talk to me about his wife's brother, 18-year-old Dov. "He needs help and no one is getting it for him," Zalman told me. "He's so depressed. He doesn't want to get up and go to yeshivah, even though he's a really smart kid and well liked, too. I try to talk to him but I can't get anywhere. His principal told my in-laws to put him on anti-depressants, so they did. But he needs to talk to someone."

I agreed to see Dov. Zalman spoke to his in-laws and was able to convince them to send him to me. A week later, when Dov arrived for his first session, he seemed to meet his brother-in-law's dire description precisely. I wondered what had pushed a smart, likable kid into such a low state.

Dov told me a little about his household. His mother, he said, was "all tension." She wanted everything to be picture perfect. Things got especially crazy before Yamim Tovim, because she insisted on hosting her married children and their growing families. "Then she can't handle it," Dov explained. "She starts panicking and crying and screaming at everyone. So my father gets furious at her and tells her, 'No more! If you can't handle it, don't invite!' Then you know what my mother does? She cooks for all my married brothers and sisters anyway and sends them the food. She still goes crazy."

Dov's parents fought constantly. Every night, they bickered about the subjects on their rotating agenda of conflicts: often money was at the core of the problem. His father felt that his mother spent too much. His mother felt that she did not have enough money to run the household properly. Other issues cropped up, too: in-laws, social plans, housekeeping, children and grandchildren, etc. Dov refused to invite any friends to his house because his parents' bickering embarrassed him.

At yeshivah, Dov was actually a sought-after *chavrusa* because of his intelligence and easygoing personality. However, he did not see himself as popular. "There are only a few guys who are my friends," he told me. "They probably just feel bad for me."

Assessing Dov through the ILA formula, we see that his inspiration is sorely lacking. He is disinterested in most of his daily activities. He can't concentrate in yeshivah, he feels little love from his parents and doubts the sincerity of his friends. His Inspiration was about a 2.

In the area of Logic, Dov functioned better. He realized he was smart, even though his performance suffered from his lack of motivation. The many days he didn't manage to make it to yeshivah were causing him to fall behind, but he knew that with a little effort, he could easily catch up again. He also understood very well the dynamics of his parents' relationship. He was perceptive and mature. His Logic was a 6.

His Actions were held back by his depression. He was spending a great deal of time in his room sleeping or reading rather than studying or playing sports. He felt almost paralyzed sometimes. "There's nothing I feel like doing and no place I feel like going," he reported. His Action rating was about 3. Altogether, Dov's rating was 2x6x3, just 36 out of a possible 1,000, far below the average of 125 (5x5x5), Dov's life was scraping along at the bottom of a deep rut.

Obviously, Dov's self-esteem needed a major overhaul in order for him to break free of his depression. Using the keys in Chapter 1 (Unlock Your Self-Esteem), we began instilling in him the encouragement he needed to believe in his own value and potential. In his parents' complete absorption in their own problems, they had found little energy to spare for building up their son. His positive traits and talents rarely won recognition at home. Therefore, we began recognizing and reinforcing them together.

We started the process by acknowledging that Dov spent a lot of energy trying to be a therapist to his parents. He would engage in shuttle diplomacy, explaining to his mother that his father was only trying to help, and then explaining to his father that his mother was only trying to be a good mother. While this was not at all a role that an 18-year-old boy should have to play, it was an indication of one of his main attributes: his deeply caring nature.

That became Number One on a list of 20 strengths that Dov was able to see in himself. Among others were his perceptiveness, borne by his need to know when trouble was brewing at home; his high level of intelligence and his sense of humor. On those rare occasions when everyone was getting along, Dov had a great gift of irony that made his family laugh.

As Dov reviewed his positive traits and focused on his many achievements, he began to believe in his own innate value. As therapy progressed, his confidence rose to the point where he was able to accept the position of *gabbai* at his yeshivah's *minyan*. "Nobody wants that job," he told me. "So I figured I'd take it. I don't mind being the one to bug people. It just doesn't bother me."

At first, he had turned down the job, reasoning that he was going into his senior year and it was too late to make changes. Working with the keys in Chapter 3 (Unlock New Beginnings), Dov came to see that anytime was a good time to reinvigorate his life with something new. Even if it was only for a year, serving as *gabbai* was bound to expand his abilities and network of friends. He visualized the nervousness he might feel the first few times he filled his new role, and learned to appreciate the feeling as evidence of courage and growth. He realized that it was worth suffering through the "learning curve" involved in starting a new job in order to gain the benefits of the experience.

Indeed, it wasn't long after he began the job that he noticed himself becoming the "go-to guy" for his fellow students and his rebbeim as well. He relished the feeling of having something to offer and being recognized for it. Dov was energized. Instead of dragging himself out of bed reluctantly each morning or skipping school altogether, he jumped up at the sound of his alarm clock to make sure he got to yeshivah on time. People were depending on him.

On another front, Dov decided that he needed to remove himself from the toxic environment of his parents' house. His sister and brother-in-law lived in the same town and had offered him a room in their house. However, his mother wouldn't hear of it. She worried that people would think she was an unfit mother if her son took up residence elsewhere, especially since it was right in the same town. Dov felt that the option was therefore closed to him.

However, as we worked through the concepts in Chapter 8 (Unlock the Power of 'No'),[7] Dov began to see that he could and should erect a boundary between his parents' turmoil and his own emotional life. He had to say "no" to engagement in their draining conflicts so that he could free up his own energy and engage fully in the healthy activities of life. His learning, his friendships and development of the *middos* he would need to become a happy, productive adult were all being suffocated by the overwhelming issues in his parents' home. He came to realize that a line needed to be drawn. The question was how to do it above his parents' objections.

I asked Dov, "Would your parents mind if you spent a few nights at your brother-in-law Zalman's house?" He answered

---

7. In this chapter, we learned that setting boundaries and saying "no" is necessary in order to productively channel our desire to help others and say "yes" to others' needs. Overextending oneself can lead to resentment, inefficiency and burnout.

that they would most likely barely notice, since he didn't get home until 10:30 at night, after Maariv, and they were usually pre-occupied with some crisis of their own. Exploring some of the keys offered in Chapter 2 (Unlock Self-Acceptance), Dov realized that he did not have to push for the perfect, complete solution of moving out lock, stock and barrel with his parents' blessing. A partial solution — staying with his sister and brother-in-law a few nights a week — would get him out of the house without forcing a confrontation with his parents. Both parents consented to his "temporary move." When he extended his stay indefinitely, no one uttered a word of objection.

Another key part of Dov's improvement came from letting go of his anger at his parents and himself. "Doesn't a kid deserve a normal home to grow up in?" he asked me. "Shouldn't parents have to grow up themselves before they have kids?"

Through the keys in Chapter 9 (Unlock Your Forgiveness), we began the work of releasing Dov from his anger at his parents. In therapy, he explored ways to emotionally detach from his parents' conflicts. He vividly imagined that his parents were just an eccentric couple living in the upstairs apartment. "Their bickering has nothing to do with me," he said. "I hear them, but it doesn't matter. It doesn't affect me. They can fight for 10 minutes or all night. It's just another sound, like the traffic noise and the sirens." I guided him to experience the lightness and freedom he would feel when he let go of his grievance. "Imagine having nothing holding you down. You're not obligated to be unhappy because of the wrongs that were done to you," I suggested. I asked him to spend five minutes a day experiencing these feelings until he could feel his tension and stress melting away.

Appealing to his logic, I asked him if he really thought that his parents purposefully behaved in ways that hurt him. "No," he admitted. "My grandparents are kind of the same way. I guess they act the way they learned to act when they were kids.

But still, it's wrong!" He also came to realize that in their own way, his parents did try to show their love for their children. There were warm memories and even in the present, acts of caring and concern. We also discussed the fact that forgiving someone's wrong does not mean endorsing it. It simply means accepting what happened, learning from it and moving forward.

Finally, we explored the grievances Dov held against himself. Like many children of conflict-ridden marriages, Dov felt somehow at fault. Deep inside him, he believed that if he were only a better son, his parents would not be angry at each other. He knew that their fights, especially of late, had sometimes revolved around his behavior. Through the keys of forgiveness, he took two giant steps: he forgave his parents and forgave himself.

After about three months of therapy, Dov began weaning off the anti-depressants he had been taking. He was living with his sister and his brother-in-law Zalman, who became his mentor and friend, fulfilling the role outlined in Chapter 7 (Unlock Your Support).[8] In the course of the six months in which Dov came to therapy, he reframed his relationship with his parents. Once he stepped away from his parents' problems, he was better able to see the love for him that each of them tried to express. He loved yeshivah and began integrating his success there into his image of himself. His Inspiration soared to a rating of 8 as he envisioned a future of more advanced learning and eventually, marriage and family.

In the area of Logic, Dov's greater enthusiasm for yeshivah brought great results. He became one of the top students in his school, and truly felt he was working at full capacity. We rated his Logic at 9.

His ability to take positive action in his life was also vastly enhanced by his new level of inspiration. His activities as *gabbai,* his move to his sister's house, his greater focus on his learning,

---

8. In this chapter, we examine the benefits of consulting with trusted friends or mentors, and establishing a circle of people who fulfill that role in our lives.

his active exploration of options for the coming year and his far-greater involvement with his friends brought his Action level up to a 7. Dov became a happy, productive, successful boy whose overall satisfaction with life had reached 504, up from the abysmal 36 at which he had started. He finished 12th grade with a bang and went out of town to an excellent *beis medrash* the following year.

Case Study #3: A Mother in Denial

Emotional Anesthesia

Leora sought therapy when one day, she realized that the center had dropped out of her extraordinarily smooth-functioning, well-ordered life. Her two married daughters had all but cut her off. Everything for which she had labored her entire life — running an efficient household and raising responsible children — seemed to have been for nothing.

What had caused the rift? "They said that they always end up feeling tense and depressed after they talk to me," Leora lamented. "They can't stand being in my home. They said it's not healthy for them or their children. I've done everything in the world for them, and now I can't even have the *nachas* of having my grandchildren over for a Shabbos. I'm a very strong person, but this is too much."

As we spoke further, Leora's "*nachas*" emerged as more of a concept than a reality. "Do you enjoy your married daughters' visits?" I asked her. She said, "Yes," but then proceeded to detail the flaws in her grandchildren's upbringing, the lack of parenting skills exhibited by her daughters and their husbands, the mess the children made and the lax attitude their parents had about cleaning up after them. "They'll be there for a whole Shabbos and I'll be picking up after the children all day. The girls tell me, 'It's no use cleaning up now. Wait until they go to bed.' What kind of thing is that?" She also objected to some of the grandchildren's picky eating habits. "Who lets a 2-year-old decide what she's going to have for dinner?" she asked. "You have to raise children, not let them raise themselves. It takes effort. I tell my daughters this, but they don't listen."

Obviously, Leora's perception of herself as a self-sacrificing mother and her daughters' perception of her as a source of toxicity needed to be reconciled. She saw herself as someone who did what needed to be done, a person of logic and action. She had no time or space in her life for emotions. When I asked her if she ever told her children that she loved them, she replied, "Every minute of my day is for them. I show them. I don't have to tell them. Words are just words."

This approach spanned her entire life's endeavor. She believed that what she felt was not important; what she did was all that mattered. She forced herself through the tasks and challenges of her life with sheer will. Shabbos was an exhausting ordeal that entailed a full menu of courses that, to her thinking, were mandatory. The day itself was often stressful for her. In her community, most of the women who were not home with small children attended shul in the morning, and so she did too. However, the prayers seemed like a long, repetitive, empty ritual. She repeatedly glanced at the clock on the wall.

Friendships, as well, were handled as a duty. She kept her thoughts and feelings to herself and conversed only about impersonal subjects. She wondered why everyone else seemed to know so much about each other's lives. She could not even name her next-door neighbor's children. However, whenever she was asked to participate in a communal project, she did her part. "Do I want to do these things? Of course not. I've got plenty to do just taking care of my own family. But it's what you have to do if you want to be part of a shul."

Inspiration in Leora's life might have been a zero: the factor that, when multiplied by the other numbers, turns them all to zero. But the very fact that her daughters' withdrawal from her did indeed prick at her emotions showed that something was still alive. Therefore, we rated her Inspiration at 1. Her Logic was excellent when it came to objective knowledge. She knew her "business" of running a household very well. However, her knowledge of how to run a home — communications, relationships, psychology, childrearing and all the other interactive aspects — were far off base. Therefore, we would give her a 3.

In the area of Action, Leora shone brightest. There was no such thing as "I don't feel like it." Anything she believed needed doing, she did. Holding her back, however, was her narrow view of what needed doing. She lacked willingness to act in ways that provided a sense of security and comfort to others. She could pick up after her grandchildren, but she would not pick them up or play with them. In Action, she was a 9. Thus, her ILA was 1x3x9, a rating of 27 out of a maximum of 1,000. She was far below the average of 125 (5x5x5), a fact borne out by her unhappiness. Here was a woman who was essentially empty inside, enjoying nothing in her life and seemingly unaware that enjoying life was even a legitimate goal.

Soon after beginning therapy, I asked Leora to bring her two married daughters to a session. I felt that it was important for them to articulate to her exactly what made their relationship with their mother so difficult. While they may not have been able to do so one-on-one with their mother, I hoped that with me present as a facilitator, they could convey their feelings in a constructive way.

The daughters agreed to meet with me and their mother. In that session, Leora learned that her ironclad self-control was experienced by her children as a lack of love. "I never yelled," Leora said. "You never smiled, either," one daughter countered. "Everything was always so dry and technical. It was like being raised in an orphanage where everything is on a schedule and the schedule is the most important thing. You never made an exception. We never felt like we were special to you. Once I thought to myself that if I went to live at my friend Raizy's house and she came to live in our house, you wouldn't notice, as long as she was dressed and at the table in time for breakfast."

Now that they were grown, their visits to their parents' house only churned up bad memories. They saw their younger siblings living under the same autopilot regimen and their hearts broke for them. Where were the laughs? The funny mishaps? The enthusiasm? Even an angry outburst would have seemed more normal than the sterility they witnessed. Most certainly, they had no desire to subject their own children to the same environment. "I feel like nothing I do is right, and nothing my kids do is right," said the other daughter. "We're walking on eggshells the whole time we're there. It's just better not to call. It's better not to come. I love you, Mommy, and I realize that in your own way, you've done everything you know how to do for us. And that's why I can't be too close. Because the closer I am, the more opportunity I have for getting upset. I'd rather keep my distance and think that, at least in theory, I know my mother loves me."

Leora was startled by her daughters' revelations. After a few starts at answering them, she fell speechless. Yet she still maintained her guard.

We needed to find the source of Leora's emotional numbness, and so, during our fourth session, we began an exploration into her subconscious and the experiences that formed it. Her earliest memories were of an impoverished childhood in Israel. She remembered being hungry and wearing shoes that pinched her feet. Her father worked hard all day and came home tired. Her mother struggled with the challenges of raising a large family. Leora, the eldest child, worked almost as hard as her mother. Despite all the difficulties, however, there was a sense of stability in those years. This was destroyed when her parents decided to move the family to America in search of a better livelihood.

Leora was 16 when her family arrived in the United States. Her mother failed to make the adjustment and gradually withdrew into herself. Leora took over. She did the shopping and handled all the interactions with the outside world. She dealt with her siblings' schools and homework. She opened the mail and paid the bills. She went to school, but was often absent. The language barrier made friendships difficult; she could not express herself fully and her classmates had no reservations about imitating her accent and affirming her sense of herself as an outsider. She had no common frame of reference with a group of America teens, either, having grown up completely removed from their culture. She was a perpetual foreigner.

"What could I do?" she recalled. "If I stopped to think about my life, I would fall apart. And then who would take care of my family? And who could I talk to anyway? My parents had enough problems and enough guilt. My father never made a living even in America. They worked so hard and had so many worries. So I let them think that everything was great for me. It didn't matter that I was lonely. Things had to get done and I did them."

As she spoke, tears began to fill her eyes. She was overcome with pity for the poor young girl she portrayed — the girl she had been — struggling so hard to be strong and brave, pretending not to mind her social isolation, keeping all her fears and pain buried under a veneer of amazing efficiency. The image of that sad, brave, lonely girl broke through Leora's emotional barriers and released her long-silenced cry. For about 20 minutes, she could barely speak through her weeping.

At the same time, she realized that she harbored a deep sadness over her "lost" childhood. "All my parents thought about was where they could make some money," she said. "They didn't think about what it would mean to rip us away from our friends and settle us somewhere where we would feel like strangers. Especially me, at 16. What an age to move a child! And it didn't even help. I'm sorry to say it, but my father just didn't have any *mazal* with money, not in Israel and not in America. Why didn't they think? Why didn't they look at the whole picture and realize how hard it was going to be?"

By the end of this session, Leora's emotional anesthetic had worn off. Unfortunately, however, that meant that she was now in pain. She fell into a depression over the next few weeks as she dealt with the issues and feelings she had managed to suppress for 35 years. Often, in the initial stages of therapy, people feel that they're "getting worse instead of better" because they are finally confronting painful, buried emotions and experiences. However, the therapist's role is not only to unearth these feelings, but to help the person process them and lay them aside. Until that happens, the buried feelings will continue to exert a negative influence on the person's life.

With Leora, on the practical level, we began working on her belief that she had to carry the world on her shoulders: a feeling that was coupled with resentment that no one ever seemed to want to share her burdens. She needed to prove to herself that she no longer had to do it all alone.

Using the keys in Chapter 10 (Unlock Your Influence),[9] I tried to help Leora see her role in the family as a leader. By encouraging the family members to take responsibility for the household's well-being, she would be able to build a far-stronger and functional home than she could ever build doing everything herself. More importantly, she could build up the members of the family, helping them discover their strengths rather than focusing in on their weaknesses. She should and could ask family members to help out. However, to be able to do so freely, she had to instill in herself the belief that asking for help was not a sign of weakness on her part. Rather, it was a sign of capable management.

---

9. In this chapter, we explore ways to move into a leadership role in life, organizing and energizing others to contribute their best to a worthy endeavor. Thus our impact can extend beyond our own personal abilities.

She began to get her children to take over some of the household responsibilities, using praise and encouragement to gain
their cooperation. She voiced a long-held desire to her husband
that he take time each night to learn with their sons, which he
gladly agreed to do. Another important part of this equation
was for Leora to learn how to assert her needs when help was
not as forthcoming as she would like. Previously, she took a
sigh or a complaint as a personal affront. Rather than persist,
she would shut down, thinking, *You see? I have to do everything myself. No one cares.* We worked on a more productive
response: pleasant, firm and insistent.

As Leora's emotions became more manageable, we began
exploring more of the natures she had been keeping under
lock and key. Using Chapter 6 (Unlock Your Natures), she took
inventory of her strengths. She discovered that she loved music
and gave herself time to listen and enjoy it. She also realized
that despite so many years of thinking of herself as asocial, she
needed and loved the company of others. She began lingering
longer after shul on Shabbos, chatting with the other women
and sharing more of her life with them. In addition, we used
the keys in Chapter 7 (Unlock Your Support) to help Leora let
go of her demand for total self-sufficiency. We decided that, as
an exercise, she would ask one neighbor for some advice. She
asked a woman known for her challah to give her the recipe. It
was simple act, but it enabled Leora to experience the feeling of
asking for and accepting advice.

The most important change, however, was in Leora's home.
She was well aware, from her daughters' revelations, that there
was a great deal of repair needed. We worked on the keys of
Chapter 2 (Unlock Self-Acceptance) to free Leora from her need
for perfection. She saw for herself how letting go of this demand
drastically reduced her level of tension and nearly eliminated the
constant criticism that had been driving her children away. The
house became a nice place to be. The children's friends began

coming over and the sterile atmosphere was replaced with noise and life.

As the barriers began to fall, Leora became more open with her family. We coined a motto: "Emotions are meant to flow." To keep her in touch with her feelings, she began keeping a journal in which she recorded each day's emotional ups and downs. She no longer feared that her children would see her as weak if she admitted to insecurity or worry. The open lines of communication were especially important to her married daughters. Now when Leora speaks to them on the phone, they speak as friends. When they come to visit, the atmosphere is relaxed. Leora has loosened her grip and learned to step back and let things unfold. Often, she recognizes that something she would have found irritating and worthy of rebuke resolves itself without her input: The toys *do* get put away. The children *do* manage to eat a nourishing meal.

Leora's life has been renewed. Although she still needs time to heal completely from her grief over her lost teen years, her Inspiration level is now at about 7. She feels the love of her husband and family as well as a far-greater connectedness with her friends. Even on the spiritual level, her dutiful rote performance of davening and Shabbos observance has begun to transform into something more meaningful.

Her Logic has improved because she has opened herself up to ideas that she formerly shut out. She is no longer afraid to learn and change. She has learned how to communicate with others in ways that are not accusatory, and she has learned to focus on the strengths and positive qualities of her children. Logic is now at 9.

In the realm of Action, Leora's strength has become much stronger. Instead of fruitlessly expending her efforts on chasing perfection, she focuses productively on building her home and family. She teaches, delegates, influences and encourages rather doing everything herself and criticizing others. Because she achieves real emotional satisfaction from her life, she is able to do more. For example, rather than waiting to be drafted, she volunteered to provide meals for a local family whose mother was ill. Her Action rating is now a 9.

Today, Leora's ILA rating is 7x9x9=567, up from 27. She described her transformation at our last session: "I feel like I came out of a coma that I've been in my whole life."

HOW TO USE THIS BOOK

Perhaps you've read this book from cover to cover. If you're like most people, however, you scanned the table of contents and zeroed in on the issues that hit a personal chord. *That's me!* or *That's my husband/wife/child/parent (fill in the blank),* you said to yourself as you flipped to the chapter and read all about it. Then perhaps you checked out another chapter and a few more after that. Reading through the case studies, you got a chance to see how the principles laid out in the chapters express themselves in real life.

My hope is that what you've read has brought you a new level of awareness and clarity about your life, your potential and the factors that may be holding you back from living your life to its fullest. But then what?

Between awareness and action is a chasm about the size of the Grand Canyon. For me as a therapist, however, there is very little satisfaction in naming a problem unless that leads to solving the problem. I'm not here to tell people what's wrong with their lives; I'm here to help them identify and use the assets they already have, or can readily attain, to fix what's wrong. The purpose of this book is to help each reader map out his own path to his own personal greatness.

This is a path that must be walked one step at a time. Think about the chapters you have read and identify the one that resonated most for you. Re-read it, trying to identify how your thoughts and habits fit into the "lock." Are you approaching your family life, relationships, job or learning endeavors undermined by this lock? How does that play out in your life? What is the personal cost to you of living with this lock? Once you have identified the specifics, you will be able to envision the opposite: a life free of this lock. For instance, if you often feel insecure at work because you fear asking for advice and guidance (Chapter 10), imagine how you would feel if you formed a mentor relationship with someone. Not only would work become more satisfying, but you would have more energy and enthusiasm for other parts of your life as well, because the drain of constant insecurity would finally be plugged. Thus, the first step to using this book is to go back to the chapters that speak to you and make them personal.

The second step is to rate yourself on the ILA scale in the particular area you want to change. How productive and helpful is your subconscious thinking? How about your ideas and knowledge in this area? Are your actions on par with your potential? You may find that you are doing exactly what you should, but feeling uninspired about it. In this case, you should concentrate on the "inspiration" keys. On the other hand, you might be motivated, inspired and burning to improve, but you lack the tools and knowledge. In that case, the "logic" keys would be most helpful. If you are someone who wants to change, knows how to change but just can't get yourself to move out of your comfort zone, then the "action" keys would be the place to apply your effort.

The third step is to take the leap across the Grand Canyon. However, it isn't such a drastic leap at all. Just start doing one of the 10 steps. Do it fully, without shortcuts, because shortcuts simply will not work when your purpose is nothing less than rewiring your mind, revising your thoughts and retraining your actions. Change works slowly, through constant repetition and reinforcement, which is what these keys are meant to provide.

Each of these keys should be taken on individually. Focus on one key for a week to 10 days, until you feel that it has been integrated into your thinking, and then move onto the next one. Make it part of your daily routine; set aside a time to work on it. If you have difficulty mastering one key, or find yourself slipping back into old habits, go back to that key and give it another week. Some of the keys are ongoing in nature, and those should be done on an ongoing basis.

Furthermore, as we have learned, a person's subconscious, his mind and his behavior all play interdependent roles in the process of change. Each reinforces the other and none can accomplish the job all alone, at least not for the long run. Even if you rate yourself as a perfect 10 on one of the ILA factors, spend some time on the keys that pertain to your strong point as well. You may find that, having improved in your areas of weakness, you can push yourself beyond your former level even in your areas of strength.

My final piece of advice in using this book is to be patient with yourself. Performing our life's mission is by definition a lifelong task. Every day we are alive is a day Hashem has given us to use for growth and accomplishment. That means there's always more we can do and further we can go. In our lives in this world, we never reach the finish line where the race is over and we can throw up our arms in triumph. My hope is that through this book, you, my readers, will discover the strength to run your best race and the illumination to see that it is a wonder, a privilege and a joy just to be able to run.

Appendix

Appendix
Chapter One

Meet Your Brain

THE NEWLYWED HUSBAND COMES HOME FRIDAY *afternoon with a large bouquet of flowers for his wife. Her heart melts: He's so considerate. He only wants to make me happy. "Thanks," she says with a sweet smile. "They're beautiful! It's so thoughtful of you!"*

"Oh, I'm glad you like them," he smiles back. "I guess my chassan teacher taught me right!"

Instantly, the young wife's euphoric bubble loses air. Her dear chassan was basically following instructions. Not bad, but not as wonderful in her eyes as a thoughtful gesture hatched in his own heart.

What we feel, what we think, what we do: Which are we? There are spiritual answers to those questions and psychological answers as well. In recent years, the far greater understanding of the workings of the brain has cast a bright light on this question from the biological perspective, and some of that understanding can be gleaned from the short tale above.

In the opening story, we witness the collision of the two major forces ruling the brain: the right side of the brain, which is the seat of our emotions, and the left side of the brain, which generates our logical thinking. When the husband buys his wife flowers, it seems as if he is showing how he feels. The wife responds to his display of emotion with emotion of her own. When she discovers that it was her husband's intelligence and logic — his adherence to the concepts he learned in his *chassan shiur* — that motivated him, she is disappointed. From his logical perspective, he doesn't understand her disappointment. What's wrong with doing what you're supposed to do? Isn't that good?

Now, if the wife's logical side were the stronger force in her mental make-up, she might have been thrilled to hear his response. What a *talmid chacham*! What a *ben Torah*! Conversely, if the husband's emotional side had been a little stronger, he might have realized that, even if he was only following instructions, his wife would feel more cherished if he allowed her to think that the gift was a spontaneous expression of his affection.

In this brief scenario, we see the operation of the two sides of our brain as each does its distinct task. Because these two sides see reality from completely different perspectives, we have the capacity to think one thing and to feel another. We reach our maximum potential when the two sides work together in a positive direction. Our emotions are what make us feel alive. They fire our imagination, sparking us to imagine what could be and to go after it. To be driven by positive emotional energy is to live with inspiration and zest. Yet none of that inspiration would result in success without the participation of our logical side. That is what harnesses our raw inspiration and channels it into productive activity. Logic provides a plan, an organized approach to our goals, the ability to analyze situations and perceive our reality. It is the part of us that fuels essential elements of achievement such as timing and consistency and reliability.

With both sides working together in a positive direction, we have it all: the passion for life and the tools to achieve. However, a great deal of human grief arises from situations that pit those two sides against each other. When negative emotions undermine what our logic tells us, we might experience feelings that are not grounded in reality. For instance, we may feel that we are failures even when we have a long list of achievements to our credit:

"I'm a loser," a boy tells his mother.

"What are you talking about? You're at the top of your class!" his mother responds.

"Sure, but that's just because it's easy. As soon as it gets harder, the rebbi will see what a loser I am."

On the other hand, when logic dominates, we might draw conclusions that are at odds with our feelings.

"My job is so boring," a young woman tells her friend. "I have such a headache by the end of the day. I really don't like working on a computer."

"So why don't you help your sister with her playgroup?" her friend suggests. "You love kids. You'd probably enjoy doing that."

"It's got no future," the girl replies. "All the good jobs now involve computers. If I want to get ahead, I have to stay with this job."

Sometimes, the fight between thoughts and feelings results in a gridlock that stops us from accomplishing that which we have the potential to accomplish. Or, we might go forward anyway, but with nagging doubts and guilt that rob us of success in our endeavors and joy in the process.

Bringing these two sides of our brain to the negotiating table, on the other hand, produces a life of personal satisfaction filled with the power to achieve. When emotion and logic work together, we can tap into the planning and the follow-through necessary to turn inspiration into action, and we can draw from our emotions the fire to keep renewing and expanding our horizons. Since the right and left sides of the brain are the two primary actors in the drama of our thinking process, we are well served by getting to know each of them and their functions.

Limbic System: The "Heart" of Your Mind

Scientists have long known that the right side of the brain controls the left side of the body. What was not known until the 1960s is that the right side of the brain also plays a more dominant role in a person's emotions and creativity. The common conception that "lefties" are more creative is based on this bit of scientific fact.

In the 1990s, researchers developed the ability to actually watch the brain's activity as it occurs in real time, through a process called the FMRI (functional magnetic resonance imaging). With this technique, researchers can observe which parts of the brain are activated by various stimuli. They can actually see what "lights up" when someone experiences a pleasant thought, does a math problem, hears music, has a fearful thought and so forth. This has given us a far more detailed understanding of a "day in the life" of the human brain.

Another Layer

While the description of the brain as it is divided between right and left brain activity gives us a good foundation for understanding how our minds work, it is not a complete picture. The FMRI reveals the interplay between the three layers of the brain. For the sake of a more complete picture, we will briefly describe these layers and their functions:

The Brain Core: This is the on-board computer for our body's automatic functions. It enables our hearts to beat, lungs to expand and contract, eyes to blink, glands to release their enzymes and hormones and innumerable other life-sustaining functions to occur without our conscious input or knowledge.

The Limbic System: This controls our emotional reactions and provides motivation to turn our thoughts into actions. This is where our gut reactions and instincts are formed. It is also the home of the mysterious and powerful subconscious. The limbic system does not operate completely free of our input as the core does, but its perceptions often seem to just rise up on their own, whether or not we want and approve of them.

The Cerebral Cortex: Our highest level of thinking and emotional awareness lies in this third brain layer. When we "use our heads," this is usually the part of the brain we are calling upon. Most of our conscious thinking goes on in the cerebral cortex. It enables us to learn and to make connections between the disparate things we learn, thereby giving us the capacity to reason, make decisions and develop new ideas based on our knowledge.

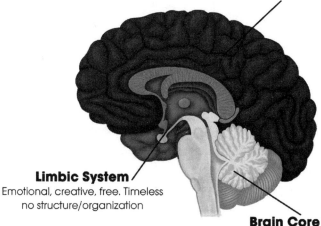

Cerebral Cortex
Time oriented. Logic. Organized. Grounded, Emotionless

Limbic System
Emotional, creative, free. Timeless no structure/organization

Brain Core
Automatic body functions, heart beat, lungs expanding and contracting, eyes blinking

Obviously, the brain is much, much more than this quick landscape we have sketched in the paragraphs above. But we can think of this landscape as a reconnaissance map of the terrain on which many people's personal battles are fought. In our quest for emotional health, spiritual growth and personal achievement, we must constantly make choices between the conflicting demands of our feelings, thoughts and actions. Understanding the layout of the brain tells us where the resistance lies, what the obstacles are and what we need to overcome in order to emerge triumphant.

The limbic system operates according to its own set of rules, and those rules are counterbalanced by the cerebral cortex's opposite approach. The first rule is that, for the limbic system, time does not exist. That might seem to be an overstatement, but most people have experienced this magical power firsthand. Artists, athletes, scholars, craftsmen — anyone who has the ability to become absorbed in his work — sometimes speak about being "in the zone," meaning they've become so emotionally engaged in their activity that they have lost track of time. However, time can disappear even in the course of ordinary activities such as having an interesting conversation or reading a good book. The right side of the brain dominates the person's awareness in these situations, so that time slips by unnoticed. Only when the left side — the side that keeps the clock — reasserts itself, do we suddenly realize just how much time has elapsed.

This trait of the limbic system packs a far-more-powerful impact than its propensity for making us late for the dentist. If time does not exist for our emotional mind, then things that happened to us in the past are, in some sense, still happening. That is why someone can meet a person who hurt his feelings 20 years earlier, and still feel raw anger. The emotional mind does not say, *That was years ago! He's changed! You've changed!* It simply registers the hurt. If that hurt is not somehow processed and disposed of, it remains intact, dormant, like a spore that is ready to sprout into a full-grown mushroom where the rain hits it.

The limbic system keeps feelings fresh and ready. It keeps the subconscious fully stocked with all the praise, love, pride, friendship and happiness — as well as the hurt, sadness, guilt, anger, criticism, bullying and disrespect — that a person has absorbed over the years. This explains why people seem to overreact to conflict and criticism. New challenges to their self-image are the "rain" that makes the old grievances sprout. People who are undone by some negative turn of events are often not reacting to the present challenge, but are feeling in real time all the shame, guilt and inadequacy stored up and kept fresh in the timeless right brain, just waiting for some stress or challenge to thrust it into the open. Thus, someone who appears calm and confident on the outside can sometimes fall apart when faced with what seems to be a perfectly manageable challenge.

Avraham was the fourth child in a family of geniuses. His three older brothers were the jewels of their elementary school: exemplary students whose names were always on the top of every "star chart" and contest. For Avraham, however, school was a constant struggle to sit still and pay attention. He would look out the window with the longing of a prisoner dreaming of freedom; he missed most of what his teachers were saying and earned a reputation as a "space cadet."

"You'll see," his parents told him. "You're going to be a big success some day. Not everyone is cut out for sitting in a classroom, but you've got lots of energy and you're a smart guy, and some day you'll be able to do something great with it."

Indeed, despite an abysmal academic record and an early departure from yeshivah after 10th grade, Avraham did make it big. He learned to bake and started a small bakery business in his home. Eventually, he expanded, opened branches in several neighborhoods and began commercial production for supermarkets. He was the "go-to guy" for many charities and a respected member of his community.

One day, Avraham's distribution manager came to his office. "Avi," he said, "I just got these new rules for trucking our refrigerated cakes. There's this whole new Department of Health policy that's going to cost us a bundle. Do you want me to read it through and figure out what we need to do?"

"No, no, give it to me. I want to look it over myself," Avraham said.

"Are you sure? It's a monster. It's got a lot of details and numbers," the manager replied.

"So what? Am I an idiot? You think I can't understand numbers? I run a business!" Avraham replied irritably.

The manager made a quick exit, but Avraham's heart was still thumping hard. "I'm not stupid," he muttered to himself. "Everyone thinks I got to this point by accident."

There's little doubt that, had Avraham not grown up feeling like the intellectual inferior of his brothers, he would not have taken offense at the manager's offer to do the detail work. He would probably have been grateful to be relieved of the tedious job of wading through new regulations. Instead, the slightest intimation that Avraham needed help understanding the rules was just enough "rain" to sprout the dormant message of "I'm stupid." Confident, competent, accomplished and admired, Avraham's right brain kept the feelings of a foundering schoolchild fresh and ready.

The second characteristic of the limbic system is that it is content with "fuzzy math." It does not need to know exactly how much is in the bank account. It is the part of the brain that lets a person say, "We'll find the money," for the child who needs tutoring or the friend who needs a loan, even though the numbers don't add up. Many a charitable organization is founded on right-brained mathematics by people who are comfortable saying, "We'll do what needs to be done and then figure out how to pay for it."

This disregard for exactitude extends to other areas as well. The rules are not necessarily the defining factor of any situation. The limbic system has no problem cutting corners if there is an emotionally valid reason for doing so. It urges us to write our own rules or does without rules altogether in order to do what we feel is good and necessary. The limbic system not only thinks "out of the box," but it actually fails to see the box.

The third defining trait of the limbic system is that emotion is its ruling principle. Things have to "feel right" to meet the limbic system's approval. For instance, a person can rush to arrive on time for *tefillah,* say every word and perform every aspect of his prayers to perfection, but if his heart was not moved as he prayed, his right brain will perceive it as a failure. The limbic system seeks connection and emotional engagement above all else.

Shlomo arrives in Jerusalem his heart brimming with good intentions. He's leaving his lackluster past behind. No more skipping out of yeshivah. No more sleeping through minyan. No more staying out late with friends. This is his chance, a golden chance his parents have given him to start fresh in a new environment, and he is determined to make the most of it. He will become not just a "solid guy," but someone his friends will describe as "amazing" and "awesome."

He decides to start the new era in his life by davening at a sunrise minyan every morning. Three days into his new routine, he is revved up like a fabulous race car, flying through the day on no sleep and little food. "This must be how the tzaddikim feel," he tells himself. His parents are worried, though, that their race car will soon run out of gas.

Indeed, one morning after three weeks of unabated intensity, Shlomo oversleeps. A few days later, it happens again. He has disappointed himself, and begins to fear that he is slipping into old habits. "It's no use trying!" he tells his parents. "Who am I fooling? I know who I am."

Shlomo's predicament has been sponsored by the limbic system. It is the result of following his inspiration/emotions to the edge of the cliff, eschewing all the useful input his more logical side might have contributed. While he clearly perceived his emotional longing to become a greater and more spiritual person, he did not hear the muted sound of his logical voice yelling, "Be reasonable!"

Nevertheless, without the limbic system, Shlomo may never have even tried to make a new start in life. If he would have relied solely on logic, he would have said, "It's too hard for me. I've been in yeshivah for 14 years and I'm still not getting anywhere. It's time to try something else." Logically, he would have been right. Emotion has the power to push us over the hump, past our limitations and into new territory.

Even someone who is functioning well in life needs the spark that emotion provides. An "A" student is not happy if his success comes from dogged determination alone. If the process of learning does not nourish his heart, his success in learning does not fulfill him. Similarly, a woman can run a perfect home and raise perfectly groomed and behaved children, but if her daily routine leaves her feeling bored and empty inside, she does not feel successful on a deep level. Emotion can change the outward success of someone who is "doing well" into the inner success of someone who is truly happy.

Obviously, a person operating with only the right side of his brain will not succeed in living a balanced, successful life. The right side is like a charge of electricity; it is useless unless it is channeled into some kind of productive machinery. On the other hand, without an electric charge, the machinery, no matter how well designed, will sit dead and useless. The left side of the brain — the intellect, logic and rules — is essential to give limbic system's emotional charge a useful purpose.

The Cerebral Cortex: Your Thinking Mind

"Help!" screams the young mother into the phone. "My son rode his bike into a tree and there's blood everywhere!"

The ambulance arrives in moments. The EMTs run to where the boy is lying. His mother is sitting helplessly by her child's side, trying to soothe his hysterical crying.

"Oh, no! This is horrible! Look at all this blood! This poor child!" the EMT thinks, his pale face beaded with sweat. "What are we going to do?"

There are times for emotion, and there are times to shut down that sector of our minds and proceed with cool logic. If we were not able to do that, we would be unable to deal with situations such as the one above. The EMT does not have the luxury of reacting to the emergency emotionally. He must put his feelings aside and swing into action, doing what he has been trained to do. Just as there are provinces in which the right side of the brain should reign, such as in giving flowers to one's wife, there are provinces in which the left side must rule.

The cerebral cortex of the brain is the counterbalance to the perceptions of the limbic system. As mentioned earlier, it is the cerebral cortex that gives us a sense of time. It is the sense that interrupts us in the middle of an engrossing conversation and makes us jump up and say, "Oh, boy! I better get moving! I have an appointment in 15 minutes!" It urges us to care about punctuality and precision. Because of the cerebral cortex's influence, we do not bring in Shabbos at "about" the right time or end it when it's "probably over." A sincerely Shabbos-observant Jew will not be satisfied until he learns the exact times, down to the minute.

Logic also emanates from the cerebral cortex. In the story of Shlomo above, the cerebral cortex's contribution could have been just what the young man needed to make good on his new commitments. His logic would have told him, *You need to get enough sleep and make sure you eat. If you get run down, you'll fall apart. Better to run at 60 miles per hour for the entire z'man than 120 miles per hour for three weeks.* The cerebral cortex logic also informs us that we cannot spend

$1,000 if we earn $500. It sees things as they are, not as we wish things could be.

Because of the cerebral cortex, the EMT can be faced with a horrific accident scene and function efficiently. The doctor can lose a patient and, although he will no doubt feel a certain amount of sadness and regret, he will be able to go back to work the next day and continue treating people. His logic tells him that he did everything he could do to help, and that the world will benefit more by his continuing to practice his skill than his sinking into sadness and guilt.

Now that we have the map, let's move forward!

Appendix

Chapter Two

Under the Radar

Your Subconscious Mind

ARI COMMUTES FROM LAKEWOOD TO BROOKLYN. IT'S *an hour-and-a-half ride, and he's been driving the route every morning from Monday to Friday for the past 12 years. One Sunday afternoon, he and his wife get into their car to go out to dinner in a town about a half-hour away. They are enjoying their little getaway, talking to each other and listening to music as they speed along. Suddenly, the wife looks out the car window and notices the road signs.*

"Ari, where are we going?" she asks.

Ari looks around. "We're halfway to Brooklyn," he says. "I'm on autopilot!"

How did Ari safely drive about 40 miles without any real awareness of where he was going or what he was doing? He simply turned the matter over to the part of his brain that is always on duty and ever-eager to run the show: his subconscious. The power of the subconscious to influence our thoughts and actions is so real and pervasive that an entire multibillion-dollar industry — advertising and marketing — is based on it. These marketers know that our subconscious can lead us to buy something we really don't need and never knew we wanted, just because it has been stocked at eye level on the supermarket shelf. The subconscious can make us buy bottled water with suggestions that we will thus become slim and athletic, or a new snack food with the promise of novelty and delight. The fact that our subconscious exists and exerts a powerful, almost irresistible influence on our behavior is confirmed by the fortunes invested in tapping into it.

Is My Subconscious Blocking My Success?

What the subconscious does to our buying habits is only a hint of what the subconscious can do to, or for, our lives. Just as it can commandeer our wallets, it can commandeer our lives, steering us toward victory or, if the messages it creates are negative, miring us in a painful rut.

It is the habitat of our elusive bad and good inclinations — our *yetzer hara* and our *yetzer tov* — which challenge us minute by minute to make positive choices that elevate our souls and satisfy our hearts. If we wish to weaken the hold of our *yetzer hara* and fortify our *yetzer tov,* the subconscious is the part of our minds we need to access. To see where your subconscious is leading you, ask yourself the following questions:

1. Do I say that tomorrow will be different from today, but it never is?

2. Do I diet and lose weight, only to regain it three months later?

3. Do I feel that I am not really the success people think I am?

4. Am I afraid of taking on a role I know I can perform well, such as leading prayer services or organizing an event?

5. Do I distrust others for no logical reason?

6. Do I commit myself to remaining calm in a tense situation, and even prepare myself with tools and ideas to keep myself calm, only to explode when the situation arises?

7. Am I anxious about something that is years away?

8. Does the very thought of a certain person, even when he or she is not in contact with me, arouse my anger?

9. Have I tried several businesses and failed at them for no logical reason?

10. Do I feel that I have no real friends?

11. Do I tend to interpret most things that happen and things people say in a negative way?

12. Do I carry around an underlying feeling of guilt?

If you've answered yes to some of these questions, you are experiencing the power of the subconscious to defy your goals, logic and best efforts to succeed. But if you can imagine being a person who answers "no" to all those questions, you can envision the life that is possible when our subconscious does not defy us, but instead fuels us with positive energy to strive, grow and reach our potential.

The Inner Workings

The subconscious by definition operates "under the radar." We are not aware of what messages it absorbs from our surroundings or what messages it passes along to our conscious minds. It is a stealth program that influences our thoughts and behavior without leaving fingerprints. Our subconscious can be our lead cheerleader, telling us, *I'm a success, People like me, I can bounce back from this setback, People are generally good.* Positive subconscious messages keep us from quitting when we need to persist, and keep us afloat even when circumstances turn against us. On the other side, if we are finding ourselves boggled by problems that won't go away, we can detect the subconscious there as well. We may only discover its activities when we set out to unravel the confusing, counterproductive ideas that it manages to insert into our thought process.

"My wife doesn't really love me," Chaim tells his therapist.

"I don't know why he says that," says Miriam, his wife. "I try so hard to show him that I love him. I got up at 5:30 in the morning yesterday to bake him a cake for his birthday! Every day, I send him an email at work...just a little 'Hi, I hope you're having a good day.' And besides all that, I really do love him. But no matter what I do or say, if I look at him the wrong way, if I'm a little tired or irritated, he's all insulted. I can't win!"

"I can tell she's sick of me," Chaim says. "She can't cover it up with cakes and emails. I see it on her face."

With a negative program, a person can interpret even patently positive input as negative. On the other hand, a positive program can reframe what objectively appear to be failures into positive experiences.

As Dov opened the New Jersey Bar Exam webpage, he felt as though his stomach were rising up into his throat. He thought for a few long moments. "Maybe I passed it and maybe I didn't," he told himself. "I have to be prepared for either. If I didn't, then I didn't. I'll be able to stay in yeshivah for a little longer and I'll try again. But if I did! Wow! All our financial troubles would be over! Rachel wouldn't have to work so hard! We could pay our tuitions without a strain! O.K., I better not get carried away. Let's see."

He scanned the list of passing test-takers, listed according to their official number. Dov's was 3828. Scrolling down into his range, he saw 3826, and then 3830. He closed the program and opened it again; nothing changed. His heart dropped like a stone into a deep well. For the first time he could remember in many years, he felt like crying.

"All right," he said to himself. "It is what it is. I knew I needed more practice writing those essays. I'm going to put this whole thing out of my head for a week, and then sign up for the essay-writing course. I know I can pass. I'm going to pass.

"But poor Rachel, she'll be so disappointed. On the other hand, she always comes through for me. I'm sure she will this time too. O.K., we get to spend another few months as a kollel couple."

When Dov broke the disappointing news to Rachel, he was straightforward and honest. He shared her frustration at the setback in their efforts to move forward financially. After a serious discussion about how to deal with the new situation, Dov told his wife, "I knew you'd be there for me." He had work to do, but he knew he could do it, and more than ever, he knew he had a loving, supportive partner in life.

In the situations above, we learn a vital fact about the subconscious; it is preprogrammed. It reacts to the world based on the program installed in it by a person's early and ongoing experiences. This program is hardwired into us as immutably as the program that operates our telephone. If we pick up the telephone and press the number 1, the phone will register the number one. No amount of advising, pleading, shouting or urging the phone to register "2" will cause it to do so as long as we are still pressing "1." In the same way, we cannot change a person's subconscious program by telling him that it should change, must change, ought to change and it would make him so much happier if it did indeed change. Logic does not work on the subconscious.

To make the phone register "2" when we press "1," we would have to go into the circuitry and rewire it. In the same way, to alter the program operating our subconscious, we must get inside and reconstruct. While a logical argument might be quite effective in altering our ideas about ourselves and the world around us, the subconscious simply cannot be reprogrammed that way. Furthermore, even after we talk things out and fully adopt a new logical construct, if the subconscious is still churning out its old message, we will find that our new improved thoughts cannot penetrate deep enough into our mind to change the way we feel.

Nevertheless, our obligations as Jews and as human beings do not disappear simply because we carry around a negative subconscious program. Our task as Jews is to do what we must and treat others as we must, even when we are not feeling the desire to do so. The Torah tells that we have a choice (*Devarim* 30:19), and we do. However, when we work to repair the negative messages embedded in our subconscious minds, we energize our obligations, and our lives, with the priceless fuel of joy.

Who Writes the Program?

Our subconscious selves are programmed by the experiences of childhood, which create our idea of who we are and what the world is like. A child who generally feels support and love, whose world is secure and whose needs are met, carries into adulthood a subconscious belief that he is worthy of love and capable of success. If he has a setback, he sees it as something gone temporarily awry in an otherwise good world. If someone treats him unfairly, he can weather the storm.

Unfortunately, however, many people travel through life carrying a subconscious program that endlessly repeats negative messages. *You're stupid. You're lazy. You're a procrastinator.*

You're always late. You can't remember anything. You're disorganized. You're socially awkward. You're a failure and you'll never succeed.

The messages, whether positive or negative, are the seeds from which our subconscious self-image sprouts. They are planted deep within our minds, where they put down sturdy roots that keep them firmly in place. The messages that are repeated to us throughout our lives reinforce the seeds; they are like the water and fertilizer that keep them growing and spreading. Someone whose subconscious is planted with healthy seeds and nurtured with healthy input grows a vigorous and productive self-image. On the other hand, someone whose subconscious is planted with weeds and nurtured with a flow of negative messages eventually loses his self-worth in a field overgrown with those weeds.

Positive

Inspiration

I am happy
I am excited
I am a winner
I am calm
I feel peace

Logic

Life fascinates me
I can learn new information
I have so many friends
I usually succeed
People are really nice

Self talk

Keeps everything consistant

I just do what I need to
I remain consistent in my tasks
I get up easily
When it gets tough I continue moving

Action

In the case of the "unloved" husband, Chaim, his subconscious program taints the way he perceives his wife's very clear expressions of love and care. He feels unlovable, and therefore he disbelieves the loving message expressed by her birthday cake and daily emails. She is "watering" his emotions with positive messages, but it cannot bring a seed that has not been planted to sprout. Instead of absorbing her messages of love, he locks into the occasional tired or irritated look on her face and takes that as the indication of her true feelings. She could list a thousand ways that she shows her love for him, but nothing on that list could reach into his subconscious program and change it. Logic and reason are simply not the tools for altering the subconscious.

In the case of would-be lawyer Dov, we see the opposite. He has suffered a major disappointment and he knows that his wife will be disappointed too. Their plans for the future will be put on hold; their hopes for relief from financial strain are now in doubt. However, Dov's program is a positive one, and therefore, although he reacts with disappointment, he does not despair. He expects his wife's continued love because he knows he is lovable. He believes that he can succeed if he tries again, and he makes a plan of action to avoid the mistake that caused him to fail. He accepts the situation and looks for the lessons and benefits it can provide.

Going one step deeper with this theory, one of the main foundations in psychology is that we recreate the world of our subconscious over and over again throughout our lives, unless and until we heal the pain. This idea is found in many classic therapeutic methods, including the classic therapeutic psychodynamic and Rogerian theories, but it is found first in Gemara with the concept, *"Kal d'pasul b'mumo pasul"* — whoever declares something unfit does so [from the perspective of] his own blemish (*Kiddushin* 70a).

Along these lines projection means that someone who grows up feeling, for instance, that his needs are never met, will always perceive others as selfish people who would rather do anything but take care of him. He will feel he has to scratch and claw to get what he needs. Someone who grows up with a great sense of financial insecurity will never feel comfortable that he has enough. Someone who grows up in a volatile household might fear any kind of conflict because in his program, conflict leads to explosive anger. These "programs" play out in a thousand ways in our lives. Here's how it works for Mordy, a man whose subconscious theme is, *The only one who really cares about me is me.*

Mordy wakes up exhausted. His wife was up with the baby half the night, and of course, the crying kept him up as well. Now he is running five minutes late and he has to get to minyan. Just as he is about to walk out the door, the baby starts to cry again.

"Mordy, could you make him a quick bottle before you leave?" his wife calls from her bed. "I'm wiped out."

He doubles back to the kitchen thinking, "Proof again that no one really cares about me." As he makes the bottle, he silently builds his case in his mind. "She's wiped out? What about me? I have to run out to minyan and spend a whole day at work. When do I get to sleep in? I work hard to give her money, and instead of getting up and making me a cup of coffee, she makes me late for minyan." These thoughts bring his emotional temperature to a near-boil. He slams the bottle down on the kitchen table and yells, "I'm running late. I have to get to minyan and get out of there in time for a meeting. Why don't you take care of the baby? You don't have anything else you have to do all day!"

Those words cut straight through her half-asleep fog. "What are you talking about? Do you have any idea what I do all day? Of course you don't because you're never here! You'd rather be anywhere than here with me and the kids!"

A 10-minute-long nuclear war breaks out. Finally Mordy

flies out the door and rolls into shul. The prayer leader has started a few minutes early, and Mordy has missed a significant juncture in the prayers. "He knows he's not supposed to start before 7!" Mordy grumbles. "What does he care about everyone else? He just does what he wants."

On the way to his meeting, someone cuts him off in traffic. Mordy slams down on the horn and holds it while he maneuvers along 10 city blocks to cut off the driver who cut him off. "He's not getting away with this," Mordy tells himself. "He could've caused an accident!"

All day, every day, Mordy's life follows the same pattern. Somehow there's always action, always outrage around him. People are trying to cut in front of him or take advantage of him. No one cares about him or values him. This is the story he carries inside him, and it plays out wherever he goes.

Now let's imagine an alternative Mordy, a man whose subconscious program is positive and peaceful. His wife asks him to make the baby a bottle. He takes two minutes and makes it, leaves it on the table and tells her, "I've got to get to shul now. Sorry you had such a bad night. I hope you get to catch up on your sleep later. Have a good day." Without the fight, he gets to shul on time. Even if he doesn't, he will not look at the prayer leader as a selfish, heedless criminal. He will think, *Maybe the clock here is fast.* Or, *Maybe he has to leave early.* On the road, someone cuts him off. He thinks, *Crazy! Good, let him go ahead of me instead of driving on my bumper.* Rather than madly maneuvering to pass him for 10 blocks, Mordy has essentially gotten rid of the nuisance driver in a matter of a few seconds.

Alternative Mordy has very little drama in his day-to-day life. He experiences the exact same events that angry Mordy experiences, but in his view, nothing particularly noteworthy has happened. Our positive Mordy projects a different belief into the world around him. *I'm a lucky man. Good things happen to me. Good people are in my life. I like them and they like*

me. From that seed sprouts a life of achievement and content-
ment. Mordy doesn't feel inconvenienced by his wife's request;
he knows it does not arise out of disregard for his needs, and he
appreciates all his wife does for him. Therefore, his marriage is
happy. The "water" of loving actions and messages keeps nurturing the seed that says "I am loved." His entire day is a projection of his positive subconscious program: Because he arrives at
shul calm, he is able to get a spiritual boost out of his prayers.
Because he sees slow traffic as a fact of life and not a personal affront, he arrives at work focused and ready for the day.
His co-workers respect him and his superiors appreciate him.
He works hard, but he comes home feeling accomplished, not
resentful, which feeds even more positive energy into his family
life. Peaceful Mordy feels like a millionaire, while angry Mordy
feels like a beggar who must demand scraps of recognition.

How the Program Is Written and Installed

Our subconscious programs write much of our life's script, but
what data becomes part of our program? So much happens
to a person in his formative years, yet obviously, only some
of those events make their way into our permanent subconscious. One element that distinguishes these indelible experiences is emotional intensity. Whether intensely pleasant or
intensely painful, the situations that truly penetrate our hearts
are the ones that paint our subconscious world. In addition,
less intense situations can be just as powerful if they occur
repeatedly. Daily small humiliations can have the same impact
as one intense episode, and daily doses of recognition and
praise can build us up as effectively as occasional dramatic
moments of triumph.

How does this programming take place? Five-year-old Yossi
and his classmates are receiving their first *chumashim* in a special ceremony attended by parents and grandparents. Yossi has

been selected to read the first verse of *Bereishis* out loud. The big day comes and he performs his part well. When the ceremony is over, his parents and grandparents and many of the other adults in the crowd come over to him to compliment him. They shake his hand, pinch his cheeks and make a fuss over the smart, adorable little boy. Yossi's brain is now programmed to equate public speaking with approval and compliments. That equation will stick with him for life. If, on the other hand, the attention had made him uncomfortable, or he had made a mistake and felt embarrassed by it, he would be programmed to equate public speaking with peril. Throughout his life, he would avoid it whenever possible. If he found himself in a position where speaking was necessary — his bar mitzvah, for instance — he would face the task with dread even if he was perfectly capable of performing it.

Another example: Reuven is a new boy in a first-grade class. Day after day, all the kids go outside at recess to play. Reuven joins them, but because the other kids all know one another and feel comfortable with one another, they never pay much attention to Reuven. They laugh and joke with one another and he feels left out. He develops a program that says, *Other kids don't like me.* This program remains with him. Then even when others do seek him out, he is likely to make an excuse, because his program tells him that he is treading on dangerous territory. The shyness he develops might emerge in stuttering, awkwardness or even what might seem to others to be aloofness, all of which serves to keep potential friends at an even further distance. Reuven's program stating that others don't like him thus turns into a self-fulfilling prophecy.

Because these programs stick, people who are 30, 40, 50 or even 60 years old are still responding to impressions created when they were 3, 4, 5 and 6 years old. A small shul needs someone to lead the prayers on Shabbos morning. The *gabbai* turns to a 50-year-old man, already a grandfather, but the man is already shaking his head and waving his hand. "No, ask someone else," he says. "I'd rather not." He knows the prayers inside out and backward. He has a pleasant voice, a clear enough pronunciation and is at least as capable as the other men in the shul. Why does he bow out? It is because he associates public performance with criticism. Someone might catch a mistake. He might be humiliated. It's a risk, and anything our subconscious interprets as a risk will be repelled over and over again.

The subconscious can keep us stuck in our place, and it may be a place we constructed while we were still in kindergarten. Even if it becomes an uncomfortable, counterproductive place and we try to break free of it, our subconscious, like a GPS, just keeps recalculating to bring us back there. It wants us to keep traveling the old familiar roads to protect us from the dangers it perceives. Even if those dangers no longer exist in our lives, and haven't existed for the past 30 years, the GPS loyally guides us on its accustomed route.

Gershon's doctor told him he had two choices: start on blood pressure medication or start losing weight. Gershon desperately wanted to avoid the medication. He completely changed his diet and began working with a personal trainer at the gym. The doctor gave him two months to show an improvement, and when Gershon returned to the doctor two months later, the doctor was amazed at his progress.

"I feel so much better," Gershon proclaimed. "I never want to go back to the way I was eating before. I can run up the stairs! I feel 10 years younger!" By the end of the year, Gershon was a new man. His family and friends showered him with compliments and he was justifiably proud of his achievement.

Then one day, the seemingly magic self-control that had gotten him so far seemed to just disappear. It started with a small slice of a cake his daughter had baked for Shabbos. It ended five months later with Gershon having regained almost every pound he had lost. "Why did I do this to myself?" he moaned to his wife.

What happened to Gershon? Why were his old, discredited eating habits able to rally and send his new, admirable habits running away like a defeated army? The "GPS" feature of his subconscious had taken over. When the stark fear of a chronic health problem and lifelong medication began to fade, Gershon's new habits loosened their hold on his conscious thoughts and behavior. His subconscious program was only waiting to regain its power to steer Gershon back on the familiar road that led him to overeat. Perhaps this was the way he was programmed to deal with stress, or to grab a little pleasure in his hectic day, or to feel the comfort and love he felt as a child when his mother gave him a slice of chocolate cake fresh from the oven. He had worked hard to strike out on a new road, but his subconscious constantly commanded him to "take the next legal U-turn" and go back on the road he was programmed to travel. As soon as his determination flagged, he heeded the message.

For Gershon and most people, counterproductive habits rooted in the subconscious take center stage during times of stress. Few people calmly and methodically go about doing what is bad for them. It is only when the downside of the habit is so frightening or unacceptable to us that logic overrides our subconscious. Gershon allowed logic to rule his diet when he feared illness. Likewise, someone who habitually loses his temper can usually override that impulse if an outburst would mean losing his job or perhaps hurting someone he loves. But once those acute fears subside, the subconscious habits of thought are free to take the reins any time our self-control is compromised by stress, anxiety or fatigue.

Updating the Program

There are ways to redirect the "GPS" and eliminate the urge to continue performing the bidding of our subconscious, even when its directions are outdated. The most effective of these is to change the program that drives our actions, and thereby change the "destination" on our internal GPS.

In other words, we have to find a way to reach down into the part of our minds that logic cannot reach and teach it a new way to interpret the events in our lives. The person who has been programmed to react to social situations with fear must somehow create a new subconscious emotional response to social situations. The person who associates food with happiness must create a new subconscious response to food. Otherwise, the person may be able to rally the willpower to overcome his subconscious commands for a while, but eventually, his willpower will weaken and the default mode of old habits will take over.

Most of the time, logic is of very little value in reprogramming a person's subconscious. As we learned in the first chapter, the limbic system and the cerebral cortex are like two separate families with different values; what is important and motivating for one does not work for the other. As a therapist, I see this disconnect clearly in many patients who seek therapy for anxiety, anger, stress or depression. They are baffled by their own emotional pain because they *know* better. They have grown up learning all the great *mussar sefarim* and have absorbed the ideal of *bitachon* from every possible angle. They *know* that people can maintain faith and appreciation for life even as they lie ill in a hospital bed, trapped in a concentration camp or crouched in a tank on the front lines of battle. Why, they wonder, can they not be calm and content in the midst of peace and plenty?

Meira is a young wife and mother who is in a constant state of anxiety. She suffers from insomnia, a poor appetite and a sense of doom. "I just know Hashem is going to punish me," she tells me. "I can't do anything right. I know that we're not expected to be perfect, but I can't help always feeling that if I tried a little harder and paid a little more attention, I could do so much better. I'm not living up to my potential."

"What stands in your way of living up to your potential?"
I ask her.

"I give in to laziness because I feel like it's no use trying. There's always something more that needs to be done," she says. *"I have no energy for my children. I don't feel up to doing arts and crafts with them anymore or to baking healthy cookies for them like I used to. Sometimes I don't even iron their clothes."*

"Isn't it possible that right now, you're doing as much as a mother with three small children could be expected to do?"

"No, of course not," she answers in a flash. *"This is my job and I have to do it. I don't care who expects what. I expect it of myself. I know I could do it if I really wanted to."*

I could tell Meira, "You need to relax and be easier on yourself. Don't try to be perfect. It's not possible." Meira, in fact, already knows that. If she had a sister or a friend suffering from her situation, she would probably offer exactly that advice. She could probably even quote a dozen Torah sources validating that point of view. Her problem does not come from a lack of knowledge or understanding; in our well-educated generation, very few people lack the knowledge and understanding that *should* lead them to satisfying lives. The problem is a lack of balance between the emotional and logical minds. Once we reconstruct the emotional world they live in, their logic can speak and be heard.

Working with the Subconscious

In working with clients like Meira, I've tried various methods of reaching into the subconscious to uncover the roots of unproductive thinking. Therapists have various tools for accomplishing this difficult task, including classical psychoanalysis, hypnosis and other established methods. Hypnosis is one method that, when it works, can be extremely useful in this regard.

Daniel was a teenager who everyone described as an under-achiever. His experiences in yeshivah were mostly of failure and reprimand as his rebbeim and parents tried to get him to use the intelligence he clearly possessed. But Daniel did not feel that he was an underachiever; he felt that he was not smart enough to ever learn well. Weeks of talking, delving and pointing out the obvious inaccuracy of his view of himself did not bring results.

Finally, we tried hypnosis. As I was speaking to him, trying to instill images of self-confidence and competence into his subconscious, he suddenly burst out with a question. "How can I be smart? Almost everyone in my family is learning disabled! I just know there's something wrong with me!"

I spent the next 45 minutes, while he remained under hypnosis, helping him absorb a new subconscious image of himself as someone fully functional and capable. From that point on, Daniel made rapid progress.

Tempting as it might be to see hypnosis as the cure to all that ails our subconscious, there are many obstacles to its use. First, only about 10 percent of people are able to "go under" deeply enough for a therapist to reach and influence their subconscious. Second, many people balk at the idea of letting anyone into their inner mind for the purpose of making alterations. They feel that hypnosis would leave them too vulnerable and exposed. Third, even when a hypnotist is successful at reaching into the patient's subconscious, there may be nearly insurmountable obstacles to the new messages the therapist is trying to introduce.

Furthermore, unless hypnosis is used in the context of comprehensive therapy, it can only cure symptoms, not causes, of unwanted patterns of thought and behavior. We can reach into the subconscious and command it to alter a specific behavior, for instance, smoking, but without the therapy component, we are not actually eliminating the need that smoking was answering in the person's psyche. Therefore, he is likely to find another habit to fill the need, such as overeating or drinking, or he may eventually revert to smoking when the need becomes too pressing to ignore.

Because of my experience with Daniel, however, I felt convinced that some method needed to be developed that would allow me to work with the subconscious in conjunction with the logical, conscious mind. Some combination of hypnosis techniques and classical therapy, it seemed to me, would be able to do the essential work of reaching the inner, subconscious program while engaging the aware, logical mind as well. In this way, I could do more than change one counterproductive subconscious message; I could enable the person's subconscious to identify the program that was blocking his ability to move forward and help the person to change the program itself.

After about three years of researching, thinking, trying various ideas and *davening* for inspiration, I developed a method that has, *baruch Hashem,* succeeded in helping thousands of people find that balance between what they feel, what they think and what they do.

The foundation of this approach is that everything we need for a good, productive, happy life is right there, within us. Hashem sends us into this world fully equipped. We bless Hashem each morning as *"she'asah li kal tzarchi"* (the One Who has provided me my every need), and we have the task of identifying, appreciating and utilizing all we've been given. When we unblock our subconscious and balance our emotions, intellect and actions, we find that we have within ourselves everything we need to be all we are meant to be.

The Winning Formula for Success

"IF I'M SO SMART, WHY AREN'T I SUCCESSFUL?"

"If I'm so excited about my new business idea, why can't I get it off the ground?"

"If I know that it's good to get up early and I love the feeling of getting an early start, why don't I just get out of bed?"

Based on what we've learned so far, we would say that the answer to all these gripes is that something in their subconscious is blocking their progress toward their goals. If we analyze these statements a little more closely, we see that in each of them, the three factors that define a person — inspiration, logic and action — are out of synch. Their beliefs on the deepest level, their knowledge on the intellectual level and their actions on the practical level are like three horses reined together that are pulling in different directions.

Defining the Players

Before we consider how to create forward motion in these situations, let's more closely define each force at play:

Inspiration: Although this might be the hardest force to define, it's the easiest to detect. It's the subconscious fuel that propels us: It reveals itself in the things that pique our excitement and motivate our all-out efforts. If we want to know where our inspiration lies, we need only take note of that which we welcome and embrace in our lives.

Whether it is born of subconscious messages or from our limbic system's emotional reactions to the experiences of our lives, inspiration is our passion to do, strive and become successful in the ways that are meaningful to us. We can take a fairly accurate measure of our level of inspiration by assessing honestly how much we encourage and support ourselves. What are the words your mind whispers to you? Do they include words like "successful," "capable," "beloved"? Are you able to process your fears and move forward, or are you paralyzed by your worries? It doesn't matter that we *think* something is important; it is only when we feel inspired that we are to likely to succeed in that area.

Logic: This is the realm of our conscious minds and the cerebral cortex layer of our brain. Logic is what we know: facts, ideas, theories and concepts, as well as the conclusions we draw from them. It is also what enables us to learn new ideas and assimilate them into our view of reality. Sometimes, new knowledge can change the way we live. For instance, if a person reads a convincing article that explains why a particular parenting technique helps get children to do their homework, he might adopt the new technique and give up his old, ineffective method.

As we have already seen, however, logic has its limitations. If logic dictates that a job-seeker should call people who might be able to help him find employment, but his inspiration level is low (he does not really believe anyone will hire him), he is unlikely to follow the dictates of logic. He will either fail to get started at all or quickly quit if he does not see results.

Action: Since we've already dissected the workings of emotion and intellect, let's now take a look at the realm of action. Someone who is operating at full throttle in the area of action is one who jumps right into a new task, who is self-disciplined in doing whatever he has committed himself to do and persists in the face of challenges.

We can clearly see that our actions are the product of inspiration and logic; a person thinks about his sick friend alone in the hospital, feels compassion and therefore goes to visit him. What is not as obvious is that this is really a two-way street: our actions also influence our logic and emotions. For instance, by giving charity over and over again, we can override a natural stinginess and become generous. By forcing ourselves to jump out of bed and get moving each day, we can override an innate laziness and become enthusiastic. Like the slow, steady drip of water on rock, our repeated actions can carve new pathways in our personalities.

This behavioral part of the brain operates separate from intellect and emotion; it works simply on the power of repetition. We can see the impact of this part of the brain in the success of behavioral therapy to alleviate some types of dysfunction. For instance, someone with a phobia might be guided to gradually engage in the activity he fears, over and over, until he becomes so accustomed to it that he no longer reacts. This part of the brain also enables us to master skills by constant repetition. The first time a piano student tries to put his fingers on the right keys and play the notes he sees on the sheet music, he has to think through every step. By the 100th repetition, his fingers know what to do with barely any conscious thought from his brain at all.

Our "self talk," the message we tell ourselves about ourselves, is one of the most powerful forms of repetition. It solidifies our self-image for better or worse, ingraining it deeper into our consciousness with every repetition. Thinking, "I'm incompetent" dozens of times a day turns the thought into a reality. Thinking "I'm valuable" does the same. Therefore, new self-talk has the power to keep and install new programs in our subconscious. (See graph on page 281).

How to Do the Math

Success in life is a formula that contains equal portions of inspiration, logic and action. I developed the Winning Formula as a way to enable people to grasp, in mathematical terms, the degree to which each of these factors define our whole life experience, and to assess for themselves their own level of satisfaction with life.

To understand how the formula works, imagine that the highest level of intellect, emotion or action is designated as 10. A mythical person who uses all his capacities fully would have a "success rating" of 10 for inspiration x 10 for logic x 10 for action, for an overall rating of 1,000. Therefore, we can say that the highest success rating, the perfect score, is 1,000.

But no one's perfect. Most people live somewhere between the superhuman 10 and the non-functional 1. We could say that an average rating for most would be 5: not noticeably strong in that particular area, but not suffering noticeably from a lack, either. That means that a person who is average across the board has a "success rating" of 5 x 5 x 5, which equals 125. Therefore, if we are just chugging along on average intelligence, fueled by an average amount of inspiration and engaged in a mediocre level of action, we achieve a life that rates 12.5 percent of the maximum human potential for success.

There is no standard test for these ratings. It is not like IQ or any of the thousands of personality self-tests we encounter throughout the world of pop psychology. To use the Winning Formula, people rate themselves — and they do a very accurate job. I have found that people whose total rating falls below the across-the-board average of 125 are almost always suffering from the feeling that they are failures in comparison to others. Those who rate themselves above that average are generally perceived by others as successful people, whether or not they actually feel that they are living fulfilling lives.

Now let's look at Reuven, who is the man behind the opening quote of our chapter, "If I'm so smart, why aren't I successful?" Reuven is indeed very smart; he is actually a genius at mathematics and a computer wizard who breezed through school, college and graduate school. People marveled at his abilities and predicted a brilliant career for him. He planned to use his smarts to dive into a challenging career as an actuary. Intellect rating: 9.

Reuven has a problem, though. He is full of self-doubt. He has trouble applying and interviewing for jobs and ends up taking a position well below his capacity. On the job, his nervousness makes him come across as a bit odd and inept. When his boss asks him a question, his mind goes blank. He inspires no confidence in his superiors, which brings them to bypass him for promotions and raises. Because his self-doubt keeps him from displaying his brilliance, his brilliance does not help him experience success. Instead, he hates his job and feels like a failure. Inspiration rating: 2.

Despite his lack of vitality, Reuven faithfully fulfills his obligations. He is at his desk every day at 9 a.m. checking his office emails and getting ready to start his day. While he completes his work conscientiously and never cheats his company out of a minute or a dollar, he never offers his ideas or volunteers to do something outside his job description. To him, just doing what he must is quite enough. Action rating: 5.

Reuven's formula is 2 x 9 x 5 = 90. Despite his brilliant mind, he enjoys a success level lower than that of someone who is just chugging along on the average track of life. His high intelligence and average diligence don't add up to success because his level of inspiration is so low.

Now imagine how frustrated Reuven is when he compares himself to Aryeh, Mr. Slightly-Below-Average. Aryeh works for the same firm as Reuven. He squeaked through college and graduate school with the minimum grades needed to graduate. Intellect rating: 4. As far as inspiration, Aryeh is happy to have a good job. When extra help is needed, the firm's managers know they can count on Aryeh to come through, and despite his less-than-stellar command of his field, he is full of ideas and eager to offer them to his boss. They see him as capable, reliable and confident, and eventually move him up to a supervisory position. Inspiration rating: 8. Like most of the other employees in the company, Aryeh arrives a little late from time to time, leaves a little early and sometimes takes a long lunch. Action rating: 5. Aryeh's formula, 8 x 4 x 5, comes out to 160 — 70 points above Reuven. Reuven looks at his fairly lackluster colleague and wonders, why is he so much happier at work, and why was he promoted above me? *It's just a stupid, corrupt system*, Reuven concludes. *They care more about a phony smile and a "rah-rah" attitude than they do about competence.*

The Winning Formula quickly demonstrates how a marked deficit in any one of the three vital factors nearly nullifies the benefits of the other two factors. Reuven's life would be just as troubled if he had been a gung-ho employee who scored 9 on the emotion/inspiration scale, but he lacked the intellectual capacity to do his job competently. Similarly, he would be in trouble if, despite high scores in intellect and emotion, his actions were very deficient; for instance, he neglected his responsibilities at work. Each factor has an equal influence on the final product.

But the purpose of the formula is not to show us how easy it is to miss our mark. Rather, it shows us the mighty impact of a small improvement in any one factor. For instance, let's say that

Reuven goes for therapy and manages to shed some of his self-doubt. Now his brilliance is liberated from the little box Reuven kept it in. He can share his ideas with his boss. He can exhibit initiative, confidence and leadership potential that he feels will certainly lead to a position that uses more of his potential. In other words, he will find success and satisfaction where before he found failure and frustration.

As Reuven begins to feel that he has a future at this job, his level of inspiration rises from 2 to 6. Now his formula is 6 x 9 x 5= 270. He has tripled his level of success. The man who yanked himself out of bed each morning with a groan now gets up with energy, motivated by a mental to-do list which he is eager to tackle. He stands straighter, walks a bit faster, smiles a lot more and finds that his family, friends and co-workers seem a lot happier to be around him.

But a person can benefit even from slight changes. For instance, imagine Slightly-Below-Average Aryeh took a course and brought his intellectual rating up to 5. With that upgrade, he found even more enthusiasm for the job, bringing his inspiration up to 9. All of this motivated him to work just a little harder, taking on slightly more responsibility, for an action score of 6. That minimal increase in each area brings his overall success level to 270, up by more than 100 points from his previous level. Where before, Aryeh's prospects were somewhat limited by his noticeable lack of expertise, now he is up to par. This small upgrade, combined with his remarkably enthusiastic approach to his job, makes Aryeh a prized employee. He feels it; he gets the respect and acknowledgment he desires, and he feels like a success.

A Tool for Self-Knowledge

By analyzing ourselves through these three factors, we can often pinpoint what is blocking our access to the path we want to take in life. We can ask ourselves, *Is my problem that*

I don't feel emotionally inspired about my goals? That I am missing the right information? Or is it that I don't take the necessary actions? By rating each factor, we can quickly see what is holding us back and to what degree it is influencing our ability to reach our potential. We can also pinpoint the area in which a little improvement could be applied to make a big difference.

At this point the ball is in our court. How does a person actually make these improvements? As we've already discussed, most people educated in our Jewish school system have the knowledge they need to steer their lives in a productive, wholesome direction. When people are troubled, it is often because they are just not "feeling it." Their sense of dissatisfaction arises not because they lack the right knowledge, but rather because there is an underground spring of negativity running through them.

To change the nature of this negative undercurrent, we have to work on all three aspects of the formula. We have to create new subconscious images of ourselves that match our potential and aspirations; internalize the positive knowledge we already possess; and engage ourselves in actions that turn our ideas into our identity.

The fact is that many, if not most, people emerge from childhood with a negative program. That is because, as we noted above, repeated actions can shape our subconscious. What is the most repeated action in a child's life? Consider the fact that a child is corrected and /or criticized many times every day by all the well-meaning adults who are trying to teach him the right way to eat, tie his shoes, speak, spell, read and so forth; a child's mind is trained to focus on his mistakes. This criticism does not have to be a vicious dressing-down or a humiliating insult; it can be as mild as "No, Yossi, not like that. Like this!"

These necessary corrections become harmful when they comprise the vast bulk of communication to the child. When the negative messages are balanced with positive attention, the child develops resilience: *I can do something poorly or do something wrong, but I'm still lovable and valuable.* On the other hand, when there is no balance, or when criticism is unduly harsh, the child's "education" can result in a subconscious message of ineptitude and failure.

It was a peaceful evening at the Kaufman home. The older children were doing their homework. The younger children were playing with their toys in the playroom. The child whose turn it was to wash the dishes had washed them, and the child who was supposed to dry the dishes had dried them. No one was fighting. No one was complaining. And no one noticed.

It was a hectic night at the Kaufman home. "I can't stand math! I'm not doing this homework!" complained the eldest child. "Just sit down right now and put your mind to it and stop stalling," said the mother firmly. "Moishy stole my Legos!" screamed Binyamin from the playroom. "Stop fighting or it's off to bed!" the mother yelled back. "And Mindy, go to the kitchen right now and do the dishes. Tonight's your turn."

It takes a high level of awareness for a busy mother to "notice" her children behaving well, but almost no thought at all for her to notice their disruptive or improper behavior. Similarly, in school, students are likely to have their mistakes pointed out to them, but rarely do they draw praise for just doing what is expected.

Our vision is therefore fixated on the negative. A boy doesn't think about the eight great innings of baseball that he played; he ruminates endlessly about the ball he fumbled in the ninth inning. The businessman doesn't focus on the 10 great deals he made this year; he obsesses about the one that lost money. The teacher doesn't allow herself to feel satisfied over the 35 minutes of her lesson that went well; she reruns in her mind the five minutes when the students wouldn't stop talking.

I call this phenomenon the "black-glass effect." Imagine that a person walks into a room in which there stands a long dining table. Lined up across the table are 200 wine glasses. Among all those glasses, there is one black glass. Upon which glass would the person's eyes instantly land? The 199 crystal glasses would fade into the background, and if we were to ask him, "What do you see?" he would say, "A black glass."

Retraining Our Focus

Fortunately, someone trained to focus on the negative, the "black glass," can be retrained to focus on the positive. By repeatedly focusing, day after day, on the good in our lives, we can slowly instill into ourselves a subconscious program that says "Life is good, people are good and good things happen to me." As we explained earlier, these repeated messages are like the water and fertilizer of our self-image. However, for them to bring forth a positive self-image from within our subconscious, the negative "seed" buried there needs to be replaced with a positive one. The **inspiration** portion of the Winning Formula comes into play here, as we work on visualizing and mentally experiencing an image of vitality, excitement and success, picturing ourselves living a life that mirrors our own hopes and potentials.

The act of "counting our blessings," taken all by itself, rarely works. For a focus on the positive to be powerful enough to seep into the subconscious and truly change the way we perceive the world around us, it is essential that those positives be real, personal sources of happiness for us. We therefore call upon our **logic** to recall and assess the people and experiences we encounter each day and recognize what we truly value. For example, when someone says, "I'm grateful to Hashem for the sunshine today," this statement will not really help to retrain his focus unless he actually has taken a few moments to observe and enjoy the warmth and brightness of the sunshine.

The gifts that we take for granted are surely still gifts, and as a person becomes more positive in his outlook, he will begin to appreciate them more. But to do the work of transforming our interior world, we need to focus on aspects of our lives that truly give our hearts a lift. These include: a compliment on a job well done; a warm conversation with a good friend; an unexpected gift; a child's endearing remark; a new business opportunity and so forth. These are the moments we should learn to notice, absorb and remember. This is the **action** we are required to do.

What helps those moments repaint our interior selves with brighter colors is repetition: the same thing that helped to paint it battleship gray. Planting the seed of a positive self-image, finding the true positives that exist in our lives and repeating them *every day really* does transform us. It seems so simple, yet despite the simplicity of this technique, surprisingly few people are willing to give it a consistent trial. They feel that they already "know" that they have it relatively good, and since this knowledge has not thus far enabled them to find happiness and peace, they feel that the effort is futile.

But it's not futile. Let's go back to the "black-glass" theory to see how we can retrain ourselves to focus on the positive and little by little, replace that negative undercurrent with a positive one. Imagine that a person enters the room with the glasses and is told to find the 50 clearest glasses. Now his eyes are focused on the sparkling clear glasses and the one black glass fades into the background. Imagine if *every* day, he had to walk into that room and count out 50 clear glasses. Eventually, he would set his eyes directly on the clear glasses and the black one would finally settle into its proper place as one amid dozens of other glasses. Rather than dominating his perception, it would become just another feature of the landscape.

Nachum came to therapy because he could no longer generate enthusiasm for anything in his life. He had a loving wife, healthy, adorable children, a successful business, a won-

*derful shul and community and yet, when his alarm rang in
the morning, he wanted nothing more than to hide under
the blankets for the rest of the day. Everything he had was a
blessing; this he knew. But to him, every blessing was a time
bomb: a disaster or a disappointment waiting to happen. He
could not enjoy what he had without worrying about losing it.*

"List 10 good things in your life," I challenged him.

*"I have a good wife and kids. I have a business, but there's
a lot of competition now. Who knows how long I'll hold on?"*

*"Wait," I said. "You got two positives out and you're already
looking at a negative. Let's go back to the positive."*

*"O.K., I like my shul. I have good friends there. But I really
should be more involved. It seems like everyone else is raising
money and running dinners and I just..."*

"The positives," I interjected. "For now, just the positives."

And so it went. Nachum's mind was like a train hurtling along
on the same well-oiled track of negativity. Only by constantly hitting the switch was he able to reroute his thinking and actually
focus on the unadulterated good in his life. To help him shift to a
different track, we had to work on getting him to visualize a different Nachum: a man who has nothing to fear, who can handle
a setback when it comes along: a brave, courageous, proactive
man who has enjoyed great blessings in his life.

Then, he needed to take on the task of "watering" this new
image, repeating his 10 positive points to himself every day
and looking for items to add to his list. By doing this simple
exercise, he worked on increasing all three factors in the Winning Formula equation. He built his inspiration by visualizing
and mentally experiencing a successful self and connecting to
the aspects of his life that made him happy; he used his logic to
recall and acknowledge the good in his life; and he took action
by repeating the positives to himself every day.

Of these three areas, the subconscious is the most complex to
decipher and to upgrade. In therapy, we use many highly effec-

tive techniques to work on the subconscious. However, within the limited scope of this book, we will only describe the simpler techniques such as visualization.

The Winning Formula succeeds by engaging all three aspects of one's mind and using each to upgrade the others. New actions can breed new thoughts and feelings. New feelings can breed new thoughts and actions. New thoughts can breed new actions and feelings. Like three partners in a business, the success of each one is essential to the success of the whole. Likewise, the deficiencies in each one bring down the success of the whole.

That's the theory. In applying this theory, I have found that there are 10 fundamental modes of thinking that most often keep people locked into a life that is far more distressing and far less satisfying than it can and should be. In the coming chapters, we explore the Ten Keys That Unlock Your Potential: the Winning Formula approach to overcoming the thoughts, feeling and actions with which we stand in the way of our own success and happiness. I invite you to use these keys to unlock your own personal barriers and embrace the magnificent goodness, wisdom and power with which Hashem has blessed us all.

Do Your Math

The questions below can help you rate yourself in each area of the Winning Formula. Ask yourself these questions and use your answers to rate yourself on a scale of 1 to 10 in each area, with 10 being the highest rating. Then multiply the three numbers together to get your overall "success rating."

Inspiration

- What is my inspiration rating?
- Do I have goals that are meaningful to me?

- Do I believe that I can reach my goals?
- Am I interested in learning new things?
- Am I looking forward to today? Tomorrow?
- Do I smile and/or laugh on an average day?
- Do I think of myself as strong? Capable? Successful?
- Do I feel liked and loved by others?
- Do I like and love others?
- What is my reaction to a setback?
- Do I have passions in life?

Logic

- What is my logic rating?
- Do I have areas of expertise?
- Do I constantly update my knowledge in relevant areas?
- Am I generally curious?
- Is my mind open to ideas that differ from my preconceptions?
- Do I understand new information?
- Am I willing to seek clarification of things I don't understand?
- Do I have a good memory?
- Am I able to study and improve my grasp of information?
- Am I able to focus on mental tasks?
- Can I come up with creative solutions to problems?

Action

- What is my action rating?
- Do I set goals for what I want to accomplish each day?
- Do I set long-term goals?
- Do I meet most of my goals?
- Can I keep a schedule I have made for myself?

- Can I perform tasks consistently?
- Do I persist in the face of failure or setbacks?
- Would I describe myself as self-disciplined?
- Do I begin tasks as soon as possible?
- Do I finish what I start?
- Are "should have" and "ought to" prevalent in my life?
- Do I have to "feel it" in order to do it?
  Personal Life:

  I _____ x L _____ x A _____ = _____

  Professional Life:
  I _____ x L _____ x A _____ = _____

Once you've tallied your ILA numbers, you have quantified that elusive quality called fulfillment. Now you're ready to seek the keys that unlock life at a whole new level.

To register for Mordechai Weinberger's ALIVE! hands-on workshop incorporating the concepts of this book, contact us at 212-920-5719 or by email at www.winnerformula.com